**STEPHEN HOGG,
PAUL RISEBOROUGH
& KAROLINA MORYS**

Naked Banking

THE TRUTH ABOUT BANKS AND YOU

Published by
LID Publishing Ltd.
The Record Hall, Studio 204,
16-16a Baldwins Gardens,
London EC1N 7RJ, United Kingdom

31 West 34th Street, 8th Floor, Suite 8004,
New York, NY 10001, US

info@lidpublishing.com
www.lidpublishing.com

A member of:

BPR
Business Publishers Roundtable

www.businesspublishersroundtable.com

Printed in Great Britain by TJ International
ISBN: 978-1-911498-38-4

Cover and page design: Caroline Li

**STEPHEN HOGG,
PAUL RISEBOROUGH
& KAROLINA MORYS**

Naked
Banking

THE TRUTH ABOUT BANKS AND YOU

LONDON   MONTERREY
MADRID   SHANGHAI
MEXICO CITY   BOGOTA
NEW YORK   BUENOS AIRES
BARCELONA   SAN FRANCISCO

Contents

CHAPTER 1

Introduction

It's 3 o'clock in the afternoon and we are waiting around in the Cambridge store of the bank we work for. In walks a harassed-looking woman pushing a pram, with two crying babies inside. You only need to look at the woman's face to know she is having a really bad day.

As she sits down to talk to one of our customer service representatives, she pulls out not one but five credit cards, all different colours, and spreads them out on the desk like a magician about to ask an audience member to pick a card.

Even though we are some ten metres away from the desk we can hear everything she is saying. The woman – let's call her Sue – explains that she's got herself into a spot of bother.

Sue saw what looked like an amazing credit card deal on the internet – 36 months' interest-free purchases and balance transfers. As she still had some credit card debt from when she was younger she transferred the balance from her old card to the new deal. Problem was, 36 months later, she still hadn't managed to pay off the debt and the interest rate on the card reverted to a much higher one. With twins on the way she had a lot to buy so she took out another credit card and moved the balance again, only this time she kept spending on the old card too.

Three further cards later and Sue was in unsecured debt to the tune of £30,000 and she didn't know what to do. She was no longer able to get accepted for a new card at any other banks and her debts were piling up almost as high as the stack of nappies she was changing each day.

As product managers working inside a bank we see situations like Sue's nearly every day. While it might be tempting to conclude that it is Sue's fault for spending money she didn't have, we know the situation is slightly more complicated than that.

Banks have always offered financial products to customers to make money. But something has changed in the last decade or so. Back in the day, banks were largely trusted and products were simple. Today customers have to navigate a blizzard of product promotions, all with confusing terms and conditions, rip-off fees, and constant rate changes. They can and do make mistakes with their finances, but nowadays banks seem to design new products so that they can profit from these slip-ups. This book explains why banks no longer seem to want to do the right thing.

Everyone hates banks

Complaining about banks has become a national pastime. From spending hours pressing buttons trying to speak to a human being in a call centre, to being told that you have to go to a branch to do something simple that you should be able to do over the phone, banks appear not to give two hoots what we think about them.

We put up with it all, of course, because the thought of switching banks is painful. Those of us who do pluck up the courage to move quickly realize that there are not very many to choose from. The biggest five banks – Lloyds Banking Group, Royal Bank of Scotland, Barclays, HSBC, and Santander – account for some 85% of all bank accounts in the UK. One player, Lloyds Banking Group, has over 25% of the market alone, following its acquisition of the Halifax Bank of Scotland at the height of the financial crisis.

Such market concentration has not always been the case. According to a report by PwC, of the 32 banks and building societies that existed in the UK in 1960, 26 were absorbed into just six major groups by 2010: Barclays, HSBC, Lloyds,

Nationwide, RBS, and Santander. Economists call this sort of marketplace an 'oligopoly'. Oligopolistic markets are rarely good news for customers.

The banks do little to help themselves. Barely a day goes by without the big banks being in the news, asked to pay huge fines and compensation for past misdeeds. Standard and Poor's estimates that banks in the UK have paid over £48 billion in fines and compensation since 2014. These are fines and compensation payments, not losses resulting from loans going bad – a normal part of banking which involves lending money to people and organizations, some of whom may not pay you back. The bulk of pay-outs have been the result of banks mis-selling products designed to be highly profitable for the banks but with scant consideration for the customers buying them. Payment protection insurance mis-selling claims alone have accounted for over £34 billion in compensation and fines for the biggest four banks (Royal Bank of Scotland, Lloyds Banking Group, HSBC, and Barclays) in the last few years.

Beyond the headlines, it is at a personal level that the behaviour of banks causes such distress and worry. Account fees and charges are often levied for minor mistakes and slip-ups. Money is made in ways that are not always clear or understood by customers, particularly when the complexities of payments, clearing cycles, card transactions, and all the rest of it are taken into account. A 2015 study from PwC found that less than one in three customers trusted their bank and only one in ten thought that this level of trust had increased over the past 12 months.

It is often quite difficult to work out whether you will be subject to charges and, if so, how much you will pay. In the same PwC study, 31% of people surveyed said that overcharging and unfair fees were the issues they were most concerned about regarding the way banks handle their money. Do you know how much your bank charged you for using your debit card abroad last summer? Thought not.

The problem is not just that we have so few banks to choose from and that they do bad things; it is that they all offer almost exactly the same thing. Current accounts, savings accounts, credit cards, loans, insurance – what other industry would survive with four or five brands selling exactly the same thing? Sure, sometimes they offer different rates on different products but these products all do the same thing, work in broadly the same way and are designed to make money out of you.

When products all work the same way and the only difference is rate, the difference in rate has to be significant for customers to be motivated enough to switch banks. "I can't be bothered to move my banking just to earn an extra £7.32 in interest a year," is the sort of comment we often hear when we talk to customers. A recent investigation by the Competition and Markets Authority (CMA) – the regulatory body charged with ensuring the UK banking market is competitive – found that just 3% of personal customers and 4% of business customers switch to a different bank in any given year. Recent figures suggest this number might actually be falling.

Banks don't just all sell the same thing; they all operate in a very similar way and look near-identical to each other. It is remarkable that in an industry that has generated such huge profits over the years, so little has been invested in offering customers something new. The average British high-street bank branch looks pretty much the same as it did in the 1960s – small, dour, invariably beige in colour, thick plastic screens separating bank counter staff from customers paying in or withdrawing money, open Monday to Friday 9am to 5pm. We often watch customers queuing in the rain outside banks on a Wednesday morning as they wait for branch staff to complete their weekly training session before opening the bank half an hour later than normal. It is difficult to imagine customer-focused businesses like John Lewis or Marks and Spencer making customers wait in the rain once a week. Banks, on the other hand, seem curiously unconcerned what we think about them.

Taking you behind the veil

In this book we take you behind the veil of retail banking to explain how it *really* works. As industry insiders working for one of the UK's highest profile new 'challenger' banks we are perhaps uniquely placed to do so. We will show you why the big banks always seem to do the wrong thing: from designing products they know will rip customers off to cutting branches they know their customers rely on – over a thousand between 2015 and 2017 alone.

The story starts with the way banks are set up – their business models. Weighed down by lots of underutilized, poorly designed branches in the wrong places and creaking information technology infrastructure, banks have big bills to pay. To meet them and still make a good return for shareholders, banks have in recent years viewed 'product innovation' as the solution, developing more and more new products to deliver increased revenue to the bank. Simple products that everyone understands are now a thing of the past.

This is more than just a story of big banks and their product strategies. We will show you how individual customer behaviour – the way we think and act when it comes to our personal finances – actually plays into the hands of the big banks. Product managers know customers have blind spots and biases and they develop products to take financial advantage of them. We will show you how they do it.

We will also give you a sense of what it's like to be a product manager at a big bank – what they are asked to do, how they are rewarded, and the type of working environment they find themselves operating in. As serving product managers we know better than most what the big banks are up to. And we reveal why the things product managers at the big banks are told to focus on – and which are important to them progressing in their careers – are often a million miles away from the things that matter to customers.

Sometimes you just want to know how to avoid tripping up when it comes to your finances and this book will help you in that regard too. We detail the specific product management strategies used by banks to part you from your money. Some are more obvious than others. Cutting the interest rate on your savings account a few months after you opened it is annoying but at least something you can understand. But what about inverse interest-rate tiers on your current account? Or 'representative' annual percentage rates (APRs) when you apply for a loan? The truth is that product managers have dreamt up every trick in the book to slowly – sometimes imperceptibly – earn more and more out of you. We thought it was about time someone documented what these tricks are, explained why product managers use them and pointed out what you can do to avoid them, or at least use them to your advantage.

Of course, it's not just about avoiding the pitfalls. A question we get asked all the time is "how do I get the best out of my banking, then?" Here we provide some pointers as to what you can do to organize your personal finances that little bit better. Some sensible steps, and a healthy dose of personal discipline, will allow most of us to bank in a way that is simple, understandable, and worry-free.

We also make some recommendations for things that banks could and should do to put customers first. From a potentially painful move away from the fiction of 'free banking' to taking more steps to ensure we all understand how products work, the opportunities for banks to become more transparent and customer focused are many indeed. We will show you how a new relationship based on a fair value exchange between banks and their customers could point to a brighter future for both.

The future doesn't stop there though. Retail banking is in a state of flux and there are reasons to believe that something more customer focused will emerge. From the promise of open banking, where personal banking data can be shared with other financial services companies to ensure products are better tailored to specific customer needs, to more thoughtfully designed services and processes, banks are starting to think more deeply about what customers want and need. This new dawn offers banks the chance to build leaner, more agile organizations, better able to respond to customer demands and deliver new products and services quickly. We'll take you through what we think it all means.

We decided to write this book because we believe that good banking is important. Important to start-up businesses needing advice on how to finance their growth. Important to young people learning how to better manage their money and save for their futures. Important for our economy and our society so that we can grow as a country and pay our way in the world. Yet the current state of affairs is not good enough. The big banks, almost without exception, have let us all down with their too-clever-by-half products and poor service cultures. The path to redemption starts with a clear-eyed view of what has gone wrong and this is our contribution to that debate.

Should you believe anything we say in this book? We are, after all, still working in the industry, albeit for a bank that is trying hard to change the status quo. You'll be your own judge of that. Our aims for this book are modest: that you understand how banks work a bit better, grasp how the products they sell actually operate so you have a bit more money in your pocket, and that you reward the *best* banks – the banks putting customer service and simple products first – with your business, and not just the *big* banks. Because for all their gleaming headquarters, bumper profits, fancy adverts, and thousands of employees, it is you – the customer – who holds the key to better banking.

PART 1

How do you solve a problem like retail banking?

CHAPTER 2

Why retail banking isn't working

Today, in our vibrant global economy, we have retail banks, commercial banks, investment banks, merchant banks – and more than a few behemoth banks that combine all of these and more under single, giant, corporate structures. For the purposes of this book we want to talk about *retail banking* in the UK: the provision of current accounts, savings products, and loans to ordinary people. We'll talk a bit about the products and services UK banks provide to businesses as well, but our primary focus is on what banks do for retail consumers.

We believe the UK's banks are delivering poor customer service because they are so damn big and complicated that they've forgotten their customers. Their management teams are focused on matters such as regulation, cost control, and internal measures of financial performance, with little spare time to think deeply about what customers want, or to design customer service experiences to make customers' lives easier. Theoretically that should present an opportunity for competitors that are more customer focused, but we will explain why this still has not happened to any significant extent.

The structure of the market, the nature of banking itself, regulatory challenges and cultural shortcomings all have a part to play in making retail banks far more intently focused on repairing the damage of recent crises to their own businesses than on working out how to build businesses that deliver really great banking experiences for customers.

The problems
Bad service

Good customer service is easy to describe. To be a 'good business' (any business, not just a bank), a company must sell products that its customers want, at a price they're willing to pay, in a way they find easy – maybe even fun.

In the context of banking, let's say you need a mortgage to buy a house. If you could pop into a local branch on any day of the week, talk to someone who was friendly and knowledgeable without an appointment, have them explain the pros and cons of a handful of simple options and then select a competitively priced product, then you'd probably conclude that was a 'good' experience.

Alternatively, you might like to go online or log in to a mobile app and do things yourself. If you got stuck with the technology you might like to call a helpful, available call centre or switch to web chat, where your query gets handled by a real human responding in real time who can complete the task for you.

All good retail businesses aspire to operate this way – think John Lewis, Apple, Disney, or Lush. They offer products people want at prices people are willing to pay and they have spent time and money building a multichannel retail experience for their customers that adds up to a clearly perceived reputation for 'good service'.

Banks continue to be a stubborn exception to the ranks of businesses offering good service. Generally speaking, they treat their customers badly (there – we said it!). From unwelcoming (or increasingly closed) branches to infuriatingly unhelpful automated phone lines and offshore call centres with infinite wait times, banks can easily give the impression that they don't want your business at all. These shortcomings are so well rehearsed that they have become accepted wisdom.

Which?, the consumer organization, conducted a survey of thousands of current accounts in 2016 to gauge the best banks for customer service. The top bank, First Direct, scored a respectable 85% across the categories of customer service; clarity of statements; dealing with queries; service in branch, online, and on the phone. The big high street banks – RBS (54%), HSBC (56%), Barclays (58%), Lloyds (59%), and Santander (62%) – were all far behind.

One reason the big banks appear to have fared so badly is that they have been the ones shutting hundreds of branches in recent years, frustrating and exasperating customers in equal measure. While many customers like – and some prefer – to bank online, there is little getting around the fact that the combined closing of 1,046 branches between January 2015 and January 2017 has impacted customer service profoundly. Which? found that the majority of these closures have been in rural areas, leaving customers with few other banking options.

The branches that are still open are not open very long. The recent CMA investigation into retail banking found that just 36% of Barclays and 44% of HSBC branches offered weekend opening. RBS stores were open around 38 hours a week, HSBC 39, Lloyds Banking Group 40, and Barclays 36. This compares to 76 hours a week for the best bank surveyed. A survey by market research firm GfK, conducted for the 2016 CMA enquiry into retail banking, found that the three most important features of a current account were (in order of importance): the quality of the staff and customer service; quality and speed of handling problems; and convenience of location and opening times of branches.

Creaking infrastructure

We all use banks every day. We might not walk into a branch or phone a call centre but most of us use money most days to buy things like a coffee or food. Each time we do, we're creating transactions that our banks will process on our behalf. Many everyday aspects of banking work so well that we're unconscious of them, much like any other utility. The trouble with utilities, though, is that if they do go wrong the consequences are often significant. Few of us could survive very long in our house or flat if it was unable to receive water or electricity, for example.

Banks' systems and products are no exception. And many are poorly designed and poorly maintained. Little wonder, then, that system outages at banks are now a fairly regular occurrence. In 2012 RBS was fined a whopping £56m by the Prudential Regulation Authority (PRA) following systems failures that left customers locked out of their accounts. RBS's systems went haywire again in 2013, with customers unable to make card payments. Planned maintenance to Nationwide's systems in 2014 again left customers locked out of their accounts and in 2015 Barclays customers were unable to make debit and credit card payments for some time. Rather amusingly at the time, it was reported that the problems at Barclays stemmed from maintenance carried out ahead of the clocks going back at the end of British Summer Time! And then in 2016 HSBC customers joined the list of the annoyed after also being locked out of their online accounts.

All these failures were predominantly failures in regular systems that arose through poor maintenance and most of the impacts were fairly minor – cash was inaccessible from ATMs, some payments got held up and arrived a few days later etc.

But if you were one of the customers in real difficulty – say a small business customer who couldn't pay a crucial supplier, or a home buyer stuck on the driveway of a new house with the estate agent refusing to hand over the keys until the payment cleared – the impact was very significant indeed.

Poor products

Banks have also failed to provide their customers with good value products that behave in a way their customers expect. In some cases they have designed and sold products that definitively do not behave as advertised and have been a waste of money for customers. This has gained bold headlines, most notably for the payment protection insurance (PPI) scandal, but there have been other examples too, including foreign exchange options sold incorrectly to small businesses, endowment mortgages sold to retail customers – the list goes on. Stories like PPI help to explain the popular opinion that the people who work in banks are arrogant and greedy, out to fleece customers and line their own pockets.

That presumption needs a second look though. Are the products sold by banks really a 'rip-off' because all bankers are sharks who would sell their own grannies to get ahead? Working in the industry, that seems unlikely to us – we think there's more to it. People who work in banks are (mostly) just regular people. They don't appear to us to be very different from anyone else. Of the hundreds of thousands of people who work in banks, the proportion that are really bad apples is likely to be quite similar to that seen in wider society – a very small number.

Yet while all these people come to work every day, aiming to do a good job, who try hard, want to get promoted, get a pay rise, provide for their families – just like we all do

– *collectively* they manage to deliver a result that is a world away from what customers actually want. Their combined efforts deliver bad service and complicated products that are poorly understood and offer mediocre value. How is that possible? There must be something about the places they work in – the corporate entities of the banks themselves or the way the banking market works – that gives rise to this perverse outcome.

How banks work

To start to answer that question we need to take a brief look at how banks work. We don't want to dive into some complicated, academic discussion of fractional reserve banking but we do need to explore the basics of how banks operate to really understand why the business models of big banks might actually deter them from providing good service and good products.

Retail banks really only do three things for us, they: provide places to *deposit* our money so we can save it safely and get it back when we want it; provide *loans* so that we can get more money than we have right now to buy big things like houses; and they provide *access to payment infrastructure* so we can use and move our money without using cash (through debit cards, credit cards, and online payments).

These three simple-sounding things give rise very quickly to staggering complexity, magnified even more by the swathes of regulation governing everything, which is itself as much a part of the problem as part of the solution. We'll take a look at the effect of this complexity later in the chapter but first let's take a look at the three things that the banks do in a little bit more detail.

Deposits: money for (nearly) nothing

Of the three services banks provide, the only one that is exclusive to banks alone is taking deposits. Ultimately that's what a banking licence grants: the permission from the regulator to take deposits. This single fact makes banks what they are because it gives them access to a cheaper cost of funds than any other business can dream of. It is worth taking a little time to understand this as it is at the heart of what makes UK retail banking tick.

We all want to keep safe the money we earn by working hard. We don't want to carry it with us, bury it in the garden, or hide it under the mattress. None of these methods are secure so customers are in the market for a product that offers security for their money. Many of us want to earn some interest too.

We also need to *use* our money to pay for things, so as well as security we need some degree of ready access to our money when we want it. This is the function of a current account. In the UK, banks generally pay no interest on current account balances but nor do they charge any upfront fees. The implied commercial agreement between banks and customers, then, is that customers value the security the banks offer highly enough that they are prepared to forgo any interest; and banks value the act of holding this money highly enough that they are willing to provide security for deposits and access to them (in the form of payment services) free of charge. The net result is that very few customers pay upfront for current account banking services in the UK as banks carry the costs of things like fraud and measures to keep our money safe without charging customers directly (e.g. via a monthly fee) to do so. It also means that at any given point in time there are billions of pounds sitting in current accounts across the UK. This money is safe and can be used to make payments, but the average balance in those accounts is just sitting there – and the banks are getting the *use* of that money very cheaply indeed because most are paying no interest on it.

For those of us lucky enough to have more money than we need to get by every week, we can also tuck some money away into savings products of various kinds. Unlike current accounts, savings accounts do pay interest. They come in different flavours and pay different levels of interest, but ultimately their purpose is all the same – they allow us to put some money away in a separate pot from our current account so that it can earn a bit of interest and we won't accidentally spend it, as savings products are generally not connected to payment systems. To spend the money in our savings account we need to move balances into our current accounts. The interest rates paid on savings accounts still tend to be low; however, as we are still getting security from the bank as well as a degree of ease-of-saving through being able to transfer funds easily out of a current account into a savings product.

We therefore give our money to banks for free (in current accounts) or very cheaply (in savings accounts). If a bank wanted to get money from anywhere else – from private investors, from pension funds, from another bank – it would probably have to pay a good deal more for it than it pays to the retail customers who walk through the door of the bank branch and hand over their money willingly. As an illustrative example, banks can currently get money from the Bank of England itself at 0.25%, yet the lowest rate on an instant access product, at the time of writing, is 0.01%. This is important for one reason only: banks use the money we give them to lend. They manufacture loans out of the raw material that we hand over for very nearly nothing. No other manufacturing industry is so efficient in the way it sources the raw material required to make the products it sells for a profit.

Lending: credit creation – the alchemy of banking

Banks are 'credit creators'. They manufacture value in the form of loans by making judgements about timing. The simple judgement banks are making every day is that of all the billions they hold in deposit funds, the majority of depositors will not demand instant withdrawal of all of their funds at any single point in time. While they must keep enough money handy to repay anyone wishing to withdraw their deposits in full, and enough to clear any payment instructions made by their customers, the rest of the deposits are available to lend.

This principle of credit creation is central to capitalism in its broadest sense as it involves society pooling its available money ('capital') using banks so they can provide funding for investment. Individuals save their hard-earned pounds. Banks accumulate those pounds and centralize the underwriting of credit risk – a specialized task. Businesses then borrow from banks to invest in things like machines, people, and stock to produce more output. Sometimes people borrow from banks in order to have the cash to buy that output – and so the cycle continues as growth is continually fuelled by an expansion of credit.

Here's a simple example. Let's say that 10,000 customers all have instant access savings accounts, each containing £1,000. That's £10m sitting there for a rainy day. The bank pays annual interest of 0.5% on the deposits, so £50,000 per annum. Then – and here's the magic of banking – the bank says: "the probability of all 10,000 people wanting all of their money back at the same time is so low as to be basically impossible." So, it takes £8m of that £10m and lends it out at, let's say, 5%. After one year, the bank has made £400,000 in interest from money that was just sitting there. Take off the £50,000 interest it had to pay to 'rent' the deposits and the bank has made an income of £350,000.

What has happened in this (very simplified) example is that the bank has created a 'balance sheet'. There is only £10m of 'real' money, in the form of cash deposited by the original depositors, yet the bank has created an additional £8m of lending into the economy. This can be represented as a 'balance sheet', as seen in Table 1.

Table 1

Assets (Money owed back to the bank, and/or hard cash)		**Liabilities** (Money the bank owes to its customers)	
Loan Accounts	£8m	Deposit Accounts	£10m
Cash in Bank	£2m		
TOTAL ASSETS	**£10m**	**TOTAL LIABILITIES**	**£10m**

This credit creation engine is at the heart of all banks and what drives the lion's share of their income. As time goes on they learn more about how long, on average, different kinds of deposits stick around for before they are withdrawn. With this expanding knowledge of deposit durations, the banks can make ever finer judgements about what proportion of any given deposit they must retain and therefore maximize their lending. Using the example above, a bank might decide that, based on all of its experience, it could actually lend out £9m and only keep £1m back to pay customers who wanted their money. That would be worth an extra £50,000 of income, just by making a slightly riskier judgement about the proportions of cash to lend versus retain.

Payments: pumping money around the system

Deposits and lending are pretty easy to understand because they are slow moving. Our salaries are deposited into an account each month, maybe we set up a regular savings deposit each month too. Once in the savings account the money sits there until we need it. A loan is even slower moving – once a loan is made it will take months or years to pay down.

Payments though are faster moving and much more varied. In the UK alone there are already many different methods of making payments, with innovative companies trying to add to this number all the time. Banks sit at the end of all the payment systems, ultimately delivering value to where it has been instructed to go.

There are many ways of paying for things in the UK – you could use your debit card or credit card for everyday purchases, for example. You might also make a bank transfer via standing order or faster payment. If you wanted to pay someone overseas you might instruct your bank to make a SEPA[1] payment to Europe or a SWIFT[2] payment further afield. If you were putting down a deposit for a new house you'd probably move the money over to your solicitor via a CHAPS[3] payment. And if you wanted a really 'retro' payment experience you might even write a cheque or withdraw your money from the bank and pay in cash.

All of these different methods of payment ultimately do the same thing – they instruct your bank to take some money out of one of your accounts and send it somewhere else. The different types of payment generate different message types that travel via different routes to reach the destination bank and result in the value transfer or 'settlement' over different timeframes, with different levels of certainty of execution.

Essentially, banks aggregate payments and net them off against each other. As a simplified example: Customer 1 who banks with Bank A pays £10 to Customer 2 at Bank B. Then Bank A owes Bank B £10. Bank A will reduce (debit) the balance of Customer 1's account and Bank B will increase (credit) the balance of Customer 2's account. If you then have Customer 3 and 4 making a transaction of £7.50 back the other way then the net exposure looks like Table 2.

---

[1]   Single European Payment Area – this is the new standard (launched 2016) for electronic payments made within the EU.

[2]   Society for Worldwide Interbank Financial Telecommunication – this is the old standard for all international payments and remains the standard for non-EU payments.

[3]   Clearing House Automated Payment System – CHAPS is the UK payment system for high value payments. It is the only system that *guarantees* real time value for each payment instruction.

Table 2

Transaction	Bank A	Bank B
Customer 1 pays £10 to Customer 2	–£10.00	
Customer 2 receives the funds		+£10.00
Customer 3 pays £7.50 to Customer 4		–£7.50
Customer 4 receives the funds	+£7.50	
TOTAL	**–£2.50**	**£2.50**

In this example four customer balances have been updated, but the two banks settle just once through netting the funds. Netting all the transactions means that Bank A owes Bank B £2.50 in real value. This netting can happen at the end of day, or more usually now, at multiple points during the day and with an industry aspiration for all payment types to settle in real time.

The various different forms of pipework through which all payments flow tend to be owned and managed by companies that are either private or consortia of several large banks. They are dedicated to ensuring that the networks remain secure and functioning at all times. Banks are responsible for following the rules associated with each payment network since it is only through collective adherence to the prescribed standards that the integrity and efficiency of the overall payments system can be maintained. If a single bank accidentally creates errors, loses transactions, delays payment message traffic, or whatever, the whole system starts to creak as reconciliations (settling up) go out of line.

Collectively, payment systems are like the circulatory system within a human body. There are regular pulses that push money around the system. If the money flow stops, or starts to pool in one place, then it creates problems very quickly, just as a thrombosis would in an artery. There are major arteries that transmit vast quantities of payments and there are much smaller capillary networks that drive payments through specific channels for specific purposes.

Banks have to understand all of this complexity and manage vast technology estates to ensure that their systems are hugely resilient, secure, and reliable. Banks also have to *reconcile* every transaction that crosses their systems to ensure that every single customer can look at their account and see an accurate reflection of all of the payment movements across their accounts.

Managing risk

Hopefully all that detail on *what banks do* wasn't too heavy going. The point we're trying to make is that while these high-level concepts are quite simple and make banking what it is, making them happen in reality is quite complex. Now we turn to *how banks work*. Again, it's conceptually quite easy to understand but the surface simplicity masks many layers of complexity beneath. We aim to give a very brief and very simple view of how banks operate as we think this is important context that helps to explain why even banks that work 'well' as banks may very well not work so well for customers. The two mainsprings of bank operations are the management of 'liquidity' and 'capital'. If a bank gets either of these wrong then the impact on customers can be very significant, and the consequences for the bank can be potentially serious too.

Liquidity

The obvious theoretical weakness in the deposit-funded lending model described above is that a bank can misjudge how much lending it can safely create from its deposits. The primary risk is that the bank lends out too much so that when the depositors want to withdraw their money the bank does not have enough funds available. In short, the risk is that the bank temporarily runs out of money.

Running out of money is *temporary* because the value is still there in the form of loans, but the bank cannot realize this value instantly to fund deposit withdrawals. Instead it must wait until enough loans are repaid to refund the depositors. If this happens the bank is technically insolvent – it cannot meet valid payment demands made to it. Once this happens the bank fails as it cannot survive losing the trust of its customers and other banks. For the system to work, customers and banks must have total confidence in the bank's ability to repay them on demand. This ultimately (and again in simplified terms) is what went wrong at Northern Rock. Too many customers wanted their deposits back at once. Northern Rock had plenty of loan assets and, given time, would have been able to repay customers in full. But at a given point in time it had insufficient cash to make full repayments to all those demanding it.

The amount of cash a bank is required to have on hand at any given time to meet its immediate liabilities is called 'liquidity'. There is – nowadays – detailed and voluminous regulation attached to how banks manage their liquidity so as to avoid failure. It is the primary risk that all banks manage and one that occupies a not inconsiderable amount of senior management time.

A helpful way to think about liquidity is to imagine an upside-down pyramid. The very narrow base of the pyramid is physical cash – notes and coins. This is the most liquid form of value in any economy as it can be instantly exchanged for goods and services or other forms of value. At the other end of the scale are things like mortgage loans where the bank will only have received back its original loan amount in full after many years. The existence of the mortgage is an 'asset' i.e. it has real value to the bank as the bank is contractually owed that money. But, for example, if the bank has £250,000 of instant access deposits only, and it uses them to lend out one £250,000 mortgage for 25 years then it is not managing liquidity sensibly at all. There is in essence no liquidity pyramid as the bank has converted *all* the depositors' liquid cash into a 25-year loan. One saver attempting to withdraw a single £1 the day after the loan was made would technically break the bank as all £250,000 is tied up in a mortgage that won't be repaid for many years.

To stop banks doing silly things like the example above, the government and the Bank of England impose detailed regulations which govern the dimensions of each bank's liquidity pyramid, by establishing what proportion of each deposit a bank is allowed to transform into other less liquid assets like loans. The regulations also require each bank to understand in detail all of the payment flows through its business and to prepare plans to cover scenarios of varying levels of liquidity 'stress' – moderate through to severe stresses from 30 through to 90 days. The purpose of these regulations is, first, to set a hard limit on what proportion of deposits banks can lend out and, second, to ensure that in a stress event – e.g. many more depositors than normal all ask for their money back at once – then the bank is well prepared and can meet the increased demand through a predetermined liquidity management plan. Assuming that the levels of liquidity required by the regulations are suitably conservative, a bank could arguably run its business without risk of failure, turning the maximum allowed proportion of its deposits into loans and retaining the rest as cash. In other words, liquidity regulation is a *preventative* measure. If banks follow the rules and there aren't too many surprises then things should work out fine.

While banks are generally very attentive to following the rules (really!) we are just coming to the end of a decade of persistent surprises for the banking industry, from the 2008 crisis onwards. Banks were following the rules on liquidity, such as they were, but in a world where all banks are to a greater or lesser extent dependent on each other, a contagion event, or an 'externality' as some economists term it, where fear spreads like a virus can result in everyone asking for their money back at once.

This highly unusual set of circumstances created a cascading series of liquidity events in 2007 and 2008 that ultimately resulted in the fall of Lehman Brothers, Northern Rock, and many other financial services businesses. While events of this nature are exceptionally rare, they can happen. The financial crisis has resulted directly in new, and significantly more stringent, liquidity regulations which require banks to hold *more* liquidity than before, i.e. the proportion of deposits that banks can use to lend out has fallen as regulators force banks to be more conservative. This in turn has made banks less profitable, but theoretically more safe, than before. This is a crucial point: well-intentioned regulation is acting as a structural drag on profitability, which in turn is driving some increased pressure into product teams to make more money out of their customers.

Capital

The section above included a simple example of breaking a bank through poor management of liquidity risk. The bank turned £250,000 of instant access deposits into one £250,000 mortgage for 25 years, and then failed when one saver attempted to withdraw £1 the day after the loan was made. In this example though, we assumed that the loan would be repaid. So the only problem was timing. In reality, not all borrowers repay their loans. So this is another source of risk for the bank to manage – it's called *credit risk*.

In the example above it's equally possible to break the bank through an absolute shortage of money, not just a problem with timing. Let's assume that all the depositors were happy to leave their money untouched for 25 years: if the loan repaid everything would be fine. The bank would have been exposed to massive liquidity risk for 25 years running, but through sheer good fortune it survives. However, if the single mortgage borrower fails to repay his loan the bank has the same problem again – it no longer has the right amount of money to repay its depositors. In this case the bank doesn't have a timing problem, it has an absolute lack of money problem as the money will *never* be recovered, so while the risk is different, the outcome is the same: the bank fails.

An unfortunate truth though is that credit losses are a natural occurrence in the business of lending money. Broad fluctuations in the economy, borrowers experiencing one of the 'three Ds' (divorce, disease, death) – all of these are likely to cause some shortfall in expected repayments. But banks cannot avoid lending; it's a key part of their business model, so how do they manage credit risk to avoid a critical failure? The most common answer is that they use some of their *own* money to fill up any gaps created by borrowers failing to repay.

In very simple terms, a bank can finance its operations and its lending either through deposits (or other forms of borrowed money) or with its own money, also known as 'capital'. Capital is defined as the value of the bank's assets minus its liabilities. Assets are the loans the bank has made and the bank's own cash. Liabilities are the customers' deposits placed with the bank, and the money the bank owes to anyone else (e.g. other banks via the payment systems). If all borrowers repaid their loans, and the bank returned all deposits to customers then whatever money left over would be 'capital'.

Where can a bank get money from other than deposits, then? There are a number of answers to this, but for the purposes of this book we'll stick with the very simplest one: from investors. Anyone can buy shares in companies. In return for an investment in a company you are entitled to a share of that company's profits (in the form of a 'dividend') and you also hope that the value of your share in the company will rise over time. People invest in banks for the same reasons – they hope to gain income from dividends as the banks make profits over time, and they hope the banks grow and get more profitable so they increase in value as companies. If so, the shares themselves will increase in value over time. The amount of money a bank has received in return for shares is called 'capital'. This capital can be used to absorb credit losses if loans are not repaid – it can act as a buffer to keep a bank running even when times are tough.

During times of economic stress like a major recession, many individuals and businesses will struggle to repay their loans and bank losses will rise. Banks therefore need a strong capital base to ensure they can absorb these losses and continue to operate. In the simple balance sheet example we looked at earlier there is no capital to absorb losses (Table 3).

Table 3

Assets (£s owed to the bank and/or cash)		Liabilities (£s the bank owes to its customers)	
Loan Accounts	£8m	Deposit Accounts	£10m
Cash in Bank	£2m		
TOTAL ASSETS	**£10m**	**TOTAL LIABILITIES**	**£10m**

If the loans go bad, then depositors will not get their money back. The bank would fail instantly. Thankfully this is not a realistic scenario!

A more typical scenario is that the bank will make some losses and absorb them using its own money (i.e. capital). Assuming the bank has enough capital, the bank will not fail. The more a bank can finance itself through capital, as opposed to customer deposits, the safer it is. If credit losses eat up capital then what happens ultimately is that the shareholders in the bank take the loss. Their share of the bank is worth less as some of that value has gone towards absorbing the credit losses on loans. Banks' share prices fluctuate and shareholders know the risks they are running – a bank will generate unhappy shareholders by making lots of credit losses, but it will not necessarily fail. However, if the bank's losses cause a liquidity issue that stops it repaying deposits to customers then it will definitely fail – as we explained above.

A revised balance sheet example is given below to demonstrate this effect. The bank starts off the same as before, but with £5m of capital added into the balance sheet (Table 4).

Table 4

Assets		Liabilities	
Loan Accounts	£8m	Deposit Accounts (ordinary customers)	£10m
Cash in Bank (relating to deposits)	£2m		
Cash in Bank (relating to capital)	£5m	Capital (shareholders in the bank)	£5m
TOTAL ASSETS	**£15m**	**TOTAL LIABILITIES**	**£15m**

Let's say the bank earns no interest on its loans, and instead makes a £2.5m loss. This would mean that it would only get back £5.5m of the £8m of loans. The bank now has a big problem. On the asset side of the balance sheet it now only has £12.5m (£5.5m of loans, £7m of cash), but it owes £15m on the liability side of the balance sheet (Table 5).

Table 5

Assets		Liabilities	
Loan Accounts	~~£8m~~ £5.5m	Deposit Accounts	£10m
Cash in Bank (relating to deposits)	£2m		
Cash in Bank (relating to capital)	£5m	Capital	£5m
TOTAL ASSETS	~~£15m~~ £12.5m	**TOTAL LIABILITIES**	£15m

But by using some of the capital it is possible to repay the depositors their £10m in full. The bank remains solvent because it has repaid its depositors on demand. However, to accommodate this the value of the shareholders' capital must fall from £5m to £2.5m to keep the balance sheet balanced. The final picture looks like Table 6.

Table 6

Assets		Liabilities	
Loan Accounts	£5.5m	Deposit Accounts	£10m
Cash in Bank (relating to deposits)	~~£2m~~ £4.5m		
Cash in Bank (relating to capital)	~~£5m~~ £2.5m	Capital	~~£5m~~ £2.5m
TOTAL ASSETS	**£12.5m**	**TOTAL LIABILITIES**	~~£15m~~ **£12.5m**

A bank losing money on its loan book is *always* a bad thing for the bank. But providing those losses can be absorbed by its capital base the bank will survive to fight another day, hopefully having learned a lesson about how to make more prudent loans in future. Certainly the shareholders will be reading that lesson out very loudly to the bank's senior management team!

As with liquidity, the government and the Bank of England impose a range of regulations to ensure that all banks *must* hold an appropriate level of capital to absorb reasonably foreseeable credit losses. Essentially, regulators set simple ratios between the amount of capital a bank has on its balance sheet and the amount of loans it can create. For example, if the required ratio of capital to lending is

4.5% then for every £1m loan that a bank wants to lend, it must hold £45,000 in capital. The intention of the regulation is to prevent banks from lending too much and getting into a position where – if things go wrong in the economy and losses rise – the losses are so great as to break the bank.

Just as the financial crisis resulted in tightening liquidity rules, the same has occurred with capital rules. Banks are being told to hold *more* capital than before. i.e. the proportion of capital that banks must hold against their loans has increased. Capital from shareholders is much more expensive than deposit funding from customers though, as the shareholders face risks that depositors do not. If a bank loses money, the shareholders get hit first, but the depositors are protected. Retail deposits are also insured by the government up to £85,000, whereas shareholders are not. As we saw above, the security that depositors get from banks means that they do not get much (if any) interest on their deposits. However, shareholders expect a higher return, therefore this form of funding is more expensive for the bank. If capital has to make up a greater proportion of all lending then the bank's profits must fall as the cost of funding the loans increases. Again then, well-intentioned regulation is negatively impacting profitability. While undoubtedly the regulations are making banks safer overall, the unintended consequence is that the pressure on profitability inevitably translates into pressure in product teams to make more money out of their customers.

Scale vs simplicity

Banking is an extremely *simple* industry – banks sell the concept of security to customers in order to obtain their money (as deposits) very cheaply, then make profit by selling that money to other customers (as loans). Because banking is, at heart, a simple business, customers shouldn't be afraid of it, shouldn't shy away from engaging with it, and should hold out for better deals. More on this in later chapters.

Second, in practical terms, though, making a bank work is actually very *complex*. We've given potted explanations of deposits, lending, payments, and the management of liquidity and capital. For the sake of simplicity though, we've missed out things like interest-rate risk, currency risk, and a host of other things that banks have to manage.

The crucial point is that because banking is so complicated it has become necessary for banks to become very large in order to manage this complexity. Banking has, in short, become a *scale* business. Being a small bank doesn't really work – you need to be big enough to support a balance sheet that is sufficiently resilient to economic shocks and also big enough to pay for the right people, systems, and controls to manage the vast complexity involved in being a highly regulated bank.

The first point is really important. Even if you don't buy all of the arguments contained in this book, or disagree with our analysis of banking, we would really, really, like you to walk away believing that banks should exist to serve their customers. In particular, they need and must do three simple things well: hold deposits, offer loans, and run payments. If your bank doesn't do this very well then you should feel empowered to hold your bank to account and ultimately switch to a new bank that does.

The second point supports our argument that there's something unique about the very nature of banks and banking in the UK that precludes good customer service and requires scale. Banks need to be big to be successful and this is why just a handful dominate the market.

These days, banks are not just managing the liquidity risk associated with transforming simple deposits into simple loans. There are multiple other cash flows to account for. For example, the banks will make interest from the loans they provide to their customers. That's incoming cash to the bank that could be used to cover some expected deposit outflows. There are different types of payment transaction, all with different clearing cycles. A payment keyed online will clear within minutes (usually), a cheque may take days. A bank may choose to add other sources of liquidity other than customer deposits – for example, it may borrow in its own name from other banks and then lend those funds out to customers too. At any given point all the banks owe each other money as their underlying customers are all making and receiving payments. The banks must net these millions of transactions out and settle them accordingly. Managing the liquidity risks of all of these flows is a secondary task. The primary task is *understanding* what all these flows are in the first place and how they will shift over time.

Our examples above are only frozen snapshots of (very simplified) balance sheets at given points in time. The real risk in banking comes when you run the clock forward in real life – all of the ins and outs on even a single customer's deposits, loans, and payment flows start to multiply over the days, months, and years. If you then scale the example from one customer to millions of customers you can see how even the three simple elements of deposits, loans, and payments can become vastly complex to manage.

This management requires investment in people, systems, and regulatory governance – all of which is expensive.

All banks are required to achieve the same minimum standard of control and compliance. Therefore, the larger the bank is, the smaller the proportion of its cost base will go on unavoidable fixed costs. A small bank would have much less left over to spend on discretionary projects like investment to fund new growth or improvements to the customer experience.

Besides fixed costs, there is another factor that drives banks to becoming large in scale, that is the fact that it is their best defence against liquidity issues or capital adequacy shortfalls. The bigger a bank is, and the more distributed its base of deposits and spread of assets, the less likely that any single event will knock it over.

Exaggerating to make the point: imagine a small bank that specializes intently, let's say, on aircraft loans to multinational airlines which it funds through deposits from large oil companies. Any wobble in the airline or oil industries (which are in fact closely connected) would be likely to spell disaster for the bank. Compare this to a very large bank that takes deposits from retail customers, small businesses, and the odd large company. It lends to all of the same customers in the form of mortgages, credit cards, overdrafts, business loans, and so on. Localized problems among its customers in a particular town (e.g. large redundancies from the primary local employer) or industry (e.g. metal working) are unlikely to bring down the bank, as its risk is widely spread across many areas.

Now imagine what level of *service* the specialist bank provides to its airline clients. That bank will have built expertise in the aviation industry, its loan officers will have deep experience of the risks involved and will have seen many different business cases. They will be able to add value to the clients through sharing that specialist knowledge – ultimately to the benefit of both the bank and its clients.

Conversely, the larger bank has made a virtue of generalization – it is now more resilient as its risk is spread, but so is its attention. The needs of its customers are more diverse, the likelihood of its staff providing specialised expertise is much less.

Here is the first and most important inherent tension in banking, then: *scale* reduces risk, but it also makes it more challenging to deliver good customer service. Specialist knowledge and value-adding customer service can therefore give way to a lowest-common-denominator approach to banking service.

Remembering the customer

So how do big companies avoid getting too remote from their customers? There are lots of books on this, lots of academic studies, too, and there are probably hundreds of people employed right now in jobs with titles like Customer Experience Manager that are theoretically supposed to achieve this according to some measurable outcome or other. Boiling that ocean down a bit we think that unless a large company has one or more of the following it is very likely to turn in on itself and forget its customers:

- sustained, intense competition that forces it to innovate and focus on retaining existing customers and beating competitors to win new ones;
- a really differentiated product offering that makes it near-unique versus its competition; and
- a really strong, deeply embedded culture that has customer experience and customer service at its heart.

Without one or more of these things, large companies tend to get distracted, spending time worrying about a corporate agenda of regulatory compliance or shareholder returns. They become internally focused – falling into the trap of ignoring the ultimate reason for their existence and the point of the entire enterprise: the customer.

This is unquestionably true when it comes to the UK banking market – a toxic environment in which great cultures, differentiated products, and sustained competition have been either absent or struggle to survive.

The banking oligopoly: full of big beasts trampling competition and customers alike

The banking market is absolutely dominated by a handful of banks. It doesn't really matter which particular measure one picks: whether it's share of the current account market, size of deposit balances, size of loan balances, and so on. As we've seen, in the UK, the biggest five banks account for an astonishing 85% of all personal and business current accounts. As we mentioned earlier, there's a technical term for this sort of thing: oligopoly. An oligopoly is a market structure in which a small number of firms hold the large majority of market share. Oligopolies are usually also characterized by some or all of the following conditions: entry to the industry is restricted; products are all very similar; and customer demand is not very responsive to changes in price. The fact is that the UK banking market meets every one of these conditions. Let's take a look at why that is likely to lead to poor customer service.

High barriers to entry

If you want to be a retailer in the UK (a nation of shopkeepers, once upon a time) then all you really need is stock to sell – satchels, party hats, whatever. Advertising could be by word of mouth, the 'shop' could be your front room your 'shop window' a website created free of charge using an online tool, your sales ledger and accounting system could be a notepad and two pens (one black, one red). There isn't much regulation governing what you're doing, little in the way of infrastructure required, and you can get going very quickly and cheaply. That is not to belittle the idea of starting a business, it is always very hard work, but compare the shopkeeper example to what must be done to start a bank…

If you want to start up a bank you have to get a licence from the PRA. The PRA is part of the Bank of England and its job is to ensure that banks and building societies operate safely and compete effectively. On 20 January 2016 it created the "New Bank Start-Up Unit" to assist such ventures. The purpose of the unit is to make starting a bank *easier*. Before the unit existed the whole process was less defined, less well managed, and much, much harder to complete. Now, however, there are two defined ways of starting a bank: the 'fully authorized upfront' route whereby everything is ready before you open the doors to customers; or 'mobilization route' where it's more of a rolling start.

Table 7 shows what a new bank must have in place to get authority from the PRA to operate. If the mobilization route is chosen, then only a very limited amount of business can be conducted initially on a test basis. Only by completing the steps to get to 'fully operational' authorization can a new bank obtain full permission to start trading normally.

Table 7

Assessment area	Fully operational at authorization	Mobilization route authorization
Business plan/viability	Fully developed	Fully developed
Financial resources Sources of funding Internal Capital Adequacy Assessment Process Internal Liquidity Adequacy Assessment Process	Fully developed	Fully developed
Corporate governance Structure Board Senior management	Fully developed Substantially in place All key senior management identified	High-level structure Key 'guiding minds' in place with senior roles critical to mobilization identified and ready to be recruited
Customer journey including details of products, pricing, and on-boarding arrangements	Fully developed	Near final
Recovery Plan	Fully developed	Draft
Business Continuity Plan	Fully developed	Draft
Risk management and control structures	Fully developed	High-level outline
IT infrastructure and systems	Fully developed	High-level outline
Material outsourcing arrangements	Fully developed	High-level outline
Policies and procedures	Fully developed	Not required but development should be planned
Mobilization plan	n/a	Fully developed and signed off by the board

Just employing enough highly skilled, credible senior bankers to prepare all the above would be very expensive – running into the millions of pounds. You'd be paying them for at least one to two years before you had a banking licence and could open the doors to your first customer.

In addition to that you'd have to raise the initial shareholder funds required to capitalize the bank. Another several million pounds would likely be required as a minimum. In order to offer *only* a current account, you would need to have built or bought systems capable of recording and transacting all the major UK payment types, including interfaces with the debit card, faster payment, and cheque systems as well as the Bank of England. Those systems would have to be sufficiently well tested, scalable, and robust to pass regulator inspection and cope with the exacting standards of the settlement banks and central clearing infrastructure. Running it all on a server in the corner of the office would not cut the mustard.

For anyone to know about your bank you'd also need to create a brand and do some marketing – a website would probably be a prerequisite. To be a serious contender you'd also need a good quality online banking service for customers and probably a mobile banking app too. This is only the very tip of the iceberg of what is *required* to offer a compelling current account proposition today.

Any new bank is also likely to be a target for fraudsters who will target newer, inexperienced banks to test their security systems. Small banks cannot absorb substantial fraud losses as easily as a big bank that is already making a profit, so until the bank has substantial scale, its investors must be prepared to cover fraud costs too.

Anyone starting a bank in the UK therefore needs tens of millions of pounds, a great relationship with the regulators, some highly skilled senior bankers and a massive amount of positive energy and perseverance to see it all through. There cannot be many industries on earth where the barriers to entry are quite so high. If competition is required to keep large companies focused on their customers, then clearly high barriers to entry are dangerous as they discourage competition.

There is a further sting in the tail to the high barriers to entry with regards to UK banking. To risk a substantial quantity of start-up capital, investors expect a substantial return. Sinking tens (or even hundreds) of millions of pounds into a bank requires that bank to grow a balance sheet of many hundreds of millions, or more likely billions, in order to justify the return on investment.

So even a start-up competitor needs to achieve substantial scale as a matter of strategic necessity. In the unlikely event that a new start competitor manages to overcome the barriers to entry and win a substantial market share it runs the very real risk of becoming part of the problem and extending the oligopoly. In other words, the lack of material competition becomes self-perpetuating as the only banks who have a realistic prospect of surviving long term are the bigger ones.

Products are all the same

We explore the nature of banking products more thoroughly in Part 2, including some of the frequent pricing practices that banks employ to extract value from customers. Suffice to say here, though, that banking products are not highly differentiated. Apple customers queue outside to be the first to get the newest model of the iPhone. When was the last time you saw customers queuing outside a bank so they could be first to open a new kind of deposit account? The very concept is absurd. Banking products, on the whole, all look, feel, and operate the same and the only queues one is likely to see arise because the big banks are not open at sensible times so people queue at opening time and lunch time to get in when it suits them.

If banks cannot compete through product design then what's left? Imagine there was no difference between Samsung's handsets and Apple's. The only differences left would be price and marketing. If the Samsung handset was 20% cheaper, all other things being equal, it would probably sell more than Apple's offering.

But if the price too was the same then marketing is really the only possible differentiator left. If Apple's marketing budget was ten times that of Samsung's then, arguably, more people would know about the Apple phone and more people would want it, so Apple would sell more than Samsung. Such a thought experiment feels a bit ludicrous in relation to smartphones because we all know that they have very different product features, operating systems, cost bases, marketing budgets, and prices.

This is pretty much exactly the case when it comes to banking products though. In some ways, this is not a bad thing – society needs its money to circulate efficiently, so a degree of commonality is required across the banks. Yet while there are many obvious upsides to standardising across enough areas of banking for it to work efficiently, the similarity of most banking products also creates downsides for customers. Companies operating in markets where products are highly differentiated (whether that's mobile phones, cars, or vacuum cleaners) *must* focus intently on what customers want. If they don't their rivals will take their market share.

Nokia is a good example of this. Nokia famously missed the significance of the emergence of smartphone technology and their products continued to be produced even though customer demand had shifted in a different direction. Apple, Samsung, and HTC, for example, were all beneficiaries of this error as they designed differentiated products that customers wanted more. Yet banking doesn't have this competitive 'threat' ensuring firms continue to innovate to deliver better and better products for customers. As we see in Part 2, this means that many banking products are poor and let customers down.

Price doesn't seem to matter much

It's not just the type of products banks sell – the inertia of customers is also a problem too. A key feature of oligopolistic markets is that customer demand is 'inelastic' – it doesn't respond quickly to changes in products or their price. When banks put up their fees and charges, few of us would take action against this, such as switching banks.

What this teaches banks is that they can get away with quite a lot before they start to lose customers – something we explore at length in Part 2. So, a key factor that should dissuade banks from profiteering at their customers' expense is missing – customers fail to respond to negative stimuli quickly so the balance of power between buyer and seller is lost. Much like the fabled frog slowly boiling in the pan, the banks are able to take a bit of extra profit here, and charge a higher fee there, and the poor customer, having missed the first cue to react, gradually succumbs to the negative environment.

Culture – the last defence

The complexity involved in delivering banking products and services drives banks towards scale. They have to be big to survive. The high costs of entry discourage competition and also ensure that any successful new entrant will ultimately have to become part of the oligopoly as well, so the problem of restricted competition is likely to be an endemic feature of the market. The largely undifferentiated product set and customer inertia further entrench the oligopoly. In the absence of the need (and to some extent the ability) to compete through product differentiation big banks are deprived of key external forces that might drive them to focus on customers. If the structure of the market isn't providing an external check to banks, then the only thing that is likely to drive a focus on delivering amazing customer service and value is an *internal* stimulus. For want of a better word we call that a bank's *culture*.

A cultural focus on – or even obsession with – customer service excellence isn't common in banking. It's not actually all that common in many companies. Culture is a hazy concept too – it defies precise definition – but we think of it as the organizational context in which each bank employee operates.

It starts with the executive leadership team all signing up to a clearly defined cultural ambition, and then reinforcing it every single day, through every single action, in the certain knowledge that everything they do either adds to the culture or weakens it a little. Bit by bit that culture has to be absorbed, embraced, and reinforced by every single employee within the organization to keep it alive and fresh. Employees need to believe in what they're doing and ensure their actions are aligned to the company's vision and values.

Done wrong, it can feel like a bit of a cult that overrides individual decision-making and accountability. Done well, it boosts the effect of every individual's best efforts by providing a constant, central reference point of best practice.

If the culture is inherently 'good' – built around providing great service to customers and a great environment for colleagues – then that must surely be better than an organization that is culturally focused on making money and cutting costs.

Let's take a simple example: imagine two different bank branches. One is a bit tatty – the carpet tiles are stained and lifting at the corners, there's a chipped wooden writing stand in one corner with a pen on a chain, and behind a bulletproof plastic screen sits a single bank employee. The other branch is clean, brightly lit, with a marble floor and hotel-reception style counter, there are piles of bank-branded pens you are free to take, there is no bulletproof plastic and there are four bank employees sitting waiting to serve customers.

The appearances of the respective branches are the combined result of many individual decisions around allocation of property maintenance budget, organization of works schedules, the setting of staff-to-customer ratios. In a rational organization, one would expect costs to be minimized to the greatest possible degree in order to maximize profits. In a market lacking competition, with minimal product differentiation and customer inertia, the bank might well conclude that the value in investing in its branches was minimal, and the outcome would be the tatty branch.

The individual decisions that lead to the tatty branch must be modified to produce the shiny branch. The decisions have to be influenced by something other than rational economic principles. This is where culture comes in. Imagine if everyone making a decision in the bank was trained from their first day, and reminded every day thereafter, that the purpose of the bank was to supply great customer service. A sense of personal responsibility for that mission was drummed in to all bank employees at every turn. Every decision from the materials used in the design of new branches, through to the availability of free pens would then be informed by that all-pervading culture. The director of the branch network might be told by the executive team to cut the staff-to-customer ratio to save cost. In the tatty bank, he might just roll over and agree. In the shiny bank, he might put up a fight – and the culture would dictate that the executive team would listen carefully and try to find ways to retain the organizational commitment to great customer service as embodied in a high staff-to-customer ratio. Ultimately, they might still reduce the ratio, but at the very least their decision-making would include cultural considerations as well as economic ones.

What the management team of the tatty branch are implicitly saying to both their colleagues and their customers is that they do not care enough about customer service to make the branch a welcoming place of business. The management team of the brighter branch are stating that it's important to them to create a context in which both colleagues and customers feel welcome. All of that context comes to an apex at the point of the interaction between branch colleagues and customers. In this example, the colleagues of the shiny branch have a much higher chance of smiling, greeting the customer warmly, and initiating a great interaction, than the colleagues in the tatty branch. Multiplying those interactions up many thousands of times across many branches reinforces the culture through repetition and communication.

Unfortunately for UK banks, their cultures aren't in great shape. The legacies of the credit crunch and a series of mis-selling scandals continue to linger; the market remains in thrall to low interest rates that make it very difficult for banks to make money and pay staff as well as they have done historically; and every newspaper in the country continues to carry negative stories about big, greedy banks. Management teams are tasked with cutting costs, restructuring balance sheets, and shrinking branch estates with little time left to consider innovation and growth opportunities. With that backdrop is it any wonder that big banks' senior management teams are struggling to find the energy to reset bank culture and continually reinforce it through every layer of their organization until it becomes self-sustaining? Is it any wonder that employees at these banks are struggling to deliver great service when their working environment is characterised by redundancies, branch closures and near-daily headlines criticising their employer?

Given the scale of the challenges facing the larger, older banks this is a huge task for any leadership team. It would be a truly exceptional set of leaders who were able to come to work every day, read the various internal tales of woe on spiralling cost, falling income, more fines, more new regulation, and increasing competition and then still smile, welcome their colleagues into the office, set a clear expectation around customer service excellence, and go on to create the conditions to deliver it.

Far easier to believe is the scenario where even the strongest leaders gradually succumb to senior management and shareholder pressure to drive better financial returns for the business, to the temptation of generous incentive plans, to take advantage of the lack of competition in the market. It is a short step from here to signing off the next product like PPI.

Regulation and the perils of unintended consequences

Thus far, all of the potential sins that banks might commit could be summarized as sins of omission – distracted by one thing or another, and not held in check by market forces, they *forget* about the customer. There are however a couple of examples of forces that actually make it more likely that banks will *deliberately* act contrary to the interests of customers. Perversely, both are ultimately driven from the same source – the one thing that is supposed to really help – regulation.

As we saw from our crash course in bank capital, the more capital a bank has the safer it is. But it's not quite that simple unfortunately. Bank capital is a discretionary investment; no bank is guaranteed to find shareholders willing to invest either upfront or to continue to top up capital as required – it must convince those investors of the value of that investment.

A bank's shareholders invest in the bank to make a return. That return comes in the form of the profit the bank makes, distributed back to shareholders as dividends. If a bank must hold more capital, then, the return on capital from a given level of profit must fall. A very simple example is shown in Table 8.

Table 8

	Measure	Scenario 1 (e.g. in 2002)	Scenario 2 (e.g. in 2002)
A	Profit	£10m	£10m
B	Required Capital	£100m	£150m
C	Return on Capital (i.e. A divided by B)	10.00%	6.67%

If regulation depresses the return on capital available to shareholders of banks too far they will simply invest their capital somewhere else. Capital will move away from banks and into, for example, non-bank lenders or other industries entirely.

If banks cannot raise enough capital then they must curtail their lending – because capital regulation directly relates the amount of lending to the amount of capital banks hold. Curtailing lending means less funding into the economy. So, an increase in bank capital requirements may well result in a restriction in the availability of credit which in turn may result in falling levels of investment in productive capacity, goods and services and, ultimately, lower growth.

Capital requirements on UK retail banks have grown materially since the 2008–2009 global recession. Over the same time frame, the regulators have hammered the banks with billions in fines. The respective rationales for both the additional capital requirements and the fines are easy to understand. Greater capital buffers are a prudent defence against shocks like those which occurred in 2008 and a useful lesson to gung-ho bank executives that they need to prioritize a safer form of banking. Persistent malpractice by the banks – which led directly to customer detriment – is obviously worthy of sanction in the form of fines.

The timing of the two things together though is unfortunate as the income uncertainty produced by regulatory mega fines is making banks a uniquely *unattractive* opportunity for potential investors just at the point regulators are also requiring banks to hold more capital.

If banks do not have enough capital then they run the risk of plunging into something of a vicious circle. The regulator requires them to hold a given level of capital. If a bank is perceived to be struggling to raise this capital, then its share price is likely to fall. The reduction in share price means a reduction in the value of the capital the bank already has. As the value of the bank's existing capital is directly related to the amount it can lend, the lower the capital value falls the less the bank can lend out. The less it can lend, the less interest it can earn – meaning that its ability to earn more profit which it could retain to boost its capital (rather than distribute to shareholders) is reduced. As the problems mount, potential capital providers demand higher returns for their investment – so the bank's cost of capital increases leading to a further restriction on profitability.

Given the squeeze on profitability the banks have only two choices – they can cut costs or they can find a way to boost income. Cutting costs is very obviously detrimental to customer service and unpopular. Whether it's closing branches or reducing staff-to-customer ratios, less money being spent on the delivery of the bank's products and services means more complaints and bad newspaper headlines. More insidiously, lower budgets for internal teams like IT, quality assurance, and risk management make it more likely that banks will run too much risk with controls spread too thinly. This will then result in poor customer outcomes in the form of breakdowns of key infrastructure (such as ATM networks).

Clearly management teams don't want to make their staff redundant or take difficult decisions around cost reduction if they can possibly avoid it. So, the other way out is to boost income. If the origin of the problem is capital constraints, then more lending cannot be the answer. There is only one other way for banks to turn and that is towards increasing the income they obtain from fees and charges.

Fees and charges are catnip for banks as they do not consume capital. Every £1 a bank lends must be matched by a proportion of bank capital dictated by the regulations. By contrast, each and every fee a bank receives from a customer is simply raw income.

Clearly there's a cost to the bank for providing the service for which the fee is charged, but the marginal cost of each of these tends to be very, very low. For example, most small business customers pay for their payments. The marginal cost to the bank of making more payments is near-zero, but if the bank charges each business customer 20p per payment then from a bank's perspective this is fantastic income.

If banks can drive fee income then it is an ideal way to make more profit in a capital-efficient manner, ultimately refloating capital reserves through natural trading rather than raising capital externally which tends to be expensive.

So, the increase in regulatory capital requirements creates a very obvious incentive to drive fee income hard.

No one minds paying a fair price for a product that they need or want and which subsequently performs as expected. However, as we've seen above, banks are not well geared to providing good products or services that work well, and they also face inelastic demand – customers who are *insensitive* to price.

It is not hard to see how this context produces unfavourable customer outcomes. Of course, there are both general and specific regulatory conditions covering what can and can't be charged for and also around what information must be given about charges to the customer. But here's the thing – imagine you're a bank executive and you're being told to deliver more income, and what's more your own personal compensation is tied to this. If you don't deliver you're out of a job, your lifestyle will suffer, and your family will experience a downturn in their fortunes. You haven't got enough capital to drive more lending so you need to push fees and charges harder. What kind of interpretation of the rules are you going to make? Will you be super-prudent or will you seek to push the rules as far as they'll bend without breaking? At this point the only thing that will determine the outcome is the leadership and culture around you – which as we explored above has proven in the past to be an insufficient brake on bad behaviour.

The retail banking dilemma

UK banking is clearly in a particular bind at present. Faced with increasing capital requirements the banks must raise more capital. Access to capital is becoming harder and more expensive as investors are cautious around a scandal-hit market where real growth is minimal. Bad debts left over from the 2008 crisis and legacy regulatory fines continue to impact banks' costs and returns. Low interest rates have depressed net interest margins.

All of these factors are driving banks to look for other ways to boost income. Inevitably that is leading them to focus on fees, charges, and – potentially – more poor products. With the absence of strong, company-wide, customer-focused corporate cultures, banks have little hope of delivering great service and value-for-money products any time soon.

The situation is exacerbated by the structure of the banking market as it appears today. The standard characteristics of oligopolies – high barriers to entry, homogeneous products, and inelastic demand – all reduce the probability of good customer outcomes as meaningful, disruptive competition and product innovation is frustrated.

The good news is that we think that things are beginning to change and corners are in the process of being turned. The flood of banking scandals seems to have slowed to a trickle, senior management teams are acutely aware of the need to reform, the regulatory attitudes are moving in the right direction. It's not happening fast enough though and the main reason for this, in a word, is *cost*.

CHAPTER SUMMARY

- Retail banks provide three things:
  - Places to safely deposit our money.
  - Loans to allow us to purchase large items or help manage cash flow.
  - Access to payment infrastructure so we can use our money.

- What makes a bank a bank is the ability to gather deposits. Lending-only and payment-only businesses are subject to less regulation.

- Retail deposits in the form of current accounts or savings accounts are very cheap compared with other forms of funding.

- Banks use retail deposits to lend to other customers. This drives most of a bank's income.

- Lending fuels economic growth as businesses borrow from banks to invest in resources, and customers borrow to buy the output from those businesses. The economic cycle is continually fuelled by an expansion of credit.

- Banks offer several types of payment: card payments, direct debits, faster payments, standing orders, CHAPS, SEPA, SWIFT, cheque, and, of course, cash.

CHAPTER SUMMARY

- Rather than processing each payment individually, banks aggregate payments and net them off against each other in a settlement process.

- Delivery of deposit management, lending, and payments for millions of customers is complex in itself. Additionally, there are many types of financial risk that a bank needs to manage:
  - Liquidity: when banks lend from their base of deposits, they need to ensure that they have enough cash so that deposit customers can make cash withdrawals and payments from their money.
  - Capital: banks need to have enough capital (their 'own money') to be able to absorb losses from lending during periods of economic stress, which allows them to continue to operate.

- Banks need to be big to be successful, because:
  - A large bank can more easily absorb the high fixed cost associated with systems, people, and regulatory compliance, necessary to running a bank.
  - A large bank can better diversify its deposit and asset base to make itself less vulnerable to large-scale economic shocks.

CHAPTER SUMMARY

- The UK banking market can be described as an oligopoly, characterized by domination by a handful of players, high barriers to entry, homogeneous products, and low price elasticity of demand.

- A customer-centric culture is not common in UK banks. There is significant pressure to make money, which is sometimes more easily achieved by taking advantage of structural inefficiencies in the market and, therefore, the customer.

- Pressure on profitability has been compounded by regulation which requires banks to hold more capital against their assets to protect deposits during economic shocks.

CHAPTER 3

Costs – the heaviest cross to bear

It is impossible to understand the current predicament retail banking finds itself in without understanding the subject of costs. Investing for growth has become extremely challenging for the bigger banks. Instead, they are investing to transform their cost bases to deliver the same business as today – but at a lower cost. Think about that from the customer's perspective for a moment: here we have businesses that are trying to do only what they do today, but cheaper. And in many cases the banks are not even attempting to perpetuate what they do today. Instead they are reducing the breadth of their business to focus on a 'core' offering where they can concentrate even more on maximizing cost-efficiency.

Managing cost sensibly is undoubtedly a sound business principle, but the cost levels in some of the big banks are so high that the period of adjustment required to bring them back under control is necessarily a long one. Lloyds, for example, has been running its much publicized 'simplification' programme for several years. It is aiming to reduce its annual costs by £1.4 billion by the end of 2017 and had achieved £0.9 billion of that in 2016. But to access these cost savings it has spent £1.6 billion to December 2016 and it expects to spend £0.6 billion more before it's done. To recap those numbers: Lloyds is *spending* £2.2 billion to reduce annual costs by £1.4 billion. In the long run this will pay off, but it's going to take two years for this investment in simplifying the business to break even, *assuming* that the purported cost reductions persist over time.

Here we explore how bad the cost picture really is in some banks. We strongly believe that an out-of-control cost profile is actually the most serious threat to the banks as we know them. And the main culprits driving the issue are IT, property, and regulation as all three are expensive in and of themselves, and also drive huge indirect costs in the form of the people required to manage them.

This cost problem is having a number of impacts on big banks today which add up to a severe limitation on those banks' ability to deliver a level of customer service and range of banking products that represent good value to customers. In addition to the present-day block that outsize costs place on service and products today, the far more serious implication is how much today's costs are constraining the big banks' ability to invest in meaningful service and product design improvements to drive growth in the future.

Bank IT – the Gordian knot

In 2014, the PRA's director Sam Woods commented to a House of Commons committee, "I feel we are a very long way from being able to sit here with confidence and say that the UK banks' IT systems are robust." That's a fairly terrifying statement for a member of the main regulatory authority for banks to make. The trouble is – he was right.

Banks are stuffed full of technology these days – they have bits of software to help them do everything from accounting to task workflow, from document management to direct debit collection. At the heart of it all, though, is the banks' 'core platform'. In every bank the core platform does the donkey work of maintaining the records of balances and transactions across current accounts and savings accounts, and often some loan accounts too. This core sits in the background tirelessly working away calculating interest, recording debits and credits, and then sending that information into countless other systems around the bank to inform the bank's own processes (like accounting) as well as presenting the information back to customers via such things as online banking. It wasn't always like that, though.

A (very) brief history of bank IT

Up to about the 1950s banking was a personal service delivered by a trusted adviser working for a respected company. If customers wanted to interact with their bank, they went there in person and transacted, or sought advice. Such transactions were relatively small, usually domestic in nature, and occurred relatively infrequently as the day-to-day economy was cash based. People would go and withdraw cash, then spend it over a period before returning to withdraw more. Hopefully in between times they also deposited cheques or takings from their business, too. The bank's task was to record the debits and credits and maintain the balance. But the manual nature of the transacting meant the task of record-keeping, though onerous and exacting (think Dickens and his depiction of a counting house), was manageable.

But in the aftermath of World War Two, the population expanded, living standards started to rise again and economic reconstruction activity meant more people had more money and therefore more need for banks than ever before. As the baby-boomer generation came into being, the operational intensity of running a bank increased. Banks started to struggle with the rising tide of transactions to record, cash to reconcile, and customers to serve. Back office administration costs started to get out of control and a solution was needed. The solution to a high cost, repetitive, manual process is almost always automation. Banking was no exception.

Putting large-scale computing devices to major industrial use started around the time of World War Two. It took another decade before computing devices started to appear in private enterprises. In the UK, Barclays was the first bank to open a dedicated computer centre in 1961. It then spent the next 20 years gradually connecting up its branches to the new centralized accounting system.

As banks got more efficient at processing transactions and maintaining balances, banking quietly grew into a mass consumer utility. But, crucially, this started decades ago and happened over quite a long period of time. Cash and cheque transactions dominated well into the 1980s. The sheer volume of accounts and transactions taking place within UK banks was far, far lower than it is today. Now more than 99% of the population over the age of 15 have a bank account of some kind and transaction volumes have increased exponentially, as have the actual methods of payment possible (more on this later).

The major banks started automating around 50 years ago to solve the efficiency problems back then. This started with the gradual automation of back office ledgers and got increasingly interesting as the telephony industry made strides in developing connectivity between computers. Remember though – the internet (as we know it) was only invented in 1989. That's nearly 30 years ago, but still about 20 to 30 years after the *first* technology landed in banks.

Consider the following milestones:

- 1961 – Barclays opens first ever banking computer centre in the UK.
- 1963 – American Express is launched in the UK with an annual fee of £3 12s (around £58 in 2017) and a required income of £2,000 (around £38,500 in 2017). The card was usable in 3,000 UK outlets and 83,000 overseas outlets.

- 1967 – First cash machine in the world installed by Barclays Bank in Enfield, Middlesex. Early dispensers were designed to receive hole-punched vouchers of £10 each purchased by the customer from the bank and used in the dispenser when needed.
- 1968 – BACS launched to allow electronic transfer of funds between banks.
- 1972 – Lloyds Bank 'Cashpoint' is the first online verified ATM using plastic cards with a magnetic stripe.
- 1993 – Half of UK adults are regular users of cash machines.
- 1994 – Half of UK adults hold a debit card (only half!).
- 1998 – UK debit card payments exceed personal cheques.
- 1999 – PayPal service launched.
- 2001 – More than half of UK retail spending is on plastic. More than 100 million card payments are made online. First year that cash machine withdrawals exceeded £1 billion during the year.
- 2007 – The first contactless card transactions occur in the UK.
- 2008 – Faster Payments are launched.
- 2015 – Apple Pay and Android Pay are launched.

So, in little more than 50 years we've gone from the first computer centre in a UK bank to digital money, where you don't need cash, a cheque, a piece of plastic, or any other token to make a payment – all you need is a smartphone. As payments have become ever easier to make, they have increased steadily in volume. Figure 1 shows the volume of domestic payments in the UK between 1990 and 2016.

Figure 1:
Monthly Payment Volumes Have Grown Over Time (000s)

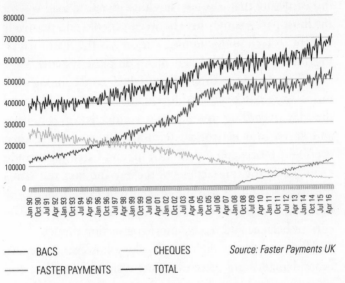

| ——— BACS | ——— CHEQUES | *Source: Faster Payments UK* |
| ——— FASTER PAYMENTS | ——— TOTAL | |

In 1990, the average number of all payments made each month was 394.4 million. In 2016, the average monthly volume was 673.9 million – a 71% increase. The BACS[4] system was launched in 1968 – very nearly 50 years ago. In the latter half of its life alone it has seen payment volume increase by over 300%. Only cheques are on a steady downward trend – the one payment method that doesn't really need a lot of technology as it's all done by pushing bits of paper around!

---

4   Bacs Payment Schemes Limited (BACS). Originally BACS stood for Bankers' Automated Clearing Services. BACS runs the Direct Debit system (as well as a number of other payment services) and the Current Account Switching Service (CASS)

The point of course is that the load being placed on banks' core IT systems is increasing at a rapid rate. The infrastructure that is supporting that increased load is – for the most part – somewhere between very old and positively ancient in technology terms. Not only is the load increasing, but so is the technical demand on those systems.

When they were originally installed, core banking platforms were batch processing engines. They would spend the day recording transactions conducted in branches and keyed into networked terminals by the tellers. Then overnight processing would kick in, and batch jobs would reconcile all the transactions of the day and kick out errors for investigation. When the branch staff came back in the next day, the system would be ready to report an up-to-date current balance and receive more transaction inputs.

With the rise of digital technology however more and more demands are placed on core systems to update and respond *in real time*. It's not only the transaction volumes going up. There are many more systems calling the data back from the core platforms than were ever envisaged when they were created. Customers can request a balance over the phone via interactive voice response technology, or via their mobile app or online banking. Even the ATM network generates a 'balance enquiry' (half the time when customers inadvertently press the Cash and Balance button instead of Cash Only). The core platforms were never designed to cope with this level of demand. So how have banks kept up? How is anything still working?

Engineering vs maintenance

The railways in the UK are problematic. They were built a long time ago. Demand has increased beyond the imagining of the original railway engineers. Sound familiar? Banks have done to their systems what Network Rail, and others, have done to our railways. They've patched, mended, maintained (sporadically), and – when they really, really needed to put something new in – they grafted it over the top of what was there already.

The analogy between the railways and the banks is actually a very apt one. The UK is a crowded little island – especially at the bottom around London and the south-east. That part of the country in particular needs new railway capacity. Ultra-modern trains on ultra-modern track controlled by ultra-modern signalling and safety systems. If we had that, trains would run faster, the network could carry more of them, commutes would get shorter, and capacity would increase. But we can't put the south-east on hold for ten years while we pick up all the old railway lines and lay down new ones in their place. People need to get around, the economy requires workers to be able to get to work. We simply cannot *stop* the trains while we fix the system.

Banking is in many respects in exactly the same position. A bank's customers will not stop spending money, or paying bills, or earning their salaries. The core systems *must* continue as chaos would ensue if they did not. Unlike the railways though, the banks *could* build new systems in parallel to the old ones. There isn't enough room for the railways to do that, but banks could buy new servers, design new systems, architect connections, and – in essence – rebuild core platforms to serve all the new ways their customers want to bank. So, why don't they?

IT costs – Hobson's choice

To maintain or to engineer afresh. If you only have enough money to do one, which do you do?

As the rate of technological progress increases it places ever greater demands on legacy systems – to the point where the fixed infrastructure of the big, old banks looks increasingly obsolete. It is staggeringly expensive now to keep some of this kit running. More and more maintenance is required to keep things working, and the resource pool of IT professionals who have the specialist skills and, more crucially, first-hand knowledge of how the systems were architected in the first place, required to maintain technology from the 1950s to the 1970s is ageing out of the workforce. With such a small resource pool available the cost of the resource is exceptionally high. This makes it ever harder and ever more expensive for banks to carry on operating.

A further complicating factor – and additional expense – is that over the years various banks have bought or merged with each other which has resulted in even greater IT complexity. Let's take Santander UK as an example – underneath that single brand is a series of older brands including Abbey National and Alliance & Leicester which were, once upon a time, significant institutions in their own right.

Assuming each had perfectly architected systems of its own (wholly unrealistic!) the three brands together would have encompassed (at least) three customer databases, three operating systems, and three transaction cores. Millions of transaction records across millions of customer accounts, dating back decades.

Now imagine integrating and reconciling all of that so that, say, consolidated financial reporting is possible. Or even just sending a simple letter to every single customer of the combined Santander Bank. These complexities are gargantuan. They are solvable – but only at enormous expense that creates a very serious cost drag on the financial performance of the banks. All of the biggest banks in the UK have this problem to one degree or another. Today some of the largest banks in the UK are sitting on the IT equivalent of catacombs – ancient, buried, labyrinthine, and with very few living people left who know their way around.

The complexity of the systems makes it exceptionally hard to know what will happen if changes are introduced. The cost of testing every change is therefore exorbitant as the cascading impact of even tiny changes has to be traced through multiple layers across a tangle of systems. There are many stories of where this has gone wrong for banks: a font change on a letterhead template that broke all letter production; a minor code change in the core that wiped out an ATM network for several days – some of these stories are a matter of public record in newspapers, others are war stories (mostly believable) shared over drinks after work when bank IT teams clock off. Every time one of these calamities occurs, more tests are added, more layers to the complexity. And the costs keep going up.

To change it all by building another version of the bank in parallel to the old systems requires investment. It's not investment that drives growth directly – the investment case for building a new platform might claim the future benefit of scalability, but this cannot be proven ahead of time. Instead the investment case must be built on the tangible costs that can be reduced. While the costs of running the old systems are massive, and rising, the costs of building new systems are equally massive.

On that basis, no sane CEO would switch on a new platform and simultaneously shut down his old one, with no parallel running contingency – the option to build a new platform would involve a period of overlap where the bank runs two different infrastructures. In that period, the costs incurred by the bank would be unbearable.

This is the definition of a vicious circle. The big banks are caught in a cost trap where the cost of continuing to maintain the old systems is so great that they cannot free sufficient income to pay for new systems and then decommission the old ones in an orderly fashion. Ironically enough, they have almost exactly the same problem with their real estate too.

The branch is dead, long live the… branch?

The big banks are in the process of closing branches. Lots of them. They are closing so many so quickly that the statistics are out of date as soon as they're published. In March 2017, RBS alone announced the closure of some 158 branches across its RBS and NatWest brands. That appears to be roughly 10% of its branch network, and is on top of about 30 branch closures in 2016. It is the result of a 43% fall in the number of in branch transactions since 2010 according to the company.

Figure 2:
Median distance to nearest other branch

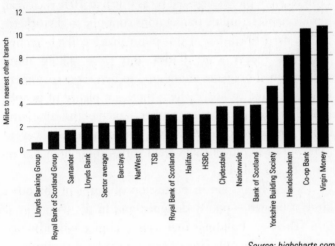

Source: highcharts.com

Of the some 10,000 branches still open in the UK, the average distance between branches of the same brand is 2.3 miles (Figure 2). However, the largest banks have acquired multiple brands – either deliberately before the financial crisis of 2008, or by necessity thereafter as smaller brands were proactively shifted into bigger brands by the PRA to avoid a bank failure.

If you consider the average distance between branches of the same *group* – you find that the distance is much lower. RBS group for example has only 1.6 miles between branches, whereas Lloyds Banking Group has only 0.6 miles between its branches. Only the big coffee chains like Starbucks can boast coverage like that. The thing with coffee shops though is that if you want coffee you have to go in a shop. You can't drink a virtual cup of coffee, while with banking it is no longer necessary to go into a branch to do most transactions. Footfall continues to drop year on year – a recent UBS research piece suggested by as much as 10% each year. Simultaneously, online transactions continue to skyrocket.

We need to confess at this point that we like branches. We think they're a good idea. But we're talking about well-designed branches configured to best serve customers' needs, situated in areas where there are plenty of people. Branches that are opposite another branch of the same bank in the high street of a small town which most people avoid in favour of an out-of-town retail park – those branches are not such a good idea.

The big banks are in possession of heaps of the other kind of branch – poorly designed and in the wrong location. These are buildings that were occupied when branch banking was the only way of serving the local community. Space was required for secure cash counting and storage. The teller lines were the main point of customer contact, and staffed to provide deposit and withdrawal services. Perhaps there was a small office or two where you could discuss a mortgage application with the bank manager.

These branches are simply not fit for purpose any more as the usefulness and role of branches has evolved. The bank branches of today and tomorrow are being used to serve customers in very different ways, including advice on mobile banking technology, a collection point for a new bank card or holiday money that has been ordered online. Face-to-face account opening and financial advice are still relevant, as are manual transactions over the counter, but they are increasingly a minority of the business done in a branch. As a result, the size and layouts of older branches need to change as no one wants to stand in a queue before shouting through a feeble microphone at bank staff behind bulletproof screens any more.

The legacy of these old-fashioned branches is causing banks a considerable problem in the form of significant cost in return for very little income. Banks know they need *some* branches, but they also know that the number they need is substantially fewer than the number they have now. They also know that the branch of the future probably doesn't look like the branches they have now. So, the banks are in a bind similar to the one involving their IT – they have a legacy position that costs a great deal to maintain, but they need to invest in new alternatives to meet modern demands. But that investment itself represents a significant cost.

It is very difficult to get a direct cost figure for what the big banks actually spend on their branches. In their annual reports the running costs of the branch network are generally wrapped up into summary lines in the financial statements. Disaggregating those summary lines is nigh on impossible. But taking Lloyds' 2016 annual report as an example, in 2016 the bank spent £672m on premises and equipment, and a further £1.8 billion on depreciation of existing property, plant, and equipment. Not all of this went on branches of course – there's a head office building, training centres, etc. But a great big chunk of that money must have gone on branches as there are around 2,000 of them in the Lloyds group.

Working back the other way it is possible to build the cost picture up from a single branch example. One branch will have a branch manager, perhaps an assistant manager, and a few staff. The cost to the bank of those staff is more than just salaries – it also encompasses pensions, national insurance contributions, and other benefits as well, along with a training budget. The branch will have a series of property costs as well – perhaps a lease, certainly maintenance, electrical and fire safety compliance, pest control in the older buildings, regular cleaning, and insurance. Inside the branch are computers, fixtures and fittings, and racks of glossy printed materials describing the products on offer. All of these things cost money to put in place and maintain. A very conservative estimate would suggest at least £0.25m per annum is required just to run a small branch. Now scale that back up to a countrywide view encompassing around 10,000 branches. The cost drain on the big banks runs into the billions.

Therefore, there's a really basic level of cost saving or 'rationalization' that needs to occur to get branch numbers down to sensible levels, but equally there are very real costs associated with doing so. In Lloyds' 2016 annual report the 'restructuring costs' line within the Staff Costs section totalled £241m in 2016. As branches close, staff redundancy must be managed. That's just the people side of it. It also costs money to vacate the property. Any remaining term on the lease must be paid off, the property must be maintained until it can be sold and the contents disposed of, or stored as required. All of this is yet more money the big banks must find to shift their branch estates from outdated, underutilized cost drains into leaner, slicker customer service channels.

This is where it gets really interesting. No one quite knows what the 'branch of the future' will look like now that digital banking is such a big thing. The first response to the cost conundrum of branches was to automate them. It is not uncommon to walk into some branches and be faced with a rank of machines for paying in cash and cheques and see just one staff member, usually with a clipboard.

This is one answer, but it cannot be the only answer. Anyone not capable of using the machines easily is not going to have a good experience. And if the only thing keeping the branch open is the tangible brand value of serving the community, this argument is quite difficult to make if the community is in fact self-serving at machines. The machines are only a marginal improvement too – even with machines instead of staff, the branch is still a high-cost outpost for processing low-value work from a bank's perspective.

If banks are going to incur the costs of being visible on the high street then they need to deliver and receive more value from customers that use them. As it stands, even in an automated branch, neither bank nor customer is getting a great outcome. Some of the buzzwords of the moment like 'bricks and clicks' and 'click and collect' feature heavily when bankers talk about how they are transforming their branches. But again, the time and effort required to create new branch strategies, and the technology required to deploy them, cost money.

The holy grail for banks is to get their high-cost staff doing high-value tasks that customers really appreciate, while the physical space of the branch is used efficiently to deliver great customer service at low cost. No one has quite worked it out yet, but experimentation requires investment, with no guarantee of return. Given the huge cost burden of their legacy stores it is very, very difficult for the big banks to justify this investment. Exactly like the problem they have with IT – the big banks are trapped in a doom loop with their branches as well: too much legacy cost to allow serious spending on designing new solutions to grow the business and win more customers.

Bad behaviour – and punishment to fit the crime

Payment Protection Insurance (PPI) can be a very useful product. It provides security that in the event of illness or injury your payments on your mortgage or loan will be maintained even if you cannot cover the cost yourself. That simple concept was bent out of shape entirely from the early 1990s by some of the big banks. The policies they structured were expensive, inappropriate for many customers, aggressively mis-sold, and deliberately made difficult to claim against. The trouble with running very high cost bases is that companies must make sufficient income to cover them. Profit targets are achieved either by winning more income or by cutting costs. If costs cannot be cut quickly enough, and banks' profit targets grow from year to year then the only place left to go to win profit is income. Scandals like PPI, however, are really only the tip of an iceberg. They are the highly visible manifestation of unmanageable costs.

The two main regulators of banks, the Prudential Regulation Authority and the Financial Conduct Authority have hit the banks hard for these visible manifestations – be it PPI, small business foreign exchange options, or unfair overdraft charges. Increasingly, the negative product strategies of the banks that were used to milk income from customers without providing value in return are being unwound through regulatory fines of truly eye-watering proportions.

For example, the total amount of redress repaid for PPI alone, between January 2011 and December 2016, was around £34 billion. So just at the time that banks are trying desperately hard to ready their IT systems for the digital age, and to transform their branch networks to meet modern requirements, they are being hit incredibly hard by regulatory fines.

We are not arguing for one moment that they should not be fined – their behaviour was wrong, customers lost out, therefore redress is payable. However, we can see that a large part of what drove banks into PPI (and similar) in the first place was profit pressure that arose from limited income growth and massive cost proliferation. The regulators layering in more massive costs has effectively returned banks to their original starting position – massive costs with limited income growth.

There is a bitter irony here however: the regulators, by fining the big banks so heavily, have impaired their ability to invest larger amounts in better technology and property assets to deliver a much-improved customer experience and better value for customers – the very things that the regulator would like to see. Of course, had the fines not been levied it is by no means certain that the big banks would have used the ensuing higher profits to improve their infrastructure or their capital positions. Perhaps they would have. Equally though they may have just paid higher dividends to their investors and carried on regardless. We cannot know; we can only observe the inherent tension between demanding banks invest in better systems and recapitalise quickly whilst simultaneously fining them billions!

Compliance

The financial crisis of 2008 shocked bankers and regulators alike. Up until that point both groups had built up some measure of pride in a global financial system that seemed to be working well. Sophisticated finance techniques were being used to allocate risk around the market to those most willing to hold it. Liquidity – in the general sense of the amount of money available to transact – across all financial products was high. Customers were getting cheap debt and spending it on a higher standard of living and bankers were making lots of money. When the bubble burst with the collapse of Lehman Brothers there was an intense period of firefighting to prevent the contagion spreading. When it was clear that things were – to some extent – under control, public attention turned to who to blame for the crisis. Meanwhile the regulators' attention turned to how to prevent it from happening again.

The purpose of regulation – in very simple terms – is to keep customers safe by keeping banks safe. A 'perfect' banker theoretically requires no regulation as he will naturally solve for an appropriate level of risk and return for his bank. As such, his bank remains well controlled and safe, and therefore its customers experience no nasty surprises. Then regulation is introduced and our perfect banker has to spend a proportion of his time ensuring he is compliant with the regulations otherwise he is open to regulatory censure and possible fines. If the regulation is well-drafted, rational, and proportionate to the risk, then the overall outcome should be positive. Our perfect banker gains little as he was good enough already, but he also loses little as not too much of his time is diverted.

Overall the industry is stronger as it has clearly defined and proportionate regulation. However, if the regulatory burden increases – in response, say, to a crisis caused by an *imperfect* banker then the outcome is different. The perfect banker still requires no regulation, but now more of his time is being spent on compliance. He must either hire staff to sort out the compliance work for him, or he must spend less of his time managing risk and serving his customers so he has time to do the compliance work himself.

Banking was already a highly regulated activity before the crisis with a substantial headcount and advisory cost impact on banks as a result (banks generally hire people to do the compliance work for them so the bankers can manage risk and serve customers). But the wave of new regulatory legislation that followed has been unprecedented in modern times. The EU and the US in particular have published significant volumes of new regulation, with UK banks subject to EU rules in all cases, and in many cases the US rules as well as many of our biggest banks have operations in other countries that bring them into contact with US regulation. As a consequence, the costs of compliance have skyrocketed for all banks. Compliance salaries keep increasing as more rules demand more resource to understand them, gauge their impact on each bank, and mandate any changes required to comply.

It would take another book to catalogue the regulatory change of the last 20 years and examine its impact on bank costs and customer outcomes in detail. We're absolutely not doing that here! Our observation though is that banks need to invest now – in innovation generally and technology in particular in order to break the chain that links them to the anchors of legacy systems and branches. Strong, clear, proportionate regulation is absolutely vital to the strength and prosperity of the banking industry. We do genuinely believe that.

We also believe that regulators need to understand the real-world implications of their legislation at the aggregate level. In other words, writing 100 rules may very well cause the industry to behave better in 100 different ways. However, the simple fact that now 100 rules exist means that *every* bank must carry the cost associated with understanding those rules, implementing any changes they prescribe, and monitoring and reporting on their ongoing compliance with those 100 rules.

The time and money they spend doing that is time and money they cannot spend investing in their businesses to make them better. Ultimately making banking better and safer for customers is in the hands of the banks, not the regulators. Just as the Football Association can manage the rules of the game, it is only the players who can play it. We think that the dialogue between regulator and industry needs to improve to promote open debate around whether the expected value of the 100 new rules is higher or lower than the cost consequence of introducing them. If it doesn't then there is a danger that regulation ends up being as much part of the problem – in the form of an excessive cost drain – as part of the solution.

The cost anchor

The topic of costs occupies a vast quantity of management time within banks – and permeates entire bank cultures, driving a sometimes depressing focus on what to shut down next. What gets lost during all this is a focus on the customer. This is the crux of the issue that the big banks face – the management time, intellectual effort, and sheer hard work that needs to be expended keeping the IT engine running, keeping the roof on the branch network, paying regulatory fines, and complying with new and existing regulation leaves very little time indeed to think about things that matter to customers.

Even if those thoughts were had – and they yielded brilliant ideas to transform the retail banking experience for the better – there's not enough money to invest in innovation as it is needed to meet rising costs. So, banks are reduced to making colossal efforts to manage existing complexity and improve incrementally. They sometimes fail and their systems sometimes break down as a result. The increasingly regular ATM outages and account access issues reported in the previous chapters are only too clear examples of this.

Pity then the poor product manager who is set an income target to deliver. That income target is set to meet the target level of profitability for the bank. But to turn income into profit one must deduct cost. The product manager is therefore fighting an uphill battle before they've even started. Are they going to build great products and services that customers want? Mostly no, as banks can't afford to and senior management are focused elsewhere.

Instead product managers must make do with whatever systems and distribution capability the bank already has, and drive income as hard as possible to cover the sprawling cost nightmare that lies behind the UK's high-street banks. Even if a product manager resists the temptation to invent another PPI, there are a whole range of lesser evils that might start to look rather tempting to hit that profit target, particularly if they are young, ambitious, and want to be promoted. This is something we will explore in the next chapter.

CHAPTER SUMMARY

- It is not possible to understand why retail banking is so poor in the UK without understanding the role of bank cost bases in distracting management attention from building better banks.

- Banks' inability to reduce their cost bases has significant impact on their ability to provide good customer service and value-for-money products.

- Banks' IT systems are struggling to cope with an exponential growth in the number of transactions flowing through the banking system in the last 50 years.

- Most banks' core platforms are very old and hard to keep up to date. Problems are exacerbated by a whole range of additional technology platforms banks use today, sending or requesting data from the core platform.

- Banks are caught in the dilemma of needing to update their systems while simultaneously keeping them running.

- Making changes to bank IT systems, particularly core banking platforms, requires extensive testing because of the complexities inherent in such old, layered systems.

- Many banks are in the process of closing multiple branches as they are a significant cost to banks.

CHAPTER SUMMARY

- Several of the high-street banks appear to have too many branches in the wrong places – some brands have branches less than a few miles apart.

- No one is quite sure what branches will look like in the future – or how many there will be – but the best guess is that they will be used for colleagues to engage in more meaningful interactions with customers, with low-value transactions and everyday banking business conducted digitally.

- Regulatory fines have soared for banks in recent years and they have had to hire an army of compliance professionals to ensure that decisions stay within the rules issued by the bank regulators.

- The extent and complexity of regulatory guidance is using up budgets banks could otherwise use to transform themselves to be better organizations and further exacerbating banks' high costs.

CHAPTER 4

The truth about us and the truth about you

The problems facing retail banks don't stop with the challenges of managing deposits and lending, and paying for vast cost bases. People play a big role too.

Product managers inside the big banks are the ones charged with designing and launching new products to the market, be they current accounts, savings accounts, credit cards, loans, or mortgages. The way product teams are organized, the objectives they are given and the incentives individual product managers labour under mean that they often fail to work in the customer's interest. In our view, much of what's wrong with retail banking goes wrong at the product team level and here we explain the reasons why.

Customer behaviour compounds the problem, as strange as that might sound. Blinded by promotions and offers, customers tend to plump for short-term gain only to suffer from long-term pain when it comes to financial products. This, alongside other psychological and behavioural biases, means that it is all too easy for product managers to design products that make money out of the ways customers think and behave. We spend some time exploring why customers are key protagonists in the saga of poor retail banking in the UK.

The truth about us

When you apply for a job in product management at a big bank, you are often attracted by the role description which promises that you will be building products that will revolutionize customers' financial lives. The bank's vision is – almost without exception – to be the 'best for customers'. You spend time looking at the savings accounts or loans that you will be managing and think about ways you might improve them. You look at the competition, and assess the customer experience offered by other banks and industries to see what you can learn. You can't wait to get going.

The reality of the role never quite matches the hype. Customers are mentioned, but you learn quickly that your ideas about making a customer process slick or building a superb budgeting tool that will help them manage their cash will likely never make the grade.

You soon see that the guy getting all the praise is the one that has come up with a great way to squeeze a bit more income from his products. And by products, we mean customers. The longer you stay, the more you notice that product managers are rewarded for coming up with new and exotic ways to make more and more money from customers. Nothing else gets the attention of management in quite the same way. You curse if you are put on a project to implement a new regulation, because no matter how well you do it, it isn't going to get quite the same kudos.

Product managers also seem to move around a lot. They stay in a team for a year or two before moving on to other products or other departments entirely. You wonder who to go to when you find a bug in the way your product was set up, because the individuals that worked on it are long gone. You ask around but it's tricky because you don't spend a lot of time with product managers outside of your product line. In fact, the mood between different product teams can be a bit hostile. You are all competing to make the most income and rarely spend time thinking about a customer's experience with the bank as a whole.

The overwhelming focus on commercial management
The way product teams are set up and organized inside the

big banks is revealing. Each product area – credit cards, loans, mortgages, savings, current accounts – is usually a *separate* team. Banks think about these products as individual profit centres for the bank, even if many customers hold multiple products.

The number of people working in each product team varies but in the big banks it is not uncommon for there to be well over a hundred people working in each product area. Within these teams, the roles – usually variations on the title 'product manager'– have different emphases.

There are product managers focused on sales – how many products the distribution channels (branches, contact centres, and online, mainly) are selling – as well as product managers focused on retention (trying to ensure that customers don't leave, or that the bank works out the behaviours correlated with your likelihood to leave so that they can intervene before you do).

But by far the biggest group of product managers focuses on managing the commercial performance of the products. Here you have product managers focused on pricing, the best way to set deposit or lending rates to win business and make money. You will have experts focused on credit risk in the lending product teams, identifying the best customers to lend to. There will be 'general' commercial product managers that decide what fees and charges to set to deliver the financial targets that the bank's finance team has set for the product area. There is also normally a small team in each product area focusing on risk – operational risk and regulatory compliance mainly. They are there to stop the product area proposing something that is not allowed under the rules that govern financial services in the UK and to ensure, supposedly, that the product is sold and operated by the bank in a way that leads to fair customer outcomes and does not pose financial or other risks to the bank.

Product teams will also have many managers focusing on activities banks euphemistically and alternately describe as 'strategy', 'business development', or 'new product development'. These guys sit around thinking about how to make even more money out of customers, through building new products, closing existing ones, or moving customers from one product to another, for example. They will spend time looking at the bank's competitors, the market share the product has, and whether any IT development is required to change the product in some way – adding a new feature, rate, or fee, for example. They will also look at the cost to the bank of providing the product and think about ways to do so more efficiently.

The point to make here is that the overwhelming majority of product managers in each product team are focused on the commercial performance of the product. There are precious few colleagues focused on the overall customer experience or working with other product areas on initiatives that might help customers to manage all their finances collectively that bit better. These colleagues do exist, but they tend to be squirrelled away in the digital teams elsewhere in the bank, or in a central 'customer experience' team which, in many banks, is seen as a sort of career graveyard, too far away from the 'hard' profit and loss management where reputations are made.

Deliver your numbers to get ahead

In our experience, the way to get ahead in a product team of a big bank is to deliver your numbers. Sales growth, income growth, cost reductions, fewer lending customers in default

– whatever it takes to deliver better income and profit performance for your product line. We can't prove it, but in our experience the product managers that tend to do well in terms of promotions are the ones that deliver superior income returns.

A lot of this is driven by the internal cycles that the big banks work to. Monthly reporting from finance is a thing to be feared and, if you are expecting a poor performance on your product, you better be prepared with a lot of additional analysis to explain why it isn't as bad as it looks.

Of course, none of this is to say that product managers – and the banks they work for– shouldn't focus on growing income and making profits. Profits ensure that shareholders are rewarded for providing the bank with equity and more income allows the bank to invest in further growth, creating new jobs, and, with a bit of luck, enhancing customer service.

Yet we know from working inside the industry that little focus in product teams is given to improving customer service and few believe that better customer service will *lead* to more income. Instead, income growth or cost reductions are viewed as something 'done to' customers and therefore banks spend a lot of time and focus working on how best to increase prices or reduce the cost of services in ways that customers won't notice.

It is this focus on making money almost imperceptibly, rather than working on things that customers would be willing to pay for – a fair value exchange you might say – that marks out banking from other industries. For BMW to sell its next million cars it has to come up with a sleek new design and some great technology. For bankers to make the next £10m in income they need to think about how to reduce the interest rate they are paying on a savings account used by millions of people by a few tenths of a percentage point, in such a way that means few of them will withdraw their money.

Risk management is an afterthought

Another area that this relentless focus on commercial management crowds out is risk management. From what we see, at the big banks you certainly don't get that big promotion by spending a lot of time on risk management or by tweaking a product to properly align with the latest regulatory guidance. Better to spend your time thinking up some new wheeze to make money. Yet few would deny that ensuring products are managed in a way that is compliant with required regulations is an essential element of product management.

While risk management is a constituent element of any bank's new product development process it is viewed by many product managers as a hurdle or barrier to overcome. The need to 'Treat Customers Fairly' by designing products that are clear, fair, and not misleading is something product managers invariably try to get around one way or another. If you don't believe us, ask yourself whether a range of three or four different paid-for bank accounts with different prices, features and benefits, containing insurance coverages with various exemptions and age restrictions, sounds like a range of products likely to be clear, fair, and not misleading. The truth is product managers make money through complexity.

This general disregard for risk management should be worrying to banks and regulators. Product managers are the experts and architects of the products they create and therefore often best placed to identify emerging risks. While risk management has increased in importance in banks following the 2008 financial recession and scandals like PPI, it continues to be a box-ticking exercise in many banks and one that product managers rush through or delegate.

Effective, long-term, customer-centric banking requires product managers to place risk assessment at the centre of everything they do, particularly because we know that customers rarely pay sufficient attention to how their banking works. Every apathetic customer is also a vulnerable one. Too often, risk management is seen as the work of a bank's risk team who can often be remote and unaware of how complex financial products work.

Consequences rarely catch up with you

Sometimes being a product manager can resemble being Leonardo DiCaprio in the movie *Catch Me If You Can*. The consequences of the decisions many product managers make rarely catch up with them, even when those decisions have sold customers short.

The first problem is that product managers do not stay in their roles very long. Many career product people move from role to role, and team to team, every two or three years. Others dip into product management for a couple of years before moving out (or back) to other departments like strategy, finance, or digital. Still others flit between the product teams at different banks, sometimes spending time as management consultants advising product teams that many of them used to work for. Such movement means that product managers work on a much shorter personal time horizon than the products they have sold customers, which they typically use for many years. If anything goes wrong with those products, it is rarely the same product managers who launched the product that end up picking up the pieces.

The second, related, problem is that it can take some time for the problems inherent in products to surface. For example, it was only when the economy started to turn downwards and people started to try and make claims on their PPI policies that many found out that they were unsuitable. By this time, the product managers that had designed the product were long gone.

This brings us on to the third problem – accountability. No one can deny that the banks have taken accountability for product scandals such as those of PPI and endowment mortgages. They have paid out billions in compensation and redress to customers. Yet the bankers that designed the product have not been censured, principally because few banks actually know who came up with the idea in the first place, and many would have simply copied the idea from another bank anyway. This inability to hold individuals to account when they design and sell bad products to millions of people is another challenging area for the industry. Customers – and the public at large – want to feel like bankers are taking responsibility when things go wrong but the vagaries of personnel moving around make that almost impossible.

High turnover means institutional knowledge is lost

High turnover of product managers – people coming and going from their jobs every couple of years – also means that important institutional memory is lost. More simply, the people who know the right answer to how a product should work or who can spot when a product is not working are often no longer around.

As a result, product managers sometimes have a less than firm handle on how the specific product they are managing does and should work. In our view, product managers should understand how their product is configured on a bank's core platform, right down to the team that developed the code base. Few, if any, do in the big banks.

The level of detail product managers must know about their product doesn't stop there. It should include obvious things like the rates and fees associated with the product but also the less obvious things like how regularly statements are sent to customers and what information they contain. These might sound like minor considerations but the FCA stipulates in some detail what customers in different scenarios must be shown on statements and letters to ensure they have the right information to make sensible decisions. When product managers move around regularly, this essential institutional knowledge gets lost, and errors become harder to spot.

This isn't just worrying for customers but also for the banks themselves. While large scandals like PPI dominate the headlines, banks regularly refund customers for minor regulatory breaches. Failing to provide an accurate annual statement for a personal loan, for example, can mean that a bank must repay that customer the interest they have paid on the loan. These sorts of breaches get less or no media attention and yet impact the financial performance of banks, and also mean that many customers have been sold products that did not work as they were supposed to.

A preference for complexity
In retail banking, the fundamental issue with an excessive focus on short-term profit is that the quickest way to make money is to make your product more complicated.

Product managers have two ways to increase income. They can create a product so tempting that it makes customers move across by the boat load. This usually means creating a juicy upfront offer to get more customers in (more on this in Part 2). These offers are of course paid for through back-ended fees or rate reductions that customers pay less attention to and are often buried deep in the product terms and conditions.

The second option open to product managers is to find a way to make more money from existing customers: that means amending interest rates or increasing fees. In both cases, the most lucrative way to do this is to increase the complexity of pricing to hide higher charges.

Complexity increases the market power of banks because it stops less-informed customers from understanding prices in the market. A small set of well-informed customers will educate themselves about their options and select the cheapest or best value provider, but less financially literate customers are effectively shopping at random, which means that banks can maintain higher prices.

This is an industry-wide problem because all banks enjoy higher revenue streams as a result of this unnecessary complexity. It is in no product manager's interests to make products simple. Making things simple would mean that customers could more easily compare prices, more easily find better value, and therefore be more likely to move to cheaper competitors, destroying profit at an industry level as banks 'race to the bottom'. No bank wants that. Many are sitting on a gold mine of millions of existing customers who won't move their banking unless they are pushed by a major event, like failing to identify and deal quickly with an account fraud.

Product managers build in complexity because everybody else does: making it simple for customers means throwing away margin and that is rarely advisable for your career. Of course, product managers do need to be careful – they can't exploit complexity so far as to ignite a media reaction or spark regulatory review, as neither of these is good news for the bank. But making things just confusing enough so you don't bother trying to compare your product to one elsewhere is par for the course.

Product silos 1: product areas compete

Most customers use multiple banking products, many of which cross over and interact with each other in some way or another. You might sweep some cash from your bank account to a savings account. You might use a faster payment to pay off an outstanding credit card balance. However, at a product management level the product teams are not only separate but also often in competition with each other. The effect on customers can be profound.

Interactions with other product teams are generally infrequent. They tend to happen when one team is creating something which might impact another, or when a product manager needs help or expertise from another area. Generally, though, the relationship between product teams is competitive. They compete for scarce resources, including investment in product development, the attention of senior management, recruitment of the best-performing product managers and focus from front-line sales teams. All these things have implications for customers.

Consider investment allocation. As it gets towards the end of the year, investment pounds need to be allocated to projects for the following year. Getting investment means the difference between being able to deliver a new product, process, or charging structure – or not – and as we have seen, your ability to create new income streams can determine your personal performance rating the following year.

As the pot is limited, you need to propose a project that is better than the alternative from another product team. You need to show that you can make juicy returns for your department. A proposal that helps customers, or increases another department's profit line at the expense of yours, like automatically offering a structured repayment loan if a customer is continuously languishing in their overdraft, is unlikely to get past your manager. Setting product teams up in competition with one another creates perverse incentives to compete. When combined with a focus on profits not customers, the best investment ideas for customers rarely get a look in.

Competition also exists for the attention of sales teams – particularly the branch network. Historically, front-line seller incentives were the primary tool used to drive product sales. Product managers and branch sales teams would meet annually or quarterly to determine sales targets for each product, as well as the size of the staff incentive for each product that an individual sold. These targeting sessions were fierce. Product managers pushed distribution channels to include higher volumes in their forecasts. Product teams fought among themselves to get the greatest slice of the incentive budget allocated to their product.

Monetary incentives were powerful in influencing sales volumes; which is why product managers fought hard to ensure that their product was the most lucrative to sell. Unsurprisingly, this encouraged the sale of products that weren't always right for the customer. Following a 2012 FCA review, and increased pressure from the public, most sales incentive schemes have now been improved or overhauled.

But the competition between product managers has simply moved on to another playing field. Now that product managers have less control over in-person sales through branches, their focus has moved to getting the most out of digital. Increasingly it is important for product owners to ensure that digital projects are prioritized for delivery and that their product gets sufficient airtime on the front page of the bank's public website, which can make a significant difference to sales. Little of this time and effort is spent thinking about customers.

Add to this the competition between product teams to steal each other's best-performing product managers and you have a generally dysfunctional organizational set up which is the case in most big banks. By setting product teams up separately, they inevitably compete, since they all have as their primary objective enhanced financial returns for the bank. This means that shared resources such as branches and digital platforms are fought over as they are key to whether a product will meet those financial return objectives each product area is provided with.

What gets lost is a joined-up view of the bank's customer and what they want and need. Not unreasonably, most customers see themselves as having a relationship with a bank as a whole. When they call up or visit a branch they expect staff to be able to see all their products in one place and help make sense of what's going on if they have a query. Yet the priorities and initiatives of the different product teams often make this more difficult, and sometimes impossible.

Product silos 2: contradictory customer service

As the product teams in big banks are set up as individual units tasked with driving their own 'segmental' profit and loss accounts, product teams make decisions that conflict with each other, which in turn means that customers receive seemingly contradictory service outcomes.

One of the most frustrating examples of where incoherence materializes relates to credit decisions. These are often made independently by product area. What this means is that customers might be offered a credit card with a high limit one day but be refused a small overdraft the next day. The bank looks silly and the customer is left confused.

While some differences might be down to the nature of each product and the price the bank is charging for that type of credit, contradictory credit score outcomes are usually down to the way the bank manages credit risk by product area. Credit scorecards are often developed and maintained separately by each product team. Each product credit risk team might follow slightly different statistical methodologies, use different data sources, or treat the data they use in different ways. In their eyes this allows them to optimize risk performance for their product, which is what they are incentivized to do. Furthermore, product teams might be pursuing different strategies as to the type of customers they are trying to attract, with some only willing to lend to the very 'best' customers while others are willing to lend to those with slightly worse credit histories. Whether this means customers are accepted for some products and not others is really not their concern.

Incoherence across product lines also manifests itself in communications. Customers in the UK receive a lot of letters from their bank: statements, marketing flyers, and notifications on charges and account changes. This information is never neatly summarized for you in a single communication which reflects the full range of products you might hold with the bank. As a result, you might receive five communications from different product teams in one month, and none the following month. Product managers and the marketing teams that they work with simply find it too complicated to coordinate messages (and to sort the data) to send you one message that reflects your whole relationship with the bank. And work that is tricky, non-income-generating, and requires commitment across product teams is unlikely to be a priority.

Product silos can occasionally work in a customer's favour though. The way banks make product teams compete means that they are often striving internally for the same customers' deposits and lending. Many banks, for example, offer high credit interest or cash back to current account customers funding their accounts every month. These deposits might have otherwise gone to a low-rate savings account within the same bank. Very occasionally, loan departments target customers with outstanding credit card balances within their own bank to offer them a lower-rate personal loan. Such initiatives can sometimes lead to poor financial outcomes for the bank but better ones for customers – simply because of the way that banks organize their product teams.

Product silos 3: change is slow

As we have described above, product silos lead to poor collaboration between teams. Relationships across product teams are pretty weak, meaning that when cross-functional projects are attempted, they are slow and expensive, and often fail.

To deliver a cross-product project, managers have to engage additional support teams (such as change, credit risk, and finance) from each product area and make sure that they are all working towards the same goal. This is not easy for several reasons.

The first is that many product teams use different IT platforms for their particular product. The loan product team might use one platform, the credit card team another, and the current account team yet another one. Any sort of project requiring these three platforms to talk to or integrate with each other will take a long time and cost a lot of money. Many core banking systems are decades old and stitched together. As different products will be held on different systems they may only be accessible through separate teams. Getting a single customer view to provide data or analysis for proposed projects is therefore tricky.

The second is the sheer number of stakeholders involved. For example, let's consider risk teams. Each product team will have its own risk team. These teams are often highly specialized sub-teams looking at different aspects of risk (credit, fraud, financial crime, financial promotions, conduct, operational, information security, and data protection to name just a few). That's a lot of people to engage for a single product project, let alone a project involving several products.

What is more, these teams might also exist (and require engagement) at the division or group level, and there are likely to be other risk teams inside the branch, telephone banking, and digital teams. Multiply this through all the different stakeholder groups that a product manager needs to engage: marketing, legal, change, IT finance, customer experience, HR, and training, and it is easy to see why stakeholder lists can run into the hundreds of people.

Moreover, it is unlikely that they are all sitting in the same office, or the same city, on the same day, meaning that coordination of meetings and sign offs can be virtually impossible. During a cross-product project, it can take a huge amount of time for managers not only to understand who their stakeholders are, but then to meet them regularly as the project evolves. What this means is that the project slows down, which means, in turn, that the changes the project was attempting to make are delayed.

This organizational complexity in big banks makes innovation slow, risky and expensive. Planning a single letter to current account customers, for example, can take six months and is considered a significant project. This sluggish pace of change is, of course, bad for customers. And, given that complex projects can take two or three years to deliver and leadership priorities and the economy can shift over that time, investment regularly gets reprioritized away from projects that have yet to complete. As the 2016 decision by RBS not to sell Williams & Glyn bank (after they had spent years trying to 'carve it out' from the main RBS bank) shows, millions of pounds and thousands of staff hours are wasted this way every year.

Culture

Given everything we've said above you might expect us to say that the culture within bank product teams sucks. You would be forgiven for having a mental image of Gordon Gecko-type characters in braces, chewing on pencils as they think up clever ways to screw customers again and again.

The paradox of retail banking products teams, though, is that they are not as bad as that. The cultures within individual product teams can, in our experience, be quite progressive. Colleagues are open-minded, come from diverse backgrounds, and have many different interests. There are good sources of data and other information available for product managers to use to make high-quality decisions. The training opportunities on offer from the big banks are usually vast and well-funded, meaning that product managers are more often than not highly skilled. Most product managers are genuinely interested in ensuring that customer service is improved. Product teams, at least on the face of it, therefore appear to have good *values*.

And yet the consequences of the actions and decisions these product teams take are, on the whole, largely negative for customers. This is because the objectives that individual managers and product teams are set are largely antithetical to good customer outcomes. Even if individual product managers want to do the right thing, the organization they are part of can't seem to make it happen.

At its core, this is down to an inherent and seemingly inescapable tension in the product manager–customer relationship. Customers want to pay as little as possible to borrow money and earn as much as they can from their savings. Product managers mostly have the opposite aims, and few, if any, believe that investing in customer service and product simplicity will make as much money as clever pricing strategies and high fees.

Product managers, regulators, and innovation

The regulators are significant stakeholders for any product manager. The FCA, PRA, and other bodies regularly publish guidance or rules on charges, product structures, and how they should be marketed or managed. In 2016 alone, the FCA delivered studies and guidance on the credit card market, packaged bank accounts, incentives in consumer credit, and rules for the mortgage market.

While tweaks to pricing happen relatively regularly, new product development is less frequent. Given the huge investment required for big, complex banks to innovate, they often want to wait for whatever the latest piece of regulatory guidance is to be announced, thereby ensuring that any new product won't fall foul of the latest rules.

What this means is that new product development often starts with what the regulator has laid out. This is completely at odds with a market where you develop a product based on customer need. It is difficult to imagine Apple, Facebook, or Dyson starting with a rule book and then thinking about what they can build next. While regulations embody sensible and much needed protections for customers, the extent and complexity of regulations in recent years has meant that product managers are now reluctant to experiment in case some new product or service contravenes regulations currently being developed.

The truth about you

One of the more interesting aspects of being a product manager in a bank is that you get to see how customers *really* behave when it comes to their finances. From spending too much to saving too little, bankers get to see the full spectrum of human behaviour. Perhaps the most intriguing aspect of this is just how often customers make decisions that are not in their interests – they act *irrationally*. As we shall see, this is down to a number of behavioural biases.

The odd effect of these biases is that it can make retail banking even tougher for product managers because – even if they appeal to customers' better instincts – there is no guarantee customers will do the 'right' thing.

Taking it lying down

Consider this scenario. You've just got your bank statement. You forgot to make a transfer from your savings account to your current account, so went overdrawn by £50 for a few days. You hadn't been organized enough to add an overdraft facility to your account, so the bank charged you £10 for the privilege of making a payment, even though the £50 they lent you for a few days cost them a lot less. And you now need to pay another £5 a day for the overdraft facility. You end up paying charges that would make a loan shark blush. So, what do you do?

If you were overcharged in this way by a shop or a restaurant you would kick up a fuss, storm out, and never darken their door again. But as it is a bank, you shrug your shoulders and carry on – invariably blaming yourself for being so disorganized.

This behaviour is the norm. In 2016, the CMA report into retail banking found that every year a quarter of UK banking customers are hit by unauthorized overdraft charges. These earn the banks £1.2 billion a year. But customers – while obviously deeply annoyed – don't vote with their feet. The proportion of customers switching accounts is tiny: anywhere between 1% and 4% most years.

This isn't rational behaviour. To make a rational decision, it is necessary to consider all information, and to act logically to maximize your benefits – be they financial or just your own general happiness. A rational decision-maker therefore puts intuition, brand loyalty, and emotion to one side and uses cold, hard logic to assess one alternative against another.

In theory, rational decision-making requires 'perfect information' about your alternatives and assumes you will have the time and skills to evaluate each option. This is tough when it comes to banking, requiring you to know the full breadth of your options, identify and understand competing products, and weigh them up against each other. You may need to consider your spending habits and variables over which you may have little control such as changes in your life or in the economy around you.

Little wonder, then, that the millions of people hit with unauthorized overdraft charges don't appear to be making rational decisions. Yet such irrationality is not isolated to overdrafts -we regularly see customers revolving high balances on credit cards while keeping money in savings accounts paying paltry rates.

The biases that impact our financial decision-making

While there are hundreds of biases that can impact rational decision-making, there are a few that have specific impacts on the way retail banking products have developed. These biases have, advertently or inadvertently, been exploited by product managers to boost the attractiveness of their products (and to hide some of the costs).

These are present bias (giving more weight than is rational to immediate paybacks and not enough to those in the future); optimism and projection bias (thinking that our financial habits won't be impacted by negative events in the future); mental accounting (treating pots of money differently, depending on where the money came from and what it is intended for) and persuasion from sellers or sales literature. Together these biases mean that customers often fall into the traps product managers build into products to make money.

Present bias

Imagine you are searching for a new TV. You have worked out that you can afford a 36-inch plasma screen. But then you see an ultra-high definition 80-inch and it's too hard to say no. You know you should be saving for a house, but this TV will make living in a rental so much better.

Of course, putting more value in what we can enjoy today is partly rational. Because of inflation, a pound now is worth more than a pound later, and if we get something now, we have longer to enjoy it. But even accounting for that, we tend to put more weight into what gives us a payoff sooner rather than later.

In banking, present bias has some interesting implications. Customers put up with poor service and rip-off charges because they don't want the short-term hassle of moving accounts, despite longer-term benefits further down the line. Similarly, customers love an offer that gives them a nice benefit today, even if it might cost them more later.

Professor Lawrence Ausubel at the University of Maryland did some research in 1999 on present bias in financial services and the results were revealing. He tested whether credit card customers were more likely to take a credit card with a lowered six-month introductory rate instead of a credit card with a reduction in its permanent rate after six months. He found that consumers were at least three times as responsive to changes in the introductory rate as compared to equivalent reductions in the post-introductory rate. In other words, we tend to opt for 'jam today' rather than 'jam tomorrow'.

Product managers design products to take advantage of this bias. It means that offers are designed to be attractive at the point of acquisition (when you take them out) rather than offering long-term good value. This is why the branch posters you see and the direct mail you get through the post often lead with things like cash incentives to switch and introductory credit card offers. In many cases, as we shall explore in Part 2, these offers are more than paid for by the fees and rates the product charges over the medium- to long-term.

Optimism and projection bias

Projection bias is the tendency to think that our financial habits won't be impacted by negative events in the future. Such optimism is generally a pretty positive thing for help- ing us enjoy our lives, of course, but it can create blind spots when it comes to assessing the risks and rewards of financial decisions.

We see projection bias in action when it comes to financial decisions like whether or not to use a payday loan company. Payday loans are typically repaid the following month, in a lump sum, with the interest payment added on. From an economic perspective, the decision to take out a short-term, high-cost loan may seem irrational. From a customer's perspective, these loans are often essential to make ends meet.

At the point of taking a payday loan, consumers are optimistic that they will be able to repay it on time. But in our experience, they consistently underestimate the likelihood that some other event will occur that will leave them unable to make the repayment. With payday loans, the interest rates and penalty charges for late payment are much greater than those for a standard fixed-rate, fixed- term loan, so the cost to a customer of missing repayment can be significant.

Payday loan companies used to get around half of their income from the one third of customers who did not repay their loans on time. Many customers paid significantly more in interest and penalty fees than they borrowed. So, customers who could barely afford the original loan – by definition most had very little money available to them – could certainly not afford punitive penalty costs. Optimism and projection bias were working full time on many customers. Payday loan companies made huge sums from people who were unlikely to be able to pay back the loan in the period that they had originally signed up for.

In 2013, the FCA stepped in with several specific regulations to protect customers from payday loan companies – one of which was to limit the amount of times a customer can roll over their loan (miss a payment and have the loan rolled into a new loan) to just twice. This helped save many customers from falling into an endless cycle of debt but, inevitably, pushed others towards the unregulated loans market – loan sharks.

Projection bias might also be exacerbated by a series of good or bad experiences that subsequently influence how we look at our lives. Put simply, we start to think that the past is a reliable guide to the future.

In the run up to the 2008 financial crisis, mortgages became more widely available than ever before, particularly in the US. Banks were lending to people with low incomes and risky profiles who had traditionally been refused credit in the past. Predictably, great numbers of people took up these mortgages. If you were poor, or had a sketchy credit history, the dream of homeownership probably seemed a distant one. But now the banks themselves were telling you that you could do it!

In virtually all cases, these mortgages were adjustable-rate products, with low starting rates. That was fine for a while. More and more people were getting mortgages, increasing demand for homes and driving up house prices, further building the confidence of those who had taken out the mortgages. Interest rates remained manageable, and many people took out further loans, using the higher value of their house as collateral.

These new homeowners failed to take into account that things might change. Inexcusably, so did the bankers. People generally didn't worry about what would happen if the bank changed the interest rate, or if the value of their home decreased. Consumers had seen years of plenty and saw no reason why the good times should not continue.

But as the financial crisis began to take hold, mortgage rates increased and repayments became unaffordable. People stopped paying and they lost their homes. Repossessions increased the supply of houses for sale, credit markets tightened, and people couldn't get lending, so demand for houses decreased. The downward spiral had begun.

The UK was not exempt from this irrational exuberance. It was not uncommon to see mortgage loans in the UK at loan-to-value percentages that exceeded 100% – banks were lending customers *more* than the value of the property they were buying with customers betting that house prices would just keep rising.

There were, of course, many reasons why the crisis happened. But at the level of personal customer decision-making, those taking out mortgages did not consider the risk and impact of a downturn, nor were they encouraged to do so by the banks. Optimism and projection bias were at work again.

Mental accounting

'Mental accounting' is a term coined by Richard Thaler, a Professor at Chicago Booth Business School and author of the popular 2008 book *Nudge*. His research has highlighted that people like to keep their money in different pots, and they value these pots differently depending on where the money came from and where it is going to. Of course, the *real* value of the money in each pot is the same. People might have a current account for day-to-day spending, use an overdraft for day-to-day overspend, unplanned purchases go on the credit card, and savings are put in accounts split by purpose: maybe one account for a holiday and another for a car.

While mentally accounting for our money in this way might help us to manage our cash, it can become a bias which causes people to make costly decisions. Nobody likes to think about using their holiday savings to pay off that credit card bill, even if they face much higher interest rates on their credit card than they get on their savings. Mental accounting actually stops you doing the financially sensible thing.

Product managers love mental accounting. You have savings so we know that you can pay your short-term debts, but you choose not to pay off your credit card balance. In other words, you are giving the bank cash that we then use to lend back to you, and charge you handsomely for doing so. It is irrational, but it happens often and it is costly for customers.

Researchers from the University of California, Davis and Dartmouth College looked at what customers paid on their current accounts and credit cards in the US, and whether the costs could be avoided. While their analysis was on US accounts, the lessons could hold equally for UK customers. They looked specifically at whether consumers could avoid costs not by changing their consumption habits, but simply by making different choices about how they pay for them. They found that at the median, almost half of consumers' costs could be avoided through a mix of moving from higher- to lower-rate products and repaying debt using available credit balances. Furthermore, almost all overdraft fees could have been avoided using a cheaper short-term source of credit – like available limits on a credit card. Why don't customers do all these things? Mental accounting means we don't like to mix up our separate pots – and of course sometimes customers find it difficult to calculate what the right thing is to do anyway.

Prominence and persuasion – packaging matters
Consumers tend to overvalue the benefits of a product if it is packaged in a nice way. For example, you might pick a current account because it offers you a lot of nice benefits: a switcher offer, credit interest, cash back, or a free gift like a magazine subscription or cinema tickets. These benefits will be detailed to you in a booklet with thick, high-quality paper, filled with pictures of happy people enjoying themselves on holiday.

Most of us like to think that we are not influenced by advertising but the reality is that many of us are. And the format is important. A study in South Africa looked at the impact of using different formats for letters sent to customers encouraging them to take out a loan. They found that showing fewer loan examples, adding a photo of an attractive woman and not suggesting a particular use for the loan actually increased demand for loans to the same extent as a whopping 25% reduction in the interest rate. In other words, advertising format was as effective at increasing sales as a significant reduction in the interest rate of the loan.

As customers flick through marketing booklets in bank branches, they can forget what they wanted in the first place – which is usually a simple account that can make and receive payments. This distraction is because we can only take in and process a certain amount of information, and so a product manager and the bank's marketing team ensure that your attention is instead drawn to all the freebies. Costs are buried in the back, or worse, in a separate leaflet or webpage altogether. For product managers, the economics of these upfront benefits only work if someone is paying the costs. Those cinema tickets aren't free at all.

Product managers often structure their products to give their salespeople the opportunity to use classic negotiating tricks, like starting with a high anchor point. In a traditional negotiation, your anchor point would be your first offer – the amount that you hope the opposing party will say yes to, even though you know they probably won't. By starting with a high anchor point, you set expectations for the customer, and evidence shows that when the initial anchor point is higher, the opposing party is more likely to end up closer to that amount than they had originally intended.

How does this play out in retail banking? Let's say a bank has three paid-for bank accounts: the bronze (£5.95 a month), the silver (£9.95 a month), and the gold (£15.95 a month). Banks often start by offering the most expensive account, explaining to you all the benefits and features of the top of the range product. When they have you interested, but you baulk at the cost, they then offer the alternatives, which seem cheap by comparison. Starting with a high anchor point resets customer expectations as to what they should pay.

Social influence

Sales people in banks want to come across as nice and trustworthy. People equate niceness with proficiency – it is one of the shortcuts we use to make quick decisions. Customers forget that branch staff might be incentivized to sell, either financially through commissions, or indirectly through pressure from their managers.

And this illusion is continued by the terminology banks use to describe front-line colleagues. The salespeople in branches will be called anything but salespeople, most likely something like 'banking advisers'. They will bring out a pad of paper with different prompts to question you about your life, during which they will seek to find hooks to sell you more products.

Salespeople in banking, like a lot of retail businesses, use tactics to build up trust which make you more likely to buy products. Small talk, for example, can be helpful in making sales representatives seem more trustworthy. They might disclose information about themselves or the bank – such sharing builds trust. They might also speak with authority about the intricacies of the product – building up their credibility in the eyes of the customer. And as we all know, if you want to open a new product at a bank, it often takes a long time. Sometimes hours. This leaves many customers feeling that they risk wasting the branch colleague's time if they pull out now and don't take out any new products.

Some of these are down to deliberate and overt tactics, others are due to the pressure most of us feel not to let people down. This is particularly true in situations where there is an imbalance of information and knowledge. Invariably bank branch colleagues know more about financial products than the average customer, putting them in a powerful position to influence us socially. "They told me it was the best thing to do," is the lament of many a customer sold a product that turned out not to fit their needs.

Customers are unable to see through the fog

Alongside the impact of our decision-making biases, financial decisions can be difficult because it is hard to understand how much banking costs. The information certainly isn't available in one place, and so it requires an investment of your time. Mentally, people file banking with other elements of boring life administration such as utilities, dry cleaning, and going to the dentist. The problem is, without understanding your costs, or the costs of the alternatives, you can't make rational choices.

But customers should not beat themselves up too much; even bankers don't know the costs of their own banking. Famously, when Helen Weir, the former head of retail at Lloyds Banking Group, was questioned on the cost of banking by a Treasury Select Committee member, she claimed that most customers had a "pretty good idea of what they are paying for their current banking". But, in an excruciating moment, when the Chair asked her how much *she* paid, she had to admit that she didn't know.

As we've seen, product managers design their products to take advantage of many customer blind spots. While they might not seek to deliberately mislead customers, they understand how customers tend to think about and use financial products, and design them to deliver the best income possible for the banks they work for. In Part 2 we will explore in much more depth just how product managers do this – looking at the role of products in how we bank, save, and borrow.

CHAPTER SUMMARY

- Product managers and the product teams they work within are overwhelmingly focused on managing products in ways that will deliver income to the bank.

- Delivering your numbers as a product manager in the big banks – increased sales, more income, less cost – is invariably the best way to enhance your career prospects.

- Risk management is thought of as a 'necessary evil' by many product managers.

- Product managers typically move roles every couple of years meaning that the consequences of previous bad decisions rarely catch up with them.

- High turnover of product managers also means that institutional knowledge ('how things work') is repeatedly lost.

- Product managers have a preference for complexity not simplicity. This is because complexity provides a smokescreen to make more money from customers.

- Product areas inside the big banks compete with each other and this can lead to contradictory service outcomes for customers.

CHAPTER SUMMARY

- Delivering cross-product projects and changes can be difficult for product managers due to the many stakeholders and interests involved.

- Product teams represent a paradox: they are open-minded, progressive environments yet the decisions these teams make invariably let customers down.

- Customers often do not act rationally when it comes to their banking, accepting poor service and high fees and rarely voting with their feet.

- A number of behavioural and psychological biases impact customers' ability to engage with banking rationally:

- Present bias means customers prefer 'jam today' when it comes to financial products and promotions, rarely looking at the long-term consequences of their decisions.

- Optimism and projection biases mean customers fail to think about 'what could go wrong', leaving them ill-prepared when circumstances change.

- Mental accounting sees customers keep their finances in mental 'pots' even when mixing those pots up would save them money.

- Prominence and persuasion biases see customers susceptible to the way products are described and packaged.

CHAPTER SUMMARY

- Social influence biases leave customers open to influencing techniques used by bank sales people.

- Customers are rarely able to compare the costs of different banking products, which means they are unable to pick better ones.

PART 2

How they make money out of you

CHAPTER 5

Banking

Bank accounts are simple, right? You pay money in and you spend it using your debit card. And unless you've signed up for what is variously described as a 'packaged' or 'premium' account with benefits like travel insurance, you probably think your current account is 'free'. Few of us give our bank account a second thought – we need it to work and we need help if anything goes wrong with a payment or other transaction.

What is simple and boring from the perspective of a customer is anything but for product managers. Bank accounts are *the* most important product they will manage. Win a customer's bank account and you have them for most of their life and you buy the right to sell them lots of other products and services in the future. They offer the bank stable and cheap funding since few accounts pay interest on credit balances. More importantly, when a bank owns your current account they know a lot about you, from how much you earn to how much you spend (and on what!). This information is increasingly valuable to product managers designing new products.

Bank accounts are complex products to manage from a bank's perspective, requiring lots of infrastructure to run, from large information technology platforms to sophisticated payment processing services. All this stuff costs money and as a result product managers are focused on ensuring that customers generate sufficient income for the bank from their account to cover these costs and hopefully leave something for the bottom line. The humble bank account has, over the last two decades, therefore, been turned into an income-generating machine for banks in ways that frequently enrage customers.

Here we lift the lid on how the bank account market

works, what bankers think about it and how they make money out of you – the customer.

The bank account market and how bankers think about it
A big market where few people switch

In 2013 it was estimated that there were around 65 million personal bank accounts in the UK, generating revenues of around £8.1 billion for providers. Given the adult population of the UK only totals around 48 million people, there are obviously a large number of us with second accounts to go with our main, 'primary' bank account. These second accounts are typically used to pay for things like groceries or a joint account with a partner. Around ten million accounts are estimated to be dormant – where no activity has been seen on the account for over ten years.

The current account market in the UK is growing, but only slowly. The main sources of growth in current accounts, such as new-to-the-UK migrants from the European Union and second accounts used for bills and other purposes, tend not to be the most profitable accounts for banks (at least initially). Due to the market being mature and low-growth, banks in the UK therefore tend to concentrate on market share – gaining a larger slice of a largely static market.

Achieving market share gains is notoriously tough though. Customers perceive switching – either transferring all their standing orders and direct debits themselves or using the new industry-wide Current Account Switch Service which guarantees to move all your regular payment instructions over to your new account within just seven days – as hassle. Many still think things are likely to go wrong. The financial consequences of regular payments like direct debits going wrong or payments being delayed are, of course, all too real for customers. While the industry might say, "It's easy!" customers are cautious. Switching figures vary depending on the definition of a 'switch' but anywhere between 1% and 4% of people are thought to switch their bank account each year.

Switching is also hampered by low 'price transparency' between banks. It is hard to compare and contrast charges and features between bank accounts because we all use our accounts in very different ways. Whether a new current account offered by one of the big banks is a great deal might depend on whether you regularly use an overdraft, sometimes exceed your account limit, have a large credit balance at the end of the month, are able to regularly fund your account with a salary or other credit, or whether you use your debit card frequently. It is therefore hard for customers to figure out whether moving will actually result in them saving money (or earning more) and this leads many customers to conclude: "they all look much of a muchness... I will stay where I am."

The CMA, the body charged with ensuring that the bank account market is competitive, concluded in 2016 that there are barriers to accessing and assessing information on current account charges and service quality, impediments to switching, and low levels of customer engagement.

To try to get things moving in the right direction, the CMA has plans to open up the data that banks hold on how customers use their accounts to allow new information providers like price comparison websites to better assist customers in calculating whether an alternative banking provider might offer a better deal, based on how they use their account. As we shall see in Part 3, it is possible these new tools will support customers to make better decisions about the best place to bank. However, it may also lead to banks focusing on the prices they offer customers for certain services, such as overdrafts, and ignoring the other things that are critical when it comes to bank accounts, such as the number and location of branches, opening hours, and the quality of digital services such as mobile apps.

There is one segment of the current account market that is competitive though. To the extent that any true competition does take place, it is between banks trying to get hold of customers' primary, main current account. Here many banks are willing to spend big as they know that winning the main current account of these customers means they are likely to stay with the bank a number of years, are highly likely to take out additional products and, on the whole, are more likely to repay anything they borrow.

The rest of the market – youth and student accounts, basic bank accounts that offer no overdraft facilities, second accounts – is of only passing interest to product managers. For these customers, the focus of product managers within banks tends to fall on ensuring the cost to serve them is as low as possible, that as much income is generated from them as feasible and that as many of them are turned into primary accounts over time as possible.

A source of cheap and stable funding

Imagine, if you will, that you are a market fruit and vegetable seller. Every day you go to the wholesaler to stock up on fresh produce, load up your van and head to wherever the best market is that day. Your happy customers wander by and smile as they choose their potatoes, carrots, and strawberries. How well your fruit stall does depends on a number of things – how much your market pitch costs, the quality of your fruit and vegetables, and, of course, what your customers are willing to pay for them. But by far the most important factor determining whether or not you will be a successful fruit and veg seller will be the price you have to pay wholesale for your fruit and veg – the *input costs* to the whole operation. You won't get very far if every potato you buy wholesale costs you £10 because you know that your regular punters will never pay that price for a spud!

Crude as this analogy may be, the same logic applies to bank accounts – just swap potatoes for funding. The cost of funding (the interest a bank has to pay us for our money) is the crucial input to whether the bank makes a healthy net interest margin. The net interest margin is the difference between what a bank charges you to borrow and the interest it pays you on your savings. Simply put, if I am paying you 2% on your savings and lending out those funds to someone else at 5% I get to make 3% net interest margin. However, if I am paying you 2% on your savings but I can only lend those funds out at 3%, my net interest margin falls to a miserly 1%.

Enter bank accounts. Bank accounts are a product manager's best friend. Most do not pay credit interest (although there are plenty of exceptions) and are therefore as close to 'free money' as a banker will get. If my cost of funds is 0% I can still make healthy net interest margin by lending out that money at 3%. This gives me a pricing advantage versus my competitors – my bank can offer the best loan rates because my funding is so cheap. Moreover, I don't need to make risky loans that charge a high rate on the expectation that some customers won't repay because I can make an acceptable return charging a lower rate to less risky customers because my funding costs are low.

The CMA found in 2013 that banks made around £3.1 billion in net credit interest, which is the difference between the interest paid out to customers on bank account deposits and the interest received on these funds by a bank's Treasury function (which uses the funds to either support the bank to lend to customers or buy other assets in the money markets).

But the good news doesn't stop there. Bank account funding is what product managers call 'sticky' – it is notoriously stable and predictable. Think about your own life – the chances are your salary goes into your bank account from your employer every month and is roughly the same amount (other than if you get a bonus or are lucky enough to be promoted). Banks can rely on this funding coming in each month. And the way you spend your money is often pretty predictable too. After rent or mortgage payments, groceries, and other typical commitments like paying for a car or a gym membership, you are (hopefully!) left with a residual balance in your account that is usually fairly similar each month.

Product managers and managers in a bank's Treasury function run models to work out this stable component of all the money flowing in and out of current accounts. This is the money they know they can rely on to fund lending and other assets the bank might choose to invest in. Current account funding is therefore hugely helpful to a bank.

A significant source of fee income

Current account customers generate fees – often more fees than any other retail financial services product with the exception of mortgages. The CMA found in 2013 that overdraft fees alone generated over £3 billion in revenue for banks. Account fees added another £1 billion or so and interchange fees (income from card payments) added just under a further £1 billion.

Banks also have a plethora of other fees for which the bank account product is the primary conduit. International payments, CHAPS fees, banker's drafts, stopped cheques – all carry fees that can add up significantly across the year. Additionally, banks have developed significant income streams from monthly account fees for packaged or premium accounts.

But it is overdraft fees that matter most of all. From charging when we go over our account limit to charging us a monthly fee for having an arranged overdraft, these fees are instrumental in deciding whether a product manager can make a profit from bank account customers or not.

A great way to understand customer behaviour

Bank accounts offer product managers many other benefits besides the cheap, stable funding and fees that these accounts deliver. This is because a current account is what is called a 'gateway product'. It is often the first account an individual opens as an adult (perhaps alongside a simple, instant-access savings account).

As we are all busy it is common for customers to choose the bank they have their current account with for any additional financial products they may need – be that a credit card, loan, mortgage, savings account, or insurance policy. From a product manager's perspective, if they win the bank account they have a good opportunity to provide these extra products, delivering more income and hopefully profit for the bank.

Current account customers are what product managers call 'inert' – they don't switch to other banks very often – so winning a current account customer offers the bank a long-term relationship through which the bank can sell additional products. Perhaps more interestingly, winning a customer's bank account also provides a window into how that individual manages their financial affairs. It is often possible to understand a customer's income from employment, and attitudes to saving, borrowing, and spending. This provides important data and information the bank can use to tailor offers to appeal to a customer or price lending products in a way that reflects the risk the customer poses to the bank (in terms of their likelihood to repay any borrowings).

Put simply, a bank account provides the bank with a front-row seat to your life – how much you earn, what you spend it on, and when. Smart banks and smart product managers make use of this information in ways that incentivize customers to take more products with the bank – increasing the bank's 'share of wallet'.

Primary bank accounts – the sweet spot

Not all current account customers are created equal. The customers that banks really care about are what product managers call 'primary' or 'main' bankers. The definition of what constitutes a primary banker differs within the product teams at each bank but, broadly stated, it is a customer who has their salary paid into the account to the tune of £800 to £1,000 a month, every month. These customers typically have three or more regular payments going from the account, be they standing orders or direct debits (and now increasingly recurring card payments). Primary bankers typically stay with their bank for over ten years. They take up to three times more products than non-primary customers. And they are usually better prospects to lend to with much better risk performance due to the fact that the account receives regular salary payments through which to service lending obligations.

Primary bankers are the sweet spot for product managers – a committed customer paying in their salary is rarely keen to uproot their financial life and move everything to another bank. This inertia – a strong desire on the part of customers to stay put – means that banks have upped the ante in their efforts to incentivize customers to switch, knowing that it takes something extra special to convince them to move. Today the switcher market is dominated by £100, £125, or even £150 cash incentives to switch as a result. This is a significant amount of money just to switch your current account and reveals just how valuable acquiring a customer's main bank account is.

These banks are all making the same calculation: they are prepared to pay you an attractive cash incentive to switch to them because they know once you switch you are likely to stick around for a long time and take lots of additional products from them. In reality, the banks are simply sharing the 'relationship premium' they earn from acquiring a primary current account with the customer themselves in order to make the sale. You will notice that in order to qualify for the many cash switch incentives on offer customers need to agree to pay in at least £1,000 a month (a 'regular credit') and often transfer or begin a number of direct debits from the account (usually two or more). Broadly translated this is the bank saying, "We want to be sure you are a committed customer before we pay you the incentive." A primary bank account customer in other words. The shorthand to guarantee this is a stipulation to use the new Current Account Switch Service that transfers all regular payments and credits within seven days.

How banks think about current account customers

No one likes to be pigeonholed but product managers inside the big banks pigeonhole customers pretty much constantly. They prefer to call it 'segmentation', identifying discrete sections of their customer base who display similar behaviours, profitability, and characteristics. The merits of segmentation are supposed to include the ability to better target offers, develop products that meet customer needs more closely, and a greater understanding of which customers are making the bank money and which are not. Too often segmentation is used to do one thing and one thing only: 'product push'. That is, identify customers with a higher propensity to buy more products from the bank.

When it comes to bank account customers, each bank will segment customers in different ways, but from our experience, banks usually divide customers into five or so categories.

The Deal-Hungry Switcher

These customers are quite happy to move all their banking, including all their direct debits, standing orders, and regular credits, for a £50 or £100 cash switching incentive. They typically seek out the current accounts that pay interest on credit balances and make sure they meet all the requirements and conditions on these accounts to access these benefits, such as funding the account with at least £1,000 a month. If they opt for a packaged account, they make sure they register for all the benefits. And they are very sensitive to banks reducing rates or curtailing any benefits on the accounts they have chosen. Moving and switching accounts regularly is the primary *modus operandi* for these guys.

For product managers, Deal-Hungry Switchers are the pits. They take the benefits and special deals offered to attract new customers but don't stick around long enough for the bank to make money out of them after the bank has reduced the benefits or cut the costs of providing the offers. The main benefit of Deal-Hungry Switchers, paradoxically, though is that they do actually move. Current account customers show little appetite to switch their banking as we have seen. For an ambitious product manager looking to 'win' market share, Deal-Hungry Switchers give credence to the view that "pay enough, and they will come". The problem, of course, is that they can leave just as quickly as they came.

The Busy Bankers

If the Deal-Hungry Switchers pose a number of significant challenges to the product manager, the Busy Bankers are a dream. These guys – by far the most common customer group – are busy living their lives and the last thing they have time for is thinking about their current account. Switching to another bank sounds painful to this group as they worry that to do so will involve lots of administrative work and in all likelihood lots of missed payments. Things might screw up. So they stay put and are typically in a current account that is less than competitive. As many in this group are younger, they make ample use of overdrafts and on the occasion they do pay penalty fees they put it down to their own disorganization.

For product managers, Busy Bankers hit the commercial jackpot. This is the customer group that is highly resistant to switching so the product manager need not worry that if they cut benefits on an account the Busy Banker is going to up sticks and leave. They pay the majority of overdraft penalty fees and have a reasonably high propensity to take additional financial products from the bank because they are busy and it's easier to go with a brand they know and already use.

The Basic Banker

Basic Bankers are in fact two distinct types of bankers. The first are young people or new-to-the-UK adults who may not have enough of a credit footprint to apply and be accepted for what bankers call a full facilities current account (one that typically offers an overdraft facility and a full debit card). Basic Bankers – as the name suggests – use basic bank accounts that do not generate much income for the bank as they do not offer overdrafts and the overdraft debit interest income and penalty fees associated with these.

This group is interesting to product managers as they are the full facilities current account customers of the future and – handled well – it is easier and cheaper to upgrade this customer segment to a full facilities current account than it is to spend lots of money on an exciting offer to tempt customers to switch who are already full facilities current account customers elsewhere. So the upgrade pathway – how I change my basic account into a full facilities account – is a critical customer journey to perfect for product managers looking to cater for this segment.

The second group within this category are those who have bad credit records or insufficient income to enable them to access a full facilities current account. Perhaps they had problems with credit in the past and have marks on their credit file. This is a customer segment that the product manager must manage very carefully, both to support them to make the right decisions and to ensure the bank doesn't contribute to further indebtedness by offering credit from other areas of the bank such as credit cards or loans.

Basic Bankers tend to use a bank's services heavily – branch, phone, balance statements at the ATMs – and therefore cost the bank relatively more to serve. At the same time, the income from Basic Bankers is limited in the main to the funding advantages provided by the balances in these accounts. But as this segment is relatively poor, these balances are small.

In truth, while banks have occasionally treated Basic Bankers poorly – such as by refusing to serve them at the branch counter and requiring them to use in-branch phones instead – on the whole banks provide a key service to the community in serving these customers, working with them to get on top of their finances, and helping them to start to build a credit record. It is unglamorous, costly, and essential work that goes largely unnoticed among the headlines of banker greed and excess.

The Long-Term Service Banker

Perhaps the most interesting customer type we meet – and one we secretly think of as the 'smartest' – are the Long-Term Service Bankers. These customers tend to be older and are most definitely wiser when it comes to banking. They know that flashy financial promotions and switching incentives are here today and gone tomorrow and rarely leave the customer in the best account. Instead, this customer segment prizes good customer service over the long term.

They look for convenient branch locations, easy-to-use online banking, and friendly and courteous bank staff. They will do some research as to which bank brands receive the best service ratings and they will track over time the banks that offer the best long-term deals. They therefore appreciate price stability – not moving pricing too often even if it is not the best at the start – as they like to know where they are. And they tend to treasure the importance of the stability and security of the bank, rarely taking a gamble on a brand they have never heard of, even if the rates are good. They regularly deposit up to the £85,000 Financial Services Compensation Scheme limit as they have peace of mind that their money is protected and often take multiple products out where they bank.

For the thoughtful product manager, the Long-Term Service Banker offers hope. Hope that there is the opportunity to build a long-term relationship with the customer not solely based on price. In a world full of Long-Term Service Bankers, no longer does the product manager constantly have to think up attractive pricing and account benefits to hook the next hundred thousand customers before going through the painful process of 'top-slicing' – reducing those benefits over time so the bank can start to make money. Instead, these customers look at what the bank offers in the round – branches, online, mobile, call centre, products, pricing, friendliness of staff, opening hours – and decides what works best for them.

Read most personal finance columns, magazines, or blogs and they will tell you that the smart thing to do when it comes to your bank account is to continually shop around, show no loyalty to banks, and find the best deal out there. Assuming you have the time in your life to do this (we certainly don't!), being attracted by cash incentives risks ignoring a range of factors that have a significant influence on your financial life, such as service quality, branch locations and opening hours, and how helpful the bank's staff are. Long-Term Service Bankers have figured this out.

The Digital Banker

A new wave of digital-only and increasingly 'app-only' banks are emerging in the UK. These banks will likely create a new customer segment; we suspect predominantly of 'millennials' or so-called 'digital natives', who are comfortable using digital technology for all their banking needs. In our experience, these customers are curiously uninterested in what interest rates their bank pays or charges, prizing a beautiful digital user experience and interface instead.

It is not too bold a statement to say that these customers appear to want their bank to become a lifestyle accessory and help them organize their increasingly fractured and complex financial lives more easily. They value 'plumbing not products', wanting things to work seamlessly across digital devices and bank channels and ideally want their bank to integrate with other aspects of their increasingly digital-only life, be that communicating with the bank through Twitter or Facebook or taking 'selfies' to identify themselves when applying for accounts via a smartphone.

Digital Bankers present something of a challenge for product managers – and banking as a whole. On the one hand, product managers are under siege from a raft of digital banks and other companies seeking to disintermediate high-street banks and pick off their most profitable lines of business – just witness the large number of electronic payments and foreign exchange companies to spring up in recent years. On the other hand, the year-on-year investment required to stay current, fresh, and relevant in digital banking is significant. It costs a lot of money to look cool in the eyes of digital natives!

Digital Bankers have the older high-street banks flummoxed. While they like the idea of reducing costs in 'human' channels like branches and call centres as customers do things on their smartphones instead, it is proving almost as expensive keeping up with the pace of technological change and the latest digital trends as it was to maintain these older channels. Add to this that the profitability of digital-only bankers over the medium and long term is less than proven and many banks aren't quite sure what to do. There's the distinct possibility that while their costs will be down so will their income.

How they make money out of you
First things first – it's not free banking

In our experience, the majority of customers think that their banking is free. That is, they pay nothing for having a current account, chequebook, and debit card. Yet banking is not free for two main reasons.

First, a small number – anywhere up to 15% of customers – will regularly pay fees, mainly overdraft paid and unpaid item fees, and overdraft debit interest. Contrary to what you may have read, these are not always the poorest customers struggling to make ends meet. Those customers are often in basic bank accounts that do not allow the account to go overdrawn or attract fees. Rather, in our experience it is the 'disorganized middle class' that tend to pay overdraft penalty fees (the Busy Bankers described above). But the point to focus on is that these fees generate income for the bank and cross-subsidize the cost of providing 'free' banking for the other 85% of customers. So free is not free after all – just free for some customers.

Except that's not the whole story. Free current accounts often pay no credit interest on the funds that customers place in the account, be that a birthday cheque from Mum or a regular salary credit. These funds are worth billions in net credit interest to the banks and this income in part pays for the provision of 'free' current accounts and all the branch infrastructure and staff required to run a bank. Customers are missing out on the interest they could be earning on their money because they need to keep it in a transactional bank account to enable them to pay for everyday bills and things using their debit card.

So again, free is not really free. Free banking is actually banking with no upfront costs, subsidized by some customers paying fees and most customers giving the bank their money for no interest in return. This lack of transparency has led to calls from many consumer organizations and some banks for a move to a more transparent, paid-for model where everyone is charged tariffs for the services they use, such as £5 a month for an account, or 20p every time they use an ATM. Paying for what you use is deemed to be more equitable and straightforward. As we shall argue in Part 3, there is much merit to this argument from a transparency perspective but customers – particularly those who don't tend to pay fees – are very attached to what they think of as 'free' banking meaning no bank has yet taken the plunge and started to charge tariffs.

Bait and hook

You'll recognize this one. You spot what looks like an incredible deal on a current account from one of the leading high-street banks. It might be a juicy switching incentive, perhaps £100 cash. What can possibly go wrong? You switch your account, move all your direct debits and standing orders, get a new card and PIN and congratulate yourself on finding the best deal out there.

From a product manager's perspective this is a 'gotcha!' moment. They've just bagged a customer for life and they'll earn that £100 back in quick order through invariably high overdraft fees and charges and low to no interest paid on your regular monthly credits into the account. This sort of 'bait and hook' routine is rife in the current account market (and much of the financial services industry).

Product managers know that customers are tempted by short-term, instant gratification rewards in the form of cash switching incentives. A tasty introductory offer often leaves customers stranded in accounts that offer poor value over the long term (and by implication great value for banks).

This is because, unlike a two-for-one offer in the supermarket, current accounts are not repeat purchases. They are long-term, relationship purchases. Many people still have their current account at the branch in the village they grew up in as a child. Not for nothing do product managers joke, "You're more likely to get divorced than move your current account!"

Inverse tiering

Banks attracting new customers with a juicy up-front offer is one thing. Designing offers to deliberately mislead customers is quite another. Perhaps the best example of this is inverse tiering. Several high-street banks offer customers what look like very high (compared to the rates offered to savings customers at least) interest rates on current accounts. From the perspective of a customer these deals look fantastic – I get to earn 3%, 4%, maybe even 5% Annual Equivalent Rate (AER) on my current account balance! Earning credit interest on your current account is attractive to customers as it appeals to their lazy side – there is no need to keep remembering to move money into a savings account if you are earning a decent rate on the money in your current account.

The problem is that only a portion of your money earns this high rate. Banks 'inversely tier' the rate. You might earn 4% AER on the first £1,500 in the account but anything over £1,500 will earn 0.00% AER. You don't need to be a maths genius to realize that banks are on to a winner here as lots of people will keep more than £1,500 in their current account at any one time and everything over £1,500 the banks are getting for nothing. The interest cost to the banks of offering a high-interest current account deal are therefore much less than the advertised rate. Add up all the funds in the account and the effective interest rate the bank is paying will be much less than the headline rate.

Aren't customers wise to this? Not in our experience. The 0.00% rate on funds over a threshold amount is not advertised heavily (on the TV adverts it is always in the very small print at the bottom of the screen) and customers tend not to bother reading the always-boring-looking terms and conditions for accounts.

Closing Products

Sometimes, reducing the credit interest or other benefits on a current account is a poor strategy if a product manager wants to reduce costs. It means you risk annoying large numbers of customers – sometimes running into the millions – and this can attract criticism. Financial journalists write stories about another broken promise from a bank; customer forums and blogs decry another bad bank.

Yet from a product manager's perspective the benefits provided on the account may become financially unsustainable so they need to figure out a way of limiting the damage of the account becoming too popular. Paying 2% AER on current account balances is fine if you have a few hundred thousand customers, as a product manager may reason that the price is worth paying to maintain an attractive offer that brings in new customers. It may not be fine when the number of existing customers enjoying the benefit is perhaps in the millions – that's a lot of interest expense for the bank to pay. The cost of paying the rate on a large number of existing customers might outweigh the benefits of being able to offer it to new customers.

The answer is to close the product to new customers. This effectively caps the bank's exposure to paying benefits to existing customers only. By taking the product off sale but allowing customers that have already taken the product out to continue enjoying the benefits, product managers limit bad headlines and perversely can make the customers who were lucky enough to have signed up feel like they got a great deal. However, this ring-fenced group of customers in a closed account are now top of the list for the product manager looking to extract some margin and hit the revenue targets the bank has set them. Cutting the rates paid to this group won't impact the latest new customer offer out there. And so the cycle repeats. The Closed Account sting – just like Bait and Hook – is one of the main reasons people don't trust banks.

Top-slicing

Closing an account is not the only means by which product managers can reduce the cost or drive additional income from a large current-account group of customers. The other strategy product managers deploy is to simply slowly reduce (or 'slice') the rates or benefits of an account over time. This 'margin management' will be a familiar experience to many people.

You start with a great rate or a great benefit like cash back or a free overdraft and over time – slowly and for the product manager hopefully imperceptibly – the rate or benefit is slowly reduced, potentially to zero. The justification often given is that a better, new customer or 'front book' product is now available and customers are free to take advantage of it.

In reality, the product manager is robbing Peter to pay Paul and creating a doom loop for customers. Customers go from being in a great product to being in a terrible product in a matter of years. The money made or saved from reducing the benefits on the once great product is simply recycled into a new product that can be used to entice more people in. This strategy is popular with product managers and successful because so few customers move once they finally decide to open a product.

What is particularly distressing is that many banks make it hard for existing customers to 'upgrade' to the new, better product from the old, no-longer-any-good product. Often products are 'for new customers only' or the upgrade process is made deliberately hard ("you need to visit a branch"). These techniques are brazen; the product manager is using money from existing customers to entice new ones. At no point is customer service or rewarding loyalty really ever considered.

Tripwires

This is an obvious ploy that won't have passed you by. The bank provides you with an additional benefit with your current account – perhaps European travel insurance or a high credit interest rate – but in exchange they ask you to fund the account with a minimum amount each month or hold a minimum balance on your current account.

Product managers know that a reasonable percentage of customers will not meet the criteria to be eligible for the new benefit. They might miss a month of regularly funding their account or let their balance drop below a required minimum. From a product manager's perspective this is great news. They get to advertise a fantastic product with lots of benefits to new customers while ensuring that not all customers qualify for it once inside the door by putting in place these small, qualifying tripwires. It's just plain annoying for customers.

Bundling

While the odd 'buy one get one free' offer in your local supermarket can be a good deal, this is rarely true when it comes to your bank account. Getting discounts or enhanced rates on other products if you have your main or primary bank account with one of the big banks is usually far less attractive than it might look.

In our experience, weird behavioural quirks take over people's brains when they are told that they "qualify for exclusive rates". Shoulders get pushed back, chins are raised, and customers start to feel that, as unlikely as it may be, the bank is finally treating them as the type of customer they always aspired to be – one able to access bespoke, special deals because they are of high quality.

Sadly, most of the time, nothing could be further from the truth. The bank is merely leveraging the fact that your main bank account is with them to offer you deals as they know you have a higher propensity to buy them if you hold your main bank account with the bank.

Why are you more likely to buy them? Well, for very human reasons – everyone is busy and likes to have everything in one place with one online bank account login and one call centre number to remember. Only those who want to seek out better deals and shop around mind having accounts in lots of different places. So if a bank can convince you that you are getting access to 'exclusive' offers on other products by having your main bank account with them, this is just enough motivation and pop psychology to make some customers choose to take out these additional products.

But how does the bank afford to offer these 'special' deals to existing main bank account customers? This is where the magic of cross-subsidization comes in. If I run a supermarket I know that there are a few products that tempt people into the store. Perhaps it's milk or cans of beans. Or nowadays those super flat screen TVs that the supermarkets sell cheaply. I discount these products sharply, perhaps just above or even below the cost I paid for them. I know this will drive people into my supermarket. And while you're in the store you're quite likely to pick up that pack of gum you need or the stain remover for the living room carpet. These products often carry higher margins than the can of beans or milk. If I add up what you've spent, and what my costs are, on *aggregate* I have made money.

Some products make higher returns for banks than others, and some as we said may even cost product managers money, but the aim of the game is to make money at a *customer* level. If your current account pays no credit interest but charges debit interest for an arranged overdraft and fees for unarranged overdraft payments, then that current account usually makes money for the bank. And I know that, as a primary main banker, you are likely to stay with the bank longer, buy more products, and perform better from a risk perspective. So I can use the margin all this good stuff provides to discount a few other products.

Maybe I discount a loan product because I know that you are less risky than a new customer and therefore I don't need to charge as much to cover my risk of losses. I might give you a bit more interest (a few extra 'basis points' in the parlance of product managers) on your savings account, but I also know that main bankers save more anyway. So I am benefiting from a higher savings deposit than I would from a normal customer and the money I am making on the free money in your current account more than compensates for the slight rate enhancement on your savings account.

Special deals for current account customers on other products – when banks manage to organize themselves well enough internally to offer them – are rarely special. They are simply paid for by your current account or the bank is able to offer them because your behaviour as a customer is better or more predictable by dint of you having your main bank account with the bank. There is nothing wrong with taking advantage of these offers, but make sure *in the round* you are getting a good deal on all your banking.

Smoke and mirrors

Sometimes the way account changes are communicated to customers is just as frustrating and opaque as the changes to the accounts themselves. OK, so your overdraft debit interest rate is set to rise. That's bad news. Product managers know this is bad news. To make this bitter pill that bit easier to swallow they wrap the bad news in a coating of good news, and some customers fail to spot the trick (believe it or not). It's the product management equivalent of the ball and three cups game. You're sure the ball is under cup number one but, alas, your mind is playing tricks on you.

Important changes to product terms and conditions, particularly pricing changes that negatively impact a customer, are made via a 'notice of variation', typically in the form of a letter or email to the customer. A typical notice of variation must state clearly what any rate is moving from and to and the date any changes will come into force. Banks are required to provide this notice well before any changes come into effect, normally 60 days beforehand. Account changes need to be clearly and unambiguously stated.

However, context and explanation for the changes is usually very brief. Letters typically start with good news up front (or another strategy is to make the letter look incredibly boring and unimportant so you throw it in the rubbish bin) before getting to the bad news which is typically briefly stated and pitched in such a way that it seems perfectly reasonable given the good news provided earlier in the letter.

For example, for an overdraft debit interest rate rise the letter might start with a lively discussion of the benefits of having an overdraft and just how your bank makes it very convenient to monitor your overdraft through their sparkling new mobile app. What's more, an overdraft is a convenient safety net for life's little unexpected emergencies. And by the way, the rate is set to rise from 15% to 17% APR in 60 days' time. The hope is that when the bad news about the rate rise is delivered you are still thinking about how you really ought to maintain your overdraft as it is a helpful safety net and hey, you're sure you'll never use it anyway.

Letters that 'hide' bad news are one of the chief causes of cynicism about banks and bankers. Customers understandably don't like receiving bad news about fees, charges, and rates moving in ways that may cost them more money. But banks hiding that information or communicating the changes obliquely is particularly frustrating.

Double jeopardy

Bankers love abusing the English language. And they do it to pull the wool over your eyes. 'Officialese' makes many customers think that what the bank is saying must be right because it sounds right. But in reality the customer can be an unwitting victim in a game of buzzword bingo designed to do one thing only: make money for the bank. A classic example is the double jeopardy sting where a customer is effectively paying for the same thing twice but under a different terminology. Overdrafts are again where this particular pitfall resides.

Here's how it happens. You run a low balance in your current account and as your bad luck would have it a large payment is presented for clearing and your bank honours the payment, taking you into an unarranged overdraft position. You will immediately start incurring debit interest (often but not always at an enhanced rate to a standard arranged overdraft interest rate). In addition, as you have created an unarranged, 'emergency' or 'on-demand' overdraft this often necessitates the payment of a monthly overdraft facility fee. And of course as the bank honoured the payment, you will also need to pay a paid item fee.

So for going overdrawn you can potentially pay up to three fees, all essentially for the same thing. But each is called something different, leading to customer confusion and frustration. This is a Kafkaesque position for customers to find themselves in, but when customers complain banks can rely on their long and complicated terms and conditions to say: "This is the service you signed up for."

Of course customer anger over rip-off overdraft fees is not new. These fees represent a major source of income for retail banks and they are loath to reduce them. In a recent report, Which?, the consumer rights organization, found that some customers who borrow £100 for 30 days through an unarranged overdraft can pay up to £180 in charges. That is higher than the interest rates typically charged by payday loan companies. Which? found that about 20% of all customers enter unarranged overdrafts and that these fees alone generate over £1.2 billion in fee income for the banks.

The issue here is a lack of clarity as to what the banks are actually charging customers for and why banks have to create lots of different types of fee for essentially the same thing. Why, for example, do I have to pay a monthly overdraft facility fee as well as debit interest? Why do I pay a higher debit interest rate if I step into an unarranged overdraft than when I use an arranged overdraft? This lack of clarity makes customers very angry and even though the 2016 CMA market investigation into competition in the current account market stopped short of imposing any price caps on overdraft charges, it has pressed banks to state the maximum monthly charge overdraft users could be subject to.

Banks will probably fight any suggestion of a price cap tooth and nail, arguing that the regulators risk tipping the current account market into a paid-for model, where 'free' banking becomes a thing of the past. It seems to us the most likely scenario is that banks will continue recent moves to make arranged overdraft facilities more expensive as a way to make up for reducing the charges associated with unarranged overdrafts.

Heads I win, tails you lose

Paying multiple fees for the same thing is frustrating, appearing to pay fees when the bank has – literally – done nothing, can be extra galling. Banks are specialists in this and the best example is unpaid item fees. Here you pay the bank a fee for them *not* making a payment from your account. Say for example you have £50 left in your account but a direct debit is due for £100 (the gas bill!). If the bank decides to pay the direct debit this will take your account into an unarranged overdraft, at a higher debit interest rate, and you will pay a paid item fee. If the direct debit is declined by the bank, well, this is banking so we will charge you for not paying the direct debit via an unpaid item fee. It is the banking equivalent of heads I win, tails you lose.

The bank decides whether to pay the item based on its own analysis of you as a customer and whether you are likely to pay them back the amount you have gone into unarranged overdraft by. And to add insult to injury, the companies whose bill the bank has not paid will also often charge you if their direct debit is unpaid. It is not uncommon for mortgage or credit card providers to charge you a late payment fee if their direct debit is returned unpaid – a double whammy.

As we have said, unpaid item fees are a form of cross-subsidisation, allowing banks to provide free banking to the majority of customers by charging a minority of customers who go over their account limit a fee. Until and unless customers are prepared to pay for a bank account, as opposed to expecting a bank account to be free, cross-subsidisation through unpaid item fees is likely to continue.

The Waterbed Effect

Frustratingly, even when product managers get caught out by public opinion or regulators they have ways of ensuring they don't lose out. When banks get told by regulators – or through persistent negative press coverage – that they can't make money one way they simply make it another way. Push the water bed down in one area and it rises in up in another.

The best example here is – yet again – overdrafts. Following regular press and customer outcries and regulatory scrutiny from the precursor to the CMA, the Office of Fair Trading, banks decided that it was becoming unpalatable to charge high, unarranged overdraft fees. In response, product managers decided they'd just make arranged overdrafts more expensive while reducing the charges associated with unarranged overdrafts.

The CMA reported in 2016 on the extent of this trend. Overdraft fees for arranged overdrafts increased by more than £161m between 2011 and 2013 while unarranged charges dropped by £220m. Throw in a slight increase in income to the banks from changes in net debit interest over the period and banks were not far off being all square. They had managed to survive a huge regulatory and public onslaught by simply moving charges from unarranged to arranged overdrafts.

Happy holidays!

Product managers love it when customers travel abroad. When you think of your next holiday you are probably thinking about beaches, cocktails, and having a well-earned rest. When product managers think about you on holiday they see pound signs! This is because everything about paying for things abroad using your bank account debit card is an income bonanza for product managers.

When you use your debit card in a foreign cash machine, you will be charged a non-sterling transaction fee which is levied as a percentage of the transaction and can be anywhere up to 3% *and* a non-sterling purchase fee, usually around £2.50 or so. If you make a card purchase abroad, typically only the non-sterling transaction fee is payable. Best of all, charges are invariably higher if you are undertaking these transactions outside Europe (or outside the Single European Payments Area – SEPA – to be precise).

While banks do incur some costs when customers transact outside SEPA and it is therefore not unreasonable that they try to pass some of these on, most banks make a killing on card transactions inside SEPA. It is another example of banks levying charges simply because they can.

In recent years, some of this income has been challenged by new entrants to the market, however. Nimble financial technology companies such as Revolut are able to offer more competitive international exchange rates and payment functionality. Yet millions of customers still see their bank as the first and most obvious port of call before they go on holiday. It's where their bank account is, making paying for the holiday currency easy, and customers find it difficult to compare currency rates leading many to conclude that they'll just pay whatever their bank charges them. Over the course of a holiday this can mean they are needlessly paying hundreds of pounds in charges.

Packaged accounts

Paid-for, packaged, premium, or added value accounts (product managers use all these names interchangeably for ostensibly the same thing) are one of the most lucrative 'innovations' product managers have developed for the current account market in the last decade. Today there are around ten million customers who have a current account for which they pay a monthly fee, according to the CMA. These paid-for accounts offer a range of benefits for a monthly fee – usually including the 'big three' insurance policies: mobile phone, car breakdown cover, and travel. Packaged accounts have proven popular with customers. However, they have been subject to controversy, including high rates of complaints to the Financial Ombudsman Service, widespread criticism of the sales process used to distribute the products to customers, and concerns over whether or not they are appropriate for all customers.

For product managers, packaged accounts represent an exciting opportunity to make even more fee income from bank account customers and they have taken advantage of this opportunity with almost indecent zeal.

High perceived value, low real cost

This is the trick most often pulled by product managers managing packaged accounts. It deploys some clever behavioural economics and is ruthlessly commercial. It goes something like this: you sign up for a paid-for account for, say, £20 a month. For that you get free travel insurance, free mobile phone insurance and car breakdown cover, and a whole host of other smaller benefits like discounts at restaurants and theme parks. It feels good – this is an account that takes the hassle out of arranging all these things individually and typically suits your busy life. However, our product manager has an annual profit target to deliver and the income he's making out of the group of customers with these paid-for accounts needs to rise – particularly as the cost to the bank of providing some of the account's benefits may also have risen.

Simply increasing the monthly fee to make more money – while straightforward – is likely to see a significant number of customers cancel their account in protest (not good news). So what product managers dream up instead are ways to add benefits to the package that have a high perceived value but at a low actual cost to justify a price rise.

A typical example here might be airport lounge access. The bank announces to great fanfare that holders of its packaged account can now enjoy free airport lounge access with their account. As anyone that has spent time waiting around in airport lounges can attest, that is a great benefit to have with your current account. At the same time, the price of the account is increased by, say, £5 a month.

Mentally, customers cross reference the two and invariably think, "Airport lounge access for a fiver? That's a great deal!" Except you don't need to be Einstein to realize that it's not £5 it's £60 (12 months paying an additional £5). And customers rarely go to an airport more than twice a year. The cost of providing this benefit for customers to the bank might be as little as £5 or £10, leaving them with a healthy £50 additional income per year.

You may be thinking that it is very dim of customers not to realize they are being swindled but, in our experience, many customers simply don't do the maths and compare the increase in the monthly account fee to the value of the new benefit that has been added. And of course there is the hassle of cancelling the paid-for account and arranging all those insurances separately if you do decide to go elsewhere.

The rule of thumb most banks work to is: "If I want to put the price up I need to find some air cover in the form of a new benefit or feature," and no matter whether that additional 'benefit' represents good value for the price rise or not.

Going for gold

It has always been our view that there is a perfectly good case for choosing a packaged account. Everything wrapped into one monthly bundle for a fee is a low-hassle way to organize some aspects of your financial life. The FCA agrees, stating on more than one occasion that they believe that paid-for accounts can offer good value and convenience for customers. Yes you can source the elements of the package individually and often for less money than you are paying for the paid-for account, but we are all busy. Paid-for accounts represent a one-stop shop and they have their uses.

It's when banks offer ranges and tiers of packaged accounts that things get dicey though. Nearly all of the big banks have at one time or another offered ranges of paid-for accounts and they use every conceivable, persuasive nomenclature to entice you to upgrade to the next account up in the range. Names like Bronze, Silver, Gold, and Platinum for each account in the range are used in the hope they will entice as many customers as possible to opt for the account that sounds the most premium.

Ranges of paid-for accounts make it confusing for customers and they frequently get 'bid up' by sales agents in a branch or over the phone into taking an account that is expensive and perhaps unsuitable for them. Sales agents in banks have in the past deployed a range of techniques to influence customers in this regard. Often this influencing is subtle, wondering out loud whether the customer is 'eligible' for the premium account in the range (when in actual fact the entry criteria for the account are usually identical to the other paid-for accounts in the range) and highlighting the discounts and benefits on other products with the bank that are unlocked if the customer takes the top-of-the-range account.

The difference in the benefits of each account in the range are often modest but the difference in cost is usually substantial – sometimes £10 or £15 a month. That's £120 to £180 a year! Less thoughtful customers appear to covet the idea that their account is the top-of-the-range one, even if they are paying an arm and a leg each month. The upgrade is never (ever!) worth the value of the additional monthly fee in our experience.

Although few will admit it, banks are worried that the sale of paid-for accounts will prove to be another payment protection insurance-type scandal which saw billions of pounds repaid to customers for insurance coverage wrongly sold to customers. These worries are for three main reasons.

First, generally speaking, record-keeping of the account-opening process in big banks is dreadful – banks would be hard pressed to evidence that you actively chose the paid-for account in the first place. In recent times several banks have moved to capture this sales process on a computer so that they have a virtual paper trail of the sales interaction for just this reason. If they can't prove you opted for the account, most rely on the fact that you have used some of the benefits to claim that you knew you had the account and therefore must have opted for it. Most banks feel they are skating on quite thin ice. Just how thin was made clear during the FCA's Thematic Review of the paid-for account market in 2016 which found that many banks did not consistently deliver fair outcomes for customers who complained that their account was mis-sold.

Second, the product itself is full of potential conduct risks. Banks must check whether customers could be 'doubly insured' if they take out a packaged account. Many customers will be covered by home insurance and credit card policies for much of the cover offered by these accounts and they could be paying for the same cover twice (often with the same bank!).

Similarly, some of the insurances contained within the paid-for accounts have exclusions (such as age or pre-existing medical conditions restrictions) or may clearly never be used by customers. It is therefore important for banks to record and notify customers about these aspects correctly. This is why the FCA recommended after its thematic review that banks check that customers are eligible for the insurance policies in the package of benefits regularly and send customers annual eligibility statements.

Third, complaints to the Financial Ombudsman Service about packaged accounts have risen in recent years. Only a cursory reading of consumer finance blogs and newspaper columns shows that there appears to be some truth in the rumour that these accounts have indeed at times been mis-sold. Examples include customers being told they had to get a paid-for account (often foreign nationals new to the UK), persuaded that taking the account was the only way to get an overdraft, and being informed that a paid-for account helped build a better credit score. All of these reasons are, frankly, total tosh.

It is revealing that in recent years many banks have all but eliminated the staff incentives in sales channels to sell packaged accounts over normal current accounts. The worry, of course, was that these incentives were encouraging staff to sell paid-for accounts to customers when it was clearly not suitable to do so.

CHAPTER SUMMARY

- The UK current account market is highly 'inert' (few people switch their accounts) and dominated by the big five banks.

- A recent Competition and Markets Authority investigation found that there are serious barriers to competition in the market, particularly in relation to how easy it is to compare the cost of overdrafts and obtain data from banks on how you use your account.

- Product managers in banks view current accounts as a cheap and stable source of funding and the start point for cross-selling customers other products that the bank offers.

- Each bank has different approaches to how they segment current account customers but broadly speaking they think of five groups: the Deal-Hungry Switcher, the Busy Banker, the Basic Banker, the Long-Term Service Banker, and the Digital Banker.

- Banks typically compete with switching offers for Deal-Hungry Switchers and make the most money out of Busy Bankers.

- Current accounts are often thought to be 'free' as they attract no upfront or monthly fees. In reality, few banks pay credit interest on balances and many customers pay significant fees for going over their account limit.

CHAPTER SUMMARY

- Bait and hook practices are where banks lure customers in on a competitive deal or offer and then reduce the offer over time.

- Closed account practices are where products are closed to new customers to contain the cost of a promotion and usually prior to the benefits on that product being reduced.

- 'Top-slicing' sees banks slowly reduce promotional pricing or other benefits on an account over time. Such margin management is the default management technique for product managers.

- Tripwires are the often-complex conditions put on accounts in order to access the stated account benefits. Typical examples include regular monthly funding or a minimum credit balance.

- 'Bundling' sees product managers use the current account to promote a range of cross-product discounts to encourage customers to take out more products with the bank, even if those additional products are not competitively priced.

- Banks are often guilty of using 'smoke and mirrors' in how they tell customers about changes to accounts, particularly if those changes are negative for the customers. Bad news wrapped up inside a veneer of good news is common.

CHAPTER SUMMARY

- 'Double jeopardy' is where a customer will pay two or sometimes three different fees for one transaction that takes them over their account limit, usually consisting of debit interest and a fee.

- Banks continue to make money from unpaid item fees, when a bank has refused to make a payment from an account due to insufficient funds. If the bank had paid the item they would have charged a paid item fee. This can leave customers feeling cheated – a 'heads you win, tails I lose' scenario.

- Using your debit card abroad can be expensive, with fees charged for using an ATM or paying at point of sale with your debit card and a further interest rate spread levied on the currency transaction.

- Paid-for or packaged accounts are a lucrative source of fee income for banks and product managers have devised a number of techniques to enhance the return they deliver:
    - Often product managers will add new benefits to the package that have a high perceived value but low actual cost, thereby providing a justification for product managers hiking the monthly fee for the account.
    - Banks that have ranges of paid-for accounts often try to get customers to take the next account up in the range, on a higher monthly fee.

CHAPTER 6

Saving

As any seasoned watcher of murder mystery shows on TV will tell you, it's always the slightly diffident chap at the back of the room that turns out to have killed the vicar with a fire poker. It's a bit like that with savings accounts. These accounts look unassuming and harmless but in the hands of product managers, incentivized to make as much money for their employers as possible, they regularly let customers down. This is, perhaps, all the more surprising given how simple they appear to be. You transfer some spare cash into a savings account each month for a rainy day. What could possibly go wrong?

Plenty, as it turns out. For when it comes to the way product managers look at savings accounts, we are reminded of the line from the movie *The Usual Suspects*: "The greatest trick the Devil ever pulled was convincing the world he didn't exist." Comparing product managers to the devil is probably a bit strong (just) but the metaphor is apt. Product managers design and manage savings accounts in ways that make it very difficult for customers to detect that they are losing out.

Why does this sad state of affairs persist? Perversely, some see it as a sign of a healthy and competitive savings market, with product managers competing to win your savings through 'product innovation'. The less charitable interpretation is that product managers have thought up clever ways to deliver savings deposits for the banks they work for in as cheap a way as possible, regardless of whether customers understand what's going on or not. Little wonder the savings market is flooded with complex 'bonus' products with the best rates usually reserved for new customers only.

As we explained in Part 1, ultimately retail banking is about taking in deposits and lending them out.[1] The cheaper the interest rate you pay customers for their deposits, the more money you stand to make when you lend those funds out. This means that all product managers have a laser-like focus on generating the bank's required amount of funding as cheaply as possible. Customers mostly have the opposite objective, of course, to earn as high an interest rate on their savings as possible (although the level of service, location, and reputation of the bank are admittedly also key). Thus the stage is set for a classic battle of wits: product managers looking to raise savings deposits cheaply and customers looking to earn as much interest as possible. As we'll see, it's not really a fair fight.

The savings market and how bankers think about it

According to data from the Bank of England from November 2016, there is around £1,276 billion held in retail deposit accounts in the UK. Of this, around £650 billion sits in easy-access savings accounts, £270 billion in cash Individual Savings Accounts (ISAs) and £180 billion in fixed-term savings accounts. More than nine in ten adults have a cash savings account of some sort.

The savings picture is not quite as rosy as these bumper figures would seem to suggest, though. A study by the Money Advice Service in 2015 found that over 16 million people in the UK have less than £100 in savings. In some

---

[1]   It's actually slightly more complicated than that. The idea that banks take in funds to lend them out is actually a shorthand way to describe the way banks create money through the provision of loans.

areas like the West Midlands, Yorkshire and the Humber, Wales, Northern Ireland, and the North-East of England, over half the adult population have savings *below* £100. According to the OECD, the UK saves less than almost every other country in the European Union.

The macroeconomic environment has not been kind to savers in recent years. Interest rates offered on savings accounts have fallen significantly since the reductions in the Bank of England Base Rate in 2008 and 2009 and due to the introduction by the Bank of the Funding for Lending Scheme in 2012 and the Term Funding Scheme in 2016. Just when savers thoughts rates couldn't go any lower, the Bank of England dropped rates again in August 2016, from 0.50% to just 0.25%. Saving for a rainy day is hard enough, without those savings earning hardly any interest.

The market is dominated by the big, high-street banks…

Just like the current account market, the savings market is dominated by just a few players, with Lloyds Banking Group, Santander, Royal Bank of Scotland, HSBC, and Barclays accounting for some 60% of the market. While there are many other smaller savings providers than in the current account market, and a lot more online-only providers in particular, the 'Big 5' banks continue to hold major sway. Only Nationwide, a building society, is anywhere close to challenging these banks' leading market shares.

…and they have a big advantage

The biggest high-street banks in the UK have considerable advantages in attracting lower cost, easy-access savings account balances because they are more likely to hold a customer's current account. Not unreasonably, many consumers like to keep their current account and savings account in one place, sweeping anything left over at the end of the month from their current account to their savings account.

The FCA conducted some research into the cash savings market in 2015 and found that the four largest personal current account providers paid on average materially lower interest rates on easy-access accounts than other providers. The reason was obvious enough: they didn't need to pay high rates to attract these funds because they knew they would likely get them anyway as customers like to keep their savings in the same place as their current account.

This impacts how competitive the savings market is, with newer firms like challenger banks and smaller building societies typically having to offer higher interest rates to win easy-access savings balances away from the larger current account providers.

The advantages to the big banks don't stop there, however. Lower cost, easy-access savings deposits give the bigger banks a 'funding cost advantage' that they can use to fund loans at lower rates to customers, thereby winning more business on the other side of their balance sheets. Again, it is hard for smaller banks and building societies to compete.

Loyalty doesn't pay

Perhaps the most significant aspect of the UK savings market is how poorly it treats loyal customers. The 2015 FCA study of the cash savings market showed that high-street banks are content to let loyal savers wallow on poor rates for years. One third of savings balances in easy-access accounts were found to be held in accounts opened more than five years ago and these were paid lower interest rates than accounts opened more recently.

Savings providers launch new products very regularly, sometimes multiple products every month, and withdraw older products from sale or no longer market them to new customers. The same FCA study showed the full extent of this, finding that 350 easy-access products were offered on the market but over 1,000 accounts were no longer on sale to new customers. This can leave customers bewildered and unsure whether they have a competitive rate or not, particularly as banks are not great at letting customers know what rate they are on very clearly or very often.

Better deals are out there, but few of us switch to get them

The big banks – and it does tend to be the big banks – have large numbers of customers sitting in savings accounts earning relatively low interest rates where the benefits of switching, even in the current low interest rate environment, could be high enough to make switching worthwhile. The FCA agrees and found in 2013 that around £160 billion of easy-access savings earned an interest rate equal to or lower than the Bank of England Base Rate (at that time 0.50%) when far better rates were available in the market. And these aren't accounts with just a few pounds in that customers can be forgiven for forgetting about – at least £145 billion of this £160 billion was held in accounts with more than £5,000.

Yet customers continue to feel that switching their savings somewhere else will be a hassle – just the same as they do for bank accounts. Well over three quarters of easy-access accounts have not been switched in the last three years and from a product manager's perspective this is great news – a stable source of funding for the bank and one that they have a good chance of reducing the interest rate on year after year.

Liquidity value

You might think that every pound deposited in a bank, be it from a personal retail customer or a commercial business, is of equal value. After all, the bank makes money by lending that money out so what does it matter where that pound came from? Well, as we saw in Part 1, banks have to hold liquidity against deposits – they have to keep some of their deposits in reserve in case customers come in asking for their money back. Lending out all the deposits a bank receives isn't smart since if enough depositors ask for their money back then the bank becomes technically insolvent – a classic 'run on the bank' scenario.

Banks have to hold different levels of liquidity depending on the type of customer depositing. Commercial and larger business customers are viewed as being generally sophisticated users of financial services and therefore likely to withdraw their money at short notice in the event of what banks call 'stress scenarios' such as the 2008 financial crash. As a consequence banks have to hold a higher percentage of deposits for commercial money in reserve, usually parked at the Bank of England and earning a low rate of return.

Retail savings customers in contrast are thought to be, on the whole, less sophisticated than larger commercial customers and therefore the bank can hold less liquidity against these deposits and use the rest to fund the bank's lending. This is why banks are generally able to offer higher interest rates on retail savings products than they are able to on commercial deposit accounts. The requirement to hold less liquidity against retail savings means they can use more of that funding to support lending activity which delivers a higher return, the proceeds of which are shared between the bank and retail savers.

The same principle applies for the different types of savings product. While higher levels of liquidity have to be held against commercial deposits than personal retail savings, higher levels of liquidity also have to be held against savings products that offer 'instant access' to money than fixed-term products. This stands to reason because, by definition, instant-access products allow customers, whether commercial or personal, to take money out whenever they want. In contrast, products that restrict access to the money for a fixed period or a given notice period provide the bank with peace of mind that this funding is in place for at least the period of the fix or notice period. As such, these products have higher 'liquidity value' than instant-access products and therefore pay a higher interest rate in the normal course of events.

What this all means is that for every £100 deposited in a bank from a retail and commercial customer, the amount a bank has to hold in reserves can be vastly different. A personal retail instant-access account will hold perhaps 10% of this sum as liquidity while a large commercial instant-access account will hold up to 100% (that's the full £100). A personal retail customer with a 12-month fixed-term deposit will see the bank hold a very low percentage as liquidity while the same product for a large commercial customer will require the bank to hold a much higher level of liquidity.

If you're wondering why any bank would offer large commercial depositors instant-access products when they have to hold all the deposit in reserves, the answer lies in the value these large commercial customers bring the bank in other ways, such as lending opportunities, and fee income from banking services such as foreign exchange and payment services. Sometimes it is also possible to make a small return, often a few basis points, between the rate paid to the commercial customer and the rate the bank can receive from placing the money at the Bank of England as part of its reserves. Even so, banks can sometimes make very little from deposits from large commercial customers.

Interest-rate risk

Because most banks offer fixed-term savings products paying a fixed interest rate for a set period, product managers also have to concern themselves with managing interest-rate risk. If a product manager offers a one-year fixed-term bond at an interest rate of 5%, the bank is committed to paying the customer that rate for a period of 12 months. A lot can happen in a year. If the economy enters a recession, interest rates may fall significantly meaning that the bank may have fewer opportunities to lend money out and the money it does lend out is likely to be at a lower interest rate return.

To get around this, product managers, working with their colleagues in the bank's Treasury team, will seek to hedge their exposure to interest rate changes through the use of swaps. These are agreements between the bank and other participants in the money markets to exchange a fixed interest rate for a floating rate (or vice versa) that moves up or down in line with a reference interest rate like the London Interbank Offered Rate (LIBOR) or the Bank of England's Base Rate. The important point to note is that these swaps cost a bank money as they are passing on the interest-rate risk to other market participants, thus the cost to a bank of a one-year fixed-rate deposit is likely to be the interest rate they are paying the customer plus the costs of the swap.

You might be thinking, why don't banks just use one-year fixed-rate deposits to fund one-year loans? The short answer is that in some cases banks do seek to 'term match' their deposits and lending. But in practice this proves quite hard. There is far more demand for five-year fixed-rate mortgages, for example, than there is for five-year fixed-rate savings bonds. That's because customers tend to like to borrow over a long period but save over a shorter time horizon.

Managing interest-rate risk is of seminal importance to banking and the relevant UK regulator, the PRA, closely monitors how much interest-rate risk banks are running to ensure they are not at risk of going bust if interest rates change suddenly.

Price elasticity

When product managers think of personal retail savers they think: 'quick funding'. This is because a relatively small number of retail savers can be relied upon to transfer significant funds to a bank if it offers a sufficiently attractive rate. Product managers tend to call this 'hot money'.

This segment of savings customers show *price elasticity*, that is if the interest rate offered increases, sometimes only marginally, there will be a large increase in demand from savers placing their money with the bank. The key determinant of just how much of this hot money a bank will gain tends to be where the interest rate offered sits in the best-buy tables, featured in the personal finance press and newspapers.

Banks often use 'multi-brand strategies' in this regard, that is they develop several different brands through which to offer savings accounts, optimizing for the price elasticity of customers. The big banks tend to use less-well-known brands rather than their 'core' brands to attract hot money. This reduces the risk of customers in their core brands getting tipped off about better rates and potentially increasing the bank's interest expense overall.

Price elasticity is useful to product managers. The bank may have identified a number of lucrative lending opportunities in the mortgage or commercial loan market and to take advantage of these the bank needs additional funding. A best-buy savings account, particularly in the closely monitored one- or two-year fixed-term market, will see a flurry of coverage in the personal finance columns of the national newspapers followed by significant inflows from customers keen to earn a higher rate on their savings. At its best, this represents banking working as it should, ensuring capital flows to areas of the economy where it can be used more productively – in this case mortgages and commercial lending. For the product manager, these customers represent a fantastic 'tap' that can be turned on and off as required.

Share of wallet

As the savings market sees customers move their savings to different banks to get the best rate, sometimes several times a year, this provides an opportunity for product managers to capture more of these customers' 'share of wallet'. It is not uncommon for product teams to do lots of analysis to identify savings customers who hold no other product with the bank and then create a range of offers and deploy a range of techniques to try to persuade these customers to take out an additional product with the bank.

For example, savings customers might receive a piece of direct mail through the post offering them an exclusive cash incentive if they switch their current account to the bank.

Or the product manager might work to ensure that lists of these customers are entered into the bank's customer service system so that if a savings customer pops into a branch to deposit some money, something called a 'prompt' will flash up on a branch colleague's screen. This prompt will let the colleague know about a targeted offer for the customer, perhaps a competitive promotion on a balance transfer for a credit card, again designed to persuade them to open another product with the bank.

Product managers go to all this effort because they know large numbers of savings customers will not have additional products with the bank and therefore offer a great opportunity for the bank to increase its market share in other product categories.

How banks think about savers

In our experience, it's remarkable how savers tend to fall into a number of neat categories in terms of how they behave. Being generally rather lazy, product managers use these categories as a form of shorthand.

Safety-First Savers

As the name suggests, these savers are a sensible, if somewhat paranoid, bunch that save for a rainy day and spread their savings around numerous providers to take advantage of the Financial Services Compensation Scheme protection of £85,000. The FSCS is the UK's statutory fund of last resort for customers of banks and pays compensation if a financial services provider is unable to repay a customer the savings they put into the provider, such as when a bank has gone bust or suffered a run on its funds.

Safety-First Savers tend to be an older demographic (50 years old plus) and have typically paid off their mortgage or are near to doing so. They are focused on maximizing the interest rate they receive from their savings as these are often an important source of additional income for them – or at least will be when they retire. Above all, they want to earn interest in a way that puts none of their capital at risk.

For the product manager, these customers are a challenge. On the one hand, they do tend to switch if a good rate is available and can therefore represent a significant source of quick funding if required. On the other, how much funding a product manager can gain from these savers is in practice effectively capped on an individual saver basis by the FSCS guarantee. A quick glance at any bank's system will likely show thousands of accounts, all with the same deposit balance of £85,000. This represents thousands of customers saying "I like your rates but I don't want to lose any of my money if your bank goes bust!" For Safety-First Savers, the FSCS guarantee is more important than the interest rate received but the interest rate has to be 'there or thereabouts' versus competitors in the market to tempt them to switch.

Jam-Jar Savers

These savers are what many product managers call 'tidy but tempted'. Tidy in that they like to set up different savings accounts for specific purposes, such as saving for a car or Christmas shopping. Tempted because more often than not the reason they divide up their savings across different accounts is because they know they will be tempted to spend the money unless it is earmarked for a specific purpose. They like the clarity of seeing how much they have saved towards a specific goal.

For the nefarious product manager Jam-Jar Savers can represent a good source of reasonably priced, stable funding as long as the bank is able to do something quite simple. It is important to Jam-Jar Savers that the bank makes it easy for them to transfer money into and out of all their different accounts. So a good mobile banking app is key, as is making it simple to set up standing orders from a current account into each savings account. What matters more, however, is offering Jam-Jar Savers the ability to put a different name on the account via online banking. Put simply, Jam-Jar Savers like to put a name on the jar they are saving into.

So an 'Instant-Access Savings Account' might be renamed 'Christmas Savings' or 'New Car Account'. The ability to rename an account seems to foster a bizarre psychological attachment on the part of Jam-Jar Savers, even if the rate offered on the account isn't that good. With all their standing orders set up every month to fund each account and each account having a specific name for a particular purpose, Jam-Jar Savers loathe switching to other providers unless absolutely necessary. This is good news for a product manager, as they know that as long as they offer a reasonable rate on these accounts, customers won't switch elsewhere.

Besides the opportunity to generate cheap, stable funding for the product manager, Jam-Jar Savers can inadvertently add some light relief. Many a customer service representative has had to pretend not to notice an account labelled 'Gambling Account' or 'Beer Money' when helping a customer make a deposit or withdrawal at the branch counter. Customers save for lots of reasons and Jam-Jar Savers often let you know what those reasons are!

ISA Fanatics

Individual Savings Accounts, or ISAs for short, matter to product managers. According to HMRC, the value of the cash ISA market was estimated to be £269 billion in 2016 with over ten million customers holding an ISA account. This was on top of the £249 billion invested in stocks and shares ISAs. ISA Fanatics are a smart bunch, realizing that the tax that you pay on your savings interest or share gains is a key part in determining the long-term returns from saving and investing.

Cash ISAs represent a significant element of the savings market and thus the funding available to a bank. You will often see a 'price war' between the high-street banks towards the end of a tax year and at the start of a new one as they try to tempt ISA savers to move their savings to them, whether they be fixed-rate cash ISAs or easy-access ISAs.

Until recently the rules governing the ISA market were quite simple. ISA Fanatics could save a few thousand pounds into an ISA each year, tax free. Many banks offered customers the ability to 'transfer in' previous years' ISAs as well so that customers could grow one big, tax-free, savings lump.

Things started to change in 2014, though. The government decided to increase the amount customers could put into a cash ISA significantly, from £5,940 to £15,000, with the limit now (the 2017/2018 tax year) at an all-time high of £20,000. This started to change the dynamics of the market materially. Banks used to pay high rates for cash ISA money because they knew the market was liquid (people would switch) and that their exposure was relatively small (a great rate offered for a small amount of savings). It was, in many ways, a price banks were willing to pay to tempt in new customers.

With the ISA subscription limits increasingly materially, however, this started to impact the returns product managers could make from other, non-ISA accounts like instant-access accounts. Why, for example, would a customer save into an instant-access account when they can save into an easy-access cash ISA account, tax free? The answer to that question used to be because customers could only put in a few thousand pounds into an ISA. But with the new higher limits being in most cases more than customers had in total savings there really was no reason not save everything in an ISA. In response, the difference in interest rates paid between ISA accounts and non-ISA accounts has started to narrow leading 2015 and 2016 to be dubbed the "worst ever years for ISAs" by many. Banks are now no longer willing to 'pay up' for ISA balances like they once were.

The increased ISA subscription limit isn't the only development to have significantly impacted the ISA market in recent times. In 2016 the UK Government introduced a new Personal Savings Allowance which permitted every basic rate taxpayer to earn up to £1,000 a year in interest, tax free, whether the savings account was an ISA or not. For higher rate taxpayers the tax-free interest allowance was £500 (and zero for additional rate taxpayers). Almost overnight, there was little incentive for most customers to use ISAs because few would earn over £1,000 a year in interest on their savings anyway given than average savings in the UK tend to be around the £10,000 mark. Coupled with the low interest rate environment which has persisted since 2009, for many customers the tax-free advantages of an ISA are now pretty irrelevant as they receive tax relief on the interest they receive in all savings accounts up to £1,000 a year anyway. Product managers have again responded by lowering the rates paid on ISAs.

Fixers

As the name suggests, these customers like to take advantage of the higher interest rates banks are willing to pay for fixed-rate and fixed-term deposits. They tend to be 'well saved' and don't mind placing money in fixed-term deposits as they have plenty of other savings available in instant-access accounts. Banks can more easily use fixed deposits to fund different types of fixed-term assets (such as mortgages) and they have a high liquidity value. As such, banks are willing to pay a little more for fixed deposits. Fixers tend to be quite financially savvy and spread a number of fixed-term deposits across a range of maturities (endpoints) so they are never without access to money for too long if needed.

Rate Tarts

To these customers, interest rate matters most. They will transfer large balances to the provider offering the best rate in the market, regardless of the product, sometimes even if that provider is not covered by the FSCS guarantee (such as banks in India or China).

Above all, Rate Tarts are active and informed. Active, because they are very prepared to switch their savings to another provider multiple times a year if it means they get the best rate. Informed, because they know what a good rate is in the market at any one time, often spending time flicking through best-buy tables and comparison websites to identify which provider is paying the best rates.

Rate Tarts can actually be quite helpful to product managers if they need to raise a lot of funding quickly. Offer a great rate and almost as if by magic the thousands of Rate Tarts out there will spot it and reward you with their deposits almost overnight. It is not unusual for product managers to have to withdraw savings products after just a few days if the interest rate offered is market leading. Too much funding can be a bad thing if the bank cannot lend those funds and Rate Tarts are quick to spot a great rate.

Regular Savers

Regular Savers are similar to Jam-Jar Savers but slightly different. They like to put aside something each month, often from their salary. They tend to take advantage of regular-saver products (more on which below) that offer a (seemingly) great rate for those willing to put, say, £50 or £100 away each month.

For product managers Regular Savers represent a somewhat funny group. Behaviourally they seem quite savvy, diligently putting money away each month, yet typically these savers don't have very many other savings and few lump sums saved anywhere. Part of the reason regular-saver products exist is because product managers have spotted that for people with few savings, regular saving was above all an attractive behavioural proposition.

Offsetters

Offsetters are an increasingly rare – but lucky – set of customers. Offset savers are actually more accurately called offset mortgage customers. An offset mortgage allows customers to forego earning interest on their savings and instead set those savings against a mortgage to ensure that less interest is paid on that debt. For example, if you had a £200,000 mortgage and £50,000 in savings, you would only be charged interest on £150,000 of your mortgage loan. In practice, most lenders that offer offset mortgages (very few still do) will calculate monthly mortgage repayments on the full £200,000 and set your repayments on this basis but this effectively means you are overpaying each month and therefore paying off your mortgage that bit quicker. With savings rates at historical lows, for many people using their savings to bring down the length of time they'll be paying a mortgage makes sense. Little wonder, then, few banks still offer offset deals.

How they make money out of you

Given the importance of reasonably priced deposits to a bank's ability to make a suitable return on its lending, it should come as no surprise that product managers spend a lot of time thinking about ways to 'game' customers into providing funding as cheaply as possible and leaving it in place as long as possible. 'Game' is a strong word and there are, in truth, plenty of regulations governing how product managers should treat savings customers. Yet it is difficult not to conclude that, despite this, unless customers keep a beady eye out, product managers will do their best to pay them less in interest over time.

Top-slicing, Part II

We encountered margin management ('top-slicing') in our discussion on banking in the previous chapter. For the product manager, margin management simply means reducing the interest paid to you on your savings in such a way that you do not move the money (unless the product manager really wants you to).

This series of events will again be dismally familiar to many readers. The bank tempts you to deposit your savings with them by offering a very competitive rate on an easy-access savings account. You deposit your funds and enjoy all the interest you receive. However, after a time, sometimes less than a year, the bank will drop the rate.

The FCA has ruled that if a bank wants to reduce the rate of interest it pays you on your easy-access savings account it generally has to give you two months' notice, in writing or via email. However, for rate reductions on other savings accounts like notice accounts and cash ISAs, the bank only needs to give you reasonable notice if it intends to make a 'material reduction'. The word 'material' is key here. A reduction is only considered material if you have £100 or more in your account. And up until December 2016 a reduction of 0.25% or less, and up to 0.50% in total each year, was not deemed material.

Yes, you read that correctly. Up until December 2016, your bank could cut your savings rate without telling you if they were planning to reduce your rate by 0.25% or less in one go, up to a maximum of 0.50% in a year. It is not an overstatement to say this was daylight robbery. Imagine if your employer decided to pay you less one month out of every six without you being told. You'd be annoyed. You'd be right to be annoyed.

Despite a long history of margin management by banks, many customers don't want the hassle of moving their savings around – no one likes the thought of having to take their identification and proof of address to a bank and go through all that admin again – so they leave their savings where they are. A little while longer, the bank writes to these customers again, informing them that the rate on their account is to fall again. Customers are busy so don't take any action. This sequence may repeat itself multiple times over many years until the rate they are being paid is very uncompetitive and the product manager has successfully 'margin managed' them.

Closing products, Part II

Sometimes, to make margin management that bit easier, product managers will close products to new customers. It's exactly the same trick product managers use for old bank account products that they want to cut the pricing of.

Very occasionally this is to reduce the impact of new customers entering a product that may be costing the bank a lot to provide (such as an account paying a great rate) after the bank has raised all the funds it wanted to raise. More often than not, it is a precursor to the product being margin managed.

Closing the product is usually done at the same time as a new product, suspiciously similar in features and sometimes with almost the same name, is opened to new customers. When the bank writes to customers in the old, closed product, to tell them their rate is to fall, they then have the option of offering those customers the new product, often priced competitively, to retain funds, if that's what the product manager wants to do. In reality, banks do this to 'save face', closing a product, reducing its rate and then meekly pointing out that there is a new product you can move to if you can really be bothered. Most customers won't be and therefore the product manager has achieved their aim, a reduction in the rate paid on an old product while maintaining a competitive rate to win the deposits of new customers.

Closing accounts as a precursor to margin managing them is endemic in the savings market. Metro Bank commissioned some analysis on this issue in 2015 with the independent research firm Savings Champion and found that 43% of savings accounts were paying rates less than those offered to new customers, sometimes in the same product. Out of 456 savings accounts reviewed, around 35% had their rates reduced by an average of 0.46%, meaning a total loss of nearly £4.7 billion in interest to savers. Of these cuts, 45% were done in increments of 0.25% or lower, meaning the banks didn't even need to tell customers at the time.

The rule is if a bank writes to you telling you a product is closed or closing, think carefully and closely monitor the rate paid on the account in the coming months. Closed accounts are typically 'old good deals' that a bank is trying to slowly margin manage down or, slightly less often, a popular product that simply caused the bank servicing issues or costs, such as passbook savings accounts which required investments in printing technology at the bank branch counter.

The FCA's 2015 Cash Savings study proposed some solutions to this problem, requiring providers to disclose key information about their product range, including products that are no longer on sale by prominently displaying online and in branch the interest rate they pay on their lowest-paying savings account. The aim was to make consumers aware of the low interest rate they may themselves unknowingly be receiving. The hope was that providers would feel shamed into improving their rates.

This 'Sunlight Remedy' (so-called but it aimed to shine a light on rates not prominently displayed by providers but which significant numbers of customers might be receiving) saw the FCA ask firms about the lowest possible rate that consumers can earn across all of their easy-access savings accounts. This took into consideration all of the conditions banks like to put in place that end up lowering a customer's interest rate, like restrictions on withdrawals. The FCA published the data to raise awareness of providers' strategies towards their long-standing customers and to allow comparison between open and closed accounts.

The results of the Sunlight Remedy were illuminating (if you'll excuse the pun), revealing huge differences in the rates providers offer on different accounts. Published in October 2016, they showed that for easy-access savings accounts offering branch access the difference between the best rates paid in the industry at 1.15% and the worst at 0.01% was therefore a whopping 1.14%. But this was just for products still open and available to new customers. For closed products, that is those products not available to new customers, the best rates available were at 0.65% with the worst again at 0.01%. Unbelievably, the worst rates seen for closed accounts that didn't offer branch access were a mind-boggling 0.00%, bringing into question whether this was a savings account at all in any meaningful sense.

Overall, the Sunlight Remedy reports have achieved their aim – shining a light on the gravy train that is banks closing accounts before cutting their rates, often precipitously. It has proved – pretty categorically in our view – that many banks continue to knowingly let customers sit in poorly paying savings accounts and often fail to let them know about better priced, often identical, new products available offering much better rates.

Teaser rates

Several banks have stopped offering bonus rates (known as 'teaser' rates by product managers) on savings accounts because they delivered such poor customer outcomes and attracted the attention of the regulator. But there are still lots of examples around (just type 'best savings deal' or similar into Google to see for yourself) and it pays to be aware of them.

A teaser rate does just what it says on the tin: it teases you. A savings account might have a rate of 1% AER but with a highly inviting introductory bonus rate of 3% for the first year. The important part of that last sentence was "for the first year". The bank is betting on you being too lazy to move your money in a year. At the end of the year, the rate on the account will fall back to 1% AER (possibly lower). You have been margin managed aggressively but, perversely, think you have got a great deal.

Bonus rates are good news if you pay close attention to your savings and move things around regularly to take advantage of the higher rates for set periods. However, if you are like the rest of us and have other things to remember like picking the kids up from football or paying the paperboy, chances are you should avoid teaser rates. Banks are obligated to give you just 14 days' notice that your bonus rate is set to end.

Interestingly, the FCA, the regulator that governs the savings market, is less concerned about these teaser rates than you might think. Their 2015 cash savings study found that many consumers switch reasonably soon after bonus rates expire – they found that over half of balances were moved out of the account 12 months after the bonus rate expired and over three quarters after 24 months. However, our view is that is perhaps a glass half-full interpretation of customer behaviour. The glass half empty version would point out that for every teaser rate promotion, banks can rely on a quarter of the funds they attract sticking round more than two years after the promotional rate has ended, providing a cheap ongoing source of funding because the rates on these accounts after the bonus period has ended tend to be dire.

Auto-rollover

An auto-rollover is where you give the bank permission to 'roll over' your fixed-term deposit when it reaches maturity into another fixed-term deposit without you needing to do anything. The 'benefits' are that you don't need to keep visiting a branch or calling the bank to reinvest in your fixed-term deposit once it has matured. As fixed-term deposits tend to demand a higher interest rate than variable, easy-access savings accounts or bank accounts as we have seen, auto-rollovers lose no time in reinvesting your money into a higher yielding account.

That's the cheery version of that story. In reality, auto-rollovers can be deployed by product managers to margin manage customers into cheaper fixed-term deposits than those on offer to new customers. Yes, your fixed-term deposit will be reinvested but there is often no guarantee you won't be paid a materially lower interest rate and often much lower than the rates offered to new customers.

For the bank product manager this is good news: cheaper longer-term funding that is automatically renewing. For you, the customer, it may be less good news as there may have been other fixed-term products with better rates available or you simply may wish to keep your savings in a more liquid (easy to get at) savings account like an instant-access account.

Once it's fixed, few providers will let you break a fixed-term deposit midway through without a hefty interest penalty (which can occasionally mean you get back less than the initial capital sum you fixed). So make sure you are fully aware of whether you signed up to auto-rollover any fixed-term deposit you opened at the bank.

The rules on the notice that banks must provide customers whose fixed-term deposits will auto-rollover are fairly woolly. The FCA's Banking Conduct of Business Sourcebook requires banks to give customers notice 'in good time' and at least 14 days before the deposit rolls over into a new fixed-term deposit. So customers often have just a couple of weeks (and remember banks are mostly shut at weekends) to move their deposit if they want to avoid it be re-fixed at a less than generous rate.

But it's my money! Withdrawal limitations

Another sneaky trick product managers play is to restrict the withdrawals on some savings accounts. A typical product will offer a pretty good interest rate but allow only 'up to two withdrawals a year'. If you do need to withdraw money more times than the permitted number of withdrawals, the bank will charge you an interest penalty (loss of interest accrued).

Product managers set these things up for two main reasons. First, they know that customers often need to access their savings more times than they hope to after placing them into a product. Unexpected bills like a broken boiler or a car repair mean that customers regularly need to dip into savings they had hoped not to touch. By limiting withdrawals, product managers benefit from either the funding being stable (because you cannot withdraw it without a penalty) or cheap (because if you really need to withdraw it there is an interest rate penalty). Yet again it's a case of heads they win, tails you lose.

Yet to be fair to product managers, besides an attempt to secure stable or cheap funding, these products exist to try and balance the inherent trade-off between the rate offered and the accessibility of the funds on the part of the customer. They provide customers with more flexibility than a fixed-term savings account – you can get to some of your money if you really need to – while still earning a better rate than you could from a simple variable easy-access account. However, they contain a sting in the tail for customers all too often – access to your money if required but a whacking great interest penalty if you do.

An aversion to reversion

One of the ways product managers can penalize customers – either for requiring access to money when they said they wouldn't need to or failing to regularly save into a product – is through account reversion rates. These are accounts where the interest rate drops to a lower rate automatically if some condition is not met. For example, a savings account might pay 4% AER but if you don't comply with the terms and conditions of the product, perhaps by keeping a minimum balance in the account, that rate drops to 2%. Therefore, 2% is the reversion rate. This rate is sometimes backdated so you do not accrue interest at 4% for the time the money was in the account but 2% instead.

Reversion rates are again an attempt by product managers to square the circle: incentivizing customers to leave funds where they are so the banker can do more with those funds on the lending side of the balance sheet and hold less liquidity in reserve. The consequence for customers, however, can be a failure to understand the implications of not complying with the terms of a savings account. All that interest accruing at a good rate can be wiped out and replaced with a lower rate the moment the customer fails to meet all the accounts' conditions, such as maintaining a minimum balance, funding the account regularly, or withdrawing funds.

What's in a name?

One trick that product managers often play is a simple one: they call savings accounts wildly inappropriate names in the hope that this alone will entice some customers to make deposits. We know what you're thinking: surely nobody falls for that? Unfortunately many customers do. Some of the very worst savings accounts, paying paltry interest rates, have in the past had names that sound like a pair of Nike trainers: advantage, plus, gold.

Some account names are plainly misleading – accounts with 'high interest' in the title sometimes pay hardly any interest at all. This is because the rates on these accounts have often been cut slowly over time ('margin management' again) leaving the account with an almost comically inappropriate name. When it comes to names the simple rule is to ignore them and focus on the features of the account and the interest it pays. Often the accounts with the most boring names are the best.

From tiers to tears

Some savings accounts have interest rate tiers. From £0 to £1,000 you might earn 1% AER, from £1,001 to £3,000 you could earn 1.5% and so on. Intuitively this looks like a fair deal. The more I deposit with the bank, the better the rate I receive. It pays to be careful here, though. The new, higher rate unlocked by the larger balance may not be paid on the whole balance. For example, you may only get 1.5% on £1,999 of your savings (from £1,001 to £3,000) and not the first £1,000 which will continue to receive just 1% AER. So the effective rate on the full £3,000 will not be 1.5% but 1.3%.

Those tiered rates that unlock a new rate on the whole balance can be an interesting and helpful proposition for the determined saver though, unlocking a better interest rate for a higher balance which feels like a good reward for those that have managed to save a bit more. It just pays to check the new interest rate tier applies to the whole balance and how this compares to other fixed and variable savings rates available.

Some relationship!

Beware of relationship pricing. While banks will make you think they are 'rewarding' you for your loyalty by, say, offering you a better rate on your savings account if you switch your bank account too, this often makes no financial sense. For product managers, the additional rate they are offering you on your savings is more than paid for by the regular funding they can expect to receive from your bank account. A bank account paying no interest is free money to the bank and this pays for the modest increase in the interest rate offered on the savings account. If I add up the interest rate I am getting on *all* my funds (bank account plus savings account) the effective rate is often uncompetitive when compared to the best savings *and* best current account rates offered in the market.

Regular-saver accounts

Regular-saver accounts are popular. They usually require a regular, monthly deposit to the account and in return the saver can expect some of the best rates around. It would be wrong to say that these accounts have a sting in the tail but they do have a few rules which many savers fall foul of, and the rate they advertise often confuses customers.

Over a year you might save £1,200 into a regular saver paying 10%, at £100 a month. A disturbingly high number of customers in our experience therefore think they'll earn £120 in interest (10% of £1,200). However, you would only earn the monthly equivalent of 10% AER on that £1,200 for one month, the last month. In month one, you would have earned the monthly equivalent of 10% only on the first £100 and in month two earned 10% on £200 and so on. So as a customer your average balance over the year would have been around £600, returning you about £60 in interest before tax. Not quite as impressive as £120, is it? Many customers understand the rules of the game. Many do not.

Regular-saver accounts also usually have some quite strict rules behind them. Miss a monthly payment and you may be hit by a reversion rate much less than the advertised rate. The accounts usually have a minimum and a maximum monthly amount you can save, typically something between £50 and £250. Save too much or too little into the account and again you may find yourself on a reversion or penalty interest rate. Occasionally providers will allow you to roll over any unused monthly saving allowance to the next month, others do not. Access to your savings during the period of a regular saver is usually limited, prohibited, or at the expense of an interest rate penalty. Many regular-saver products require you to have a current account with the same provider. The products usually only last for a year, at which point the funds are usually dumped into a lower-paying, easy-access account paying much less interest. Product managers are hoping you'll leave it there. You get the point. Regular-saver products are more complicated than they seem and a plain old easy-access, ISA, or fixed-term account might be the better option.

Stay right where you are! Blocking upgrades

Inertia is a product manager's best friend. The less active a customer is moving money around, the less price-sensitive they are and the more a product manager can rely on funds being there to support the bank's lending activities. As we've seen, this constant cat-and-mouse game between bank and customer, each searching for fundamentally different things, defines the savings market. Banks want low-cost funds. Customers want a high interest rate. Enter upgrade blocks.

One of the ways bankers make it harder for customers to move money to the highest paying savings accounts is to block or complicate upgrades. Thus your fixed-term savings account might have come to an end and your deposit is now sitting in a low-paying, easy-access account. Many banks will make it tricky – and sometimes impossible – for you to upgrade or reinvest your deposit into one of the accounts available to attract new customers that often have the best interest rates. Instead you will be offered a range of lower-paying accounts. It is typical to be told, "You can't upgrade to that account online and need to come in to the branch." Broadly translated this is a product manager telling you "I don't want you to move your money into one of our highest paying accounts as they are there to attract new customers, not retain existing ones so I am going to make it painful for you to upgrade."

Product managers are experienced at adding in these process 'rigidities' to make it difficult to take advantage of the best rates, often hiding behind excuses relating to what can and cannot be done online. If your bank denies you access to the best products or just makes it difficult for you to access them, take your money elsewhere.

Channel restrictions

In a similar vein, restricting the channels (branch, online, phone, mobile) you can deposit or withdraw funds through is another common trick used by product managers to achieve their aims of making you leave your money where it is and reducing operational costs.

The savings market is replete with 'online-only saving accounts' that stipulate that customers must deposit and withdraw funds to their account online only. This means customers are often not allowed to deposit or withdraw funds into that account via a branch. For the digitally savvy this is probably not a problem but for those that struggle with online or mobile banking and like the peace of mind provided by talking to someone face to face in a branch, this is not the account for you.

Why do banks offer these products? First, many see them as a way of reducing 'footfall' (customer numbers) in branches. Many banks still (wrongly in our view) think that serving customers in branch is undesirable as it drives up costs (in terms of colleagues to serve customers at the counter and the cost of the systems to process their requests). Online-only accounts, so the thinking goes, save costs. In reality, customers often end up in a branch to query something about their online-only account anyway meaning it can be a bit of a false economy.

Second, restricting channel usage can simply make it more difficult to move your money, full stop. A phone-based savings account that only permits deposits or withdrawals by calling the bank's call centre is often offered in the hope you will give up waiting in the long phone queue to be spoken to and leave your funds where they are. The product manager is happy when you put down the phone, exasperated.

Third, channel restrictions often have the effect of reducing 'rate recall'. We forget our telephone banking PIN or online logins and gradually over time we check our account less often, meaning we are less able to recall the rate we are being paid (see 'What rate am I on?' below).

In practice, most channel-restricted accounts nowadays typically centre on the new digital channels of online banking and mobile banking as banks are nearly all trying to reduce customer demand in branches to justify closing them. Incentivizing you to save online only means they can justify shutting your local branch because you're not using it but, in many cases, you are unable to do online what you can do in branch, leading to enormous customer frustration. That's worth thinking about the next time you walk by a branch and read their posters telling you how committed they are to customer service.

What rate am I on?

As we have said – but it merits repetition – it is a hallmark of the easy-access savings market that remarkably few people have any idea what rate they are getting on their easy-access savings. Fewer still in our experience know whether their bank or savings provider offers any better rate than the one they are on. Banks make customers work hard to find out the rate they are on, sometimes omitting rates on accounts viewed through a mobile app or online

The FCA cash savings market study found that 63% of respondents in their survey did not know whether their existing provider offered the same savings product with a different interest rate. This point is worth dwelling on. Few customers are aware whether their current bank or savings provider offers a comparable account to the one they already have but offering a better rate. Why? Because banks and savings providers have no interest in telling you that you could get a better rate without needing to move bank. It is a clear, if unsurprising, example of banks looking after their own interests before those of their customers.

CHAPTER SUMMARY

- Bank product managers are focused on and incentivized to drive the right amount of stable bank funding, at the right cost, and this has led them to treat existing savings customers poorly and confuse new ones with complicated account features, terms, and conditions.

- The UK savings market is worth over £1,276 billion, with almost half sitting in easy-access savings accounts.

- The main high-street banks, with their large numbers of current account customers, benefit from customers' tendency to keep their easy-access savings in the same place as their bank account.

- The savings market actively punishes customer loyalty – up to one third of easy-access accounts will be receiving a rate much lower than that available to new customers.

- Bankers view savings accounts through four lenses: liquidity value, interest-rate risk, price elasticity, and share of wallet.

- Safety-First Savers save up to the Financial Services Compensation Scheme protection limit of £85,000.

- Jam-Jar Savers save different amounts in different accounts for specific purposes.

CHAPTER SUMMARY

- ISA Fanatics make sure to utilize their full tax-free savings allowance every year. In recent years, the interest rates paid on ISA accounts have reduced as the government has increased the annual ISA subscription limit and due to the introduction of the Personal Savings Allowance.

- Fixers utilize fixed-term and fixed-rate savings products to get a better rate, locking their savings away for an agreed period at an agreed rate.

- Rate Tarts are guided solely by rate and will switch their savings in large volumes to providers offering 'best-buy' rates.

- Regular Savers put something aside every month.

- Offsetters use their savings to reduce the interest paid on their mortgage.

- Top-slicing sees product managers reduce the rate on savings accounts over time, often imperceptibly to customers.

- Closing products reduces the chance of new customers getting access to a great rate or as a precursor to margin managing the product.

CHAPTER SUMMARY

- Using bonus rates helps to 'bait and hook' customers – rates drop, often precipitously, after the bonus period.

- Auto-rollovers are used to recycle a customer's savings into a new fixed-term product at the end of a fixed-term maturity – often at a lower rate.

- Withdrawal limitations penalize customers if they need access to their money more times than the product terms and conditions permit.

- Reversion rates see the interest rate paid to customers drop significantly if they do not comply with a products' terms and conditions.

- Product managers often give accounts inaccurate or misleading names in the hope of tricking less-experienced savers into thinking they are getting a good deal.

- Product managers often offer tiered interest rates at different balance thresholds to lower the effective weighted average interest rate paid on the overall balance.

- Relationship pricing is used by product managers to entice customers to switch their bank account when they open a savings account.

CHAPTER SUMMARY

- Regular-saver accounts often have strict rules and the interest earned from the account is often not as much as customers expect due to the way that the balance in the account builds on a monthly basis.

- Blocking account upgrades, usually online, makes it difficult for customers to open the best accounts available to new customers.

- Channel restrictions deny customers the ability to use certain channels like branches, in the hope that they will give up and leave their money where it is.

- Customer awareness of the interest rate they are receiving, particularly on easy-access accounts, is low, leading product managers to reduce rates with little fear that customers will move elsewhere.

CHAPTER 7

Borrowing

Borrowing money is a serious business. Few of us like the thought of being in debt. Choosing the wrong type of product, at the wrong rate, can mean you end up paying more, for longer. Yet for many of us borrowing money is increasingly a way of life. Figures from The Money Charity show that the UK population owed £1.51 trillion in debt at the end of November 2016, up from £1.46 trillion the year before. When mortgages are taken out of these figures, outstanding consumer credit totalled £192 billion. That's £3,806 for every person, up by £515 from the previous year. By any measure these are eye-watering figures. We are a nation of shoppers and a nation of spenders and it is borrowing that regularly fuels both.

Often, borrowing money can be a smart decision, though. While we could all choose to pay rent while scrimping and saving enough to buy a house in 25 years' time, it is much more preferable to take out a mortgage and live in the house we want to live in while we pay down the loan. Similarly, it can make sense to take a loan in order to invest in our future, whether that be to go to university or to buy a car so that we can get to work. It is therefore wrong to think of all borrowing as in some way irresponsible or bad.

Even so, our experience as product managers has shown us that customers make a number of common errors when it comes to borrowing money. The first is that it is all too easy to borrow for a fancy holiday or to buy that killer dress you've had your eye on. Indebtedness is intimately connected to our psychology and the degree of impulse control we can muster when it comes to discretionary purchases.

The second is also behavioural, and relates to our commitment to paying off debt once we have incurred it. We like to spend but the long, hard slog of paying down debt is tough. Third, we often choose the wrong product to borrow money on for the specific thing we are trying to buy. It makes no sense to buy a car on a credit card unless you are confident you will be able to pay off the outstanding balance very quickly. It is inadvisable to take out a five-year personal loan if you are only ever a few pounds short at the end of the month before payday.

Product managers do not on the whole make matters any easier for customers. Lending money is how banks make money and they really like to make money. Product managers are focused on ensuring that they supply the right level of lending to the right customers at the right price, in order to make the best returns possible for their employer. This requires a detailed understanding of us as customers – our credit history, employment status, and past relationship with debt – but also an entrepreneurial streak. To win customers in a marketplace full of other lenders competing for business, product managers have to come up with clever ideas to make money and win our custom.

The problem is few if any of these ideas are good for customers in our experience. From upping your credit limit on a whim to enticing you to spend more on a credit card, product managers have an unsentimental focus on hitting revenue and profit targets. All too often the poor customer is simply collateral damage along the way.

The lending market and how bankers think about it

A big market…

According to the Council of Mortgage Lenders (CML), there are around 11 million mortgaged properties in the

UK with total debt of over £1.3 trillion. In 2015, we borrowed over £220 billion in mortgages, a rise of 8% on the previous year.

At the same time, British Bankers Association (BBA) data show that there were around 60 million credit cards in issue as of March 2016, relating to 50 million accounts. These were used to make over 2.5 billion purchases, totalling £146 billion. By the end of 2016 there was around £43 billion of credit card balances outstanding.

And the big numbers keep coming when we consider the personal loans market. BBA data show that there was just under £40 billion of personal loan debt outstanding in December 2016 with the market showing significant growth due to the low rates on offer from lenders following the Bank of England's Base Rate reduction in August 2016.

Scale matters

When it comes to lending, scale – the number of customers a bank has – is important. This is for two main reasons.

The first is that having large numbers of customers helps lenders better work out who to lend to and how much they should lend. Each customer's repayment behaviour and credit score provides data for lenders to analyse and explore. The more data they have, generally speaking, the more successful their lending decisions become (although there are clearly exceptions and sometimes external forces like a poor economy can impact customers' ability to service debt). Banks develop their own highly sophisticated credit 'scorecards' and these can become predictive of whether it is safe to provide a loan to a customer and, if so, just how much.

The second, related reason is that a lender with a large credit card, personal loan or mortgage book of customers is more able to absorb losses when and if any of those loans go bad. If a lender has very few mortgages, credit cards, or loans it doesn't take many customers to fall behind with their payments or not pay the bank back at all for lenders to face significant trouble. Bad debts can dwarf the income the bank makes from loans it has extended to customers who are paying them back as planned. A larger book gives bankers options to keep the overall portfolio profitable, perhaps by increasing the interest rate charged to a segment of customers to make up for the fact that another segment is falling behind in repayments. This luxury does not exist to the same extent with a very small book of customers.

Scale also offers other forms of diversification. A much larger book of customers often means customers based in different regions of the country, employed doing different things, and borrowing different amounts for different purposes. This protects lenders from being exposed if one region, industry, or sector hits tough times and customers stop paying back their borrowings.

Tightly regulated

The regulatory requirements that govern lending to consumers in the UK – both unsecured lending like credit cards and personal loans, and secured lending like mortgages – are significant and a defining feature of the market. Every bank and lender more generally faces a challenge to ensure they sell lending products in a way that does not contravene the required regulatory standards. Penalties from the regulator can be significant and the reputational damage to any lender substantial if they are found to have sold products in a non-compliant way.

In the unsecured lending market, it is the Consumer

Credit Act and the FCA's Consumer Credit Sourcebook that are of central importance. These regulations provide clear guidance on everything from how unsecured lending products should be promoted and interest calculated to the information customers should receive before and after opening a product, and the safeguard lenders must put in place to ensure customers are protected from bad practices. If product managers fail to comply with these regulations they can see their bank's permission to lend withdrawn by the regulator completely.

If anything, the regulatory requirements governing mortgage sales are even stricter than those relating to unsecured lending. The FCA's Mortgages and Home Finance Conduct of Business Sourcebook (MCOB) governs the relationship between borrowers and lenders in the UK. MCOB covers how mortgages are sold, communicated, promoted, and advised on, and what information, disclosure, and terms and conditions a customer should expect as part of their mortgage product. They also cover what customers can expect if they enter arrears on their mortgage loan or their home is repossessed. Key sections relate to how the total charge for credit and charges are stated and explained to customers at the outset and on statements throughout the life of the mortgage product.

While these requirements sound straightforward enough in principle, ensuring that every mortgage is sold and subsequently managed by the bank in a way that is entirely compliant with these requirements is a significant operational and management challenge. Mortgage teams within banks often number several hundred people, with several hundred more providing services as part of the mortgage product lifecycle, be they lawyers, valuers, or specialist mortgage-servicing providers. Front-line sellers are also regularly assessed to ensure they remain suitably qualified to sell mortgages. For any lender to enter the mortgage market, then, they need to invest heavily in ensuring that they meet the required regulatory standards.

Banks don't have it all their own way

The lending market is different from the bank account and savings markets in that there are a lot more lenders in the marketplace than just banks. These so-called "mono-line" businesses tend to be specialists in their chosen lending field, focusing on credit cards or personal loans only, for example. Others are peer-to-peer lenders, gathering funding from the public and lending those funds back out to the public through a technology platform that matches depositors with lenders directly.

Banks have competition in the mortgage market too. Strikingly, it is not the major high-street banks that actually sell the most mortgages in the UK. Instead, the market is dominated by intermediary brokers – individuals and firms who receive commission from mortgage lenders like banks for sending them mortgage applicants. In 2015, these brokers sold over 70% of first-time-buyer mortgages by value and number of loans. The figures were similar for those taking out a new mortgage while moving home and those remortgaging the property they were currently living in, with brokers accounting for 65% of these loans. Unlike nearly every other personal financial product, banks are not the major source of sales.

This is not to say, however, that banks miss out. For it is banks and building societies that provide the majority of mortgages in the UK, the brokers simply represent an extended salesforce that the banks reward for sending them business. Lloyds Banking Group, Royal Bank of Scotland, Barclays, HSBC, and Santander, along with building societies Nationwide, Yorkshire, and Coventry, and new challenger bank Virgin were the biggest lenders by value in 2015 according to the CML.

Risk-based pricing

A feature of most lending by banks to personal customers is risk-based pricing. Banks adjust the interest they charge customers to borrow based on an assessment of their risk, driven by their credit worthiness. Sometimes this can simply be broad product price categories. For example, banks might charge customers taking out a 60% loan-to-value (LTV) mortgage (where a bank will be lending money to the value of 60% of the property purchase price) 2.50% APR on a two-year, fixed-rate mortgage but charge customers taking out a 90% LTV mortgage a rate of 3.99% APR. The difference in price is related to the perceived difference in risk presented by the two customers. One has 40% equity in their property meaning if the bank was forced to take possession of the house in the event of the customer defaulting on their mortgage they would only need to achieve a resale price of 60% of the purchase price to get back the money they lent out. Conversely, for the 90% LTV customer there is just 10% equity in the house and on a forced resale there is a greater risk that the bank would be unable to recoup its losses as the housing market can fluctuate up and down by more than 10% in some areas of the country. This additional risk is reflected in the rate charged to the customer.

Risk-based pricing is a more sophisticated beast when it comes to unsecured lending. Here, risk-based pricing can be very 'fine', that is pricing can be managed right down to a customer level and defined by a range of inputs from credit score to affordability to employment status to income level. Risk-based pricing is not the whole story, though, as price elasticity – the highest rate banks think they can charge you without losing your business – also has a role to play (see the price optimization, below).

Capital

As we saw in Part 1, just as a bank has to hold liquidity to ensure it has enough money if some depositors want their money back, banks hold capital against any form of lending they do to ensure that the bank is able to absorb any losses resulting from customers not repaying their debts. How much capital is held is determined by a swathe of complex regulations set by the Bank of International Settlements in Basel and translated into UK regulations by the PRA. Capital rules are a 'hot topic' in international banking circles and have been since the 2008 financial crisis when it was shown that banks had far too little capital to cushion them from losses.

The specific amount of capital a bank has to hold against its lending differs by asset type and is calculated by reference to a 'risk weighting', a risk assessment of each type of loan. For example, a mortgage loan, secured by a property that could be sold if the borrower defaulted on their mortgage payments, is less risky than an unsecured personal loan, where the bank has no security (collateral, in banking terminology) in the form of a property to sell to pay off the debt. Therefore different lending products have different risk weightings that form part of a formula that then calculates the exact amount of capital a bank must hold. A mortgage might have a risk weighting of 35%, for example, while an unsecured personal loan might have a risk weighting of 75%, reflecting the relative difference in the risk each type of lending represents.

The amount of capital a bank has to hold against its lending can impact the return on equity its activities deliver for investors and is therefore a key measure tracked by bank analysts. Banks need to be capital efficient – ensuring they use limited capital wisely to support those activities that deliver what bankers call the best risk-adjusted return – while ensuring their capital levels do not fall below those required by the PRA.

If you're wondering why banks don't just focus on selling mortgages as they have a lower capital requirement than, say, credit cards, the reason is yield – the interest rate the bank earns on these assets. While mortgages are less risky and use less capital per loan, they offer relatively lower returns. Credit cards, while much riskier and much more capital intensive, offer much higher yields.

Bank capital is a finite resource and therefore all product managers need to understand the capital available to them to support their lending plans and figure out the optimum mix between the types of assets to fund, the return those assets will deliver, and the bank's overall customer growth plans.

Interest-rate risk

Fixed term, fixed-rate lending, in a similar way to fixed-term savings, means the bank is committing to an interest rate for a set period of time, perhaps two or five years. This creates interest-rate risk. For example, I might choose to offer you a five-year fixed-term mortgage at 4% APR. However, the funding required for that loan might increase in cost materially over five years due to interest rate increases from the Bank of England or intense market competition. If my funding costs go up but my lending income stays flat, I am exposed to interest-rate risk.

Just as we saw with savings in the previous chapter, banks tend to trade this interest-rate risk away through the use of money market hedging products like swaps. These swaps turn fixed-term assets into floating-rate assets, thereby reducing interest-rate risk.

Little differentiation

Lending products in the UK are fairly 'commoditized'. There are only minor differences in features between Mortgage A and Mortgage B, or Unsecured Loan A and Unsecured Loan B. Instead there are just three main battle-grounds on which banks and other lenders compete to win customers. The first is rate. The interest rate at which credit cards, loans, or mortgages are offered will have a significant impact on how many a lender sells as a general rule. This is because rate is one of the few meaningful things that differs between the various offers lenders put out there.

Second, banks compete on how easy it is to apply for products. A seamless, quick application process, ideally with some early indication of whether you will be accepted or not, can be a competitive advantage versus other banks in the market. If I can entice you to open a credit card 'in a couple of clicks' online, then that may well be enough to persuade you to choose my bank over another. For many product managers 'speed is a feature' (that is, a quick process is almost as good as having some other winning feature of the product itself) and they invest in making the application journey as simple as possible.

Third, firms compete on the quality of their credit analytics, that is how good they are at determining how much to lend you and at what rate. Complex models that track customer behaviour, credit worthiness, affordability, and a million other variables can help firms figure out the best customers to lend to depending on a lender's preferred strategy. These strategies straddle the full risk-appetite spectrum from a super-safe strategy of lending to customers that your analytics indicate will definitely pay you back but at a low interest rate, to a more risky strategy of targeting customers who may not pay you back but who you can charge much higher rates.

How banks think about borrowers
Credit cards
Revolvers

Revolvers use their credit card to borrow for longer than a month, usually taking advantage of interest-free purchase and balance transfer offers. There are plenty of 'serial revolvers' that have been moving credit balances from one interest-free balance transfer deal to another for many years. Other than the initial balance transfer fee percentage, these customers often have long periods of interest-free borrowing. Revolvers tend to be the most profitable type of credit card customer for banks though as many are revolving balances that attract interest.

Transactors

Transactors use their card to make payments in order to gain rewards, whether they be air miles, points to spend at a retailer, or some other benefit. They rarely carry over credit card balances from one month to the next and therefore rarely, in our experience, pay much interest, clearing their credit card balance before the interest-free period ends each month. Transactors tend to be less profitable than revolvers, but are still just about profitable overall.

These customers have, though, become less profitable to banks recently due to changes in the Interchange Fee Regulation that governs the income banks make every time a card is used. This regulation capped consumer credit card interchange fees at 0.3% of a transaction's value from December 2015. Banks' income from interchange has fallen from 0.8% of transaction value to 0.3%, which the FCA has estimated has to led to an overall 5% to 10% reduction in revenue from customers. This income helped fund many points schemes and it is for this reason that many reward-based credit cards have become a lot less generous in the last two years.

Stoozers
We like Stoozers. Or more accurately, we admire them. Collectively, Stoozers raise two fingers to banks and proclaim that they that will make money out of the relationship, not the other way round, thank you very much.

Stoozers – named after a prolific discussion board contributor called Stooz on the website Motley Fool – borrow money from credit card providers offering 0% deals for new customers and place the money in a high-interest savings account to make a profit on the interest earned. Stoozers then repay the credit card balance just before the 0% offer period is due to end.

Borrowing free money to make money like this is not for everyone – far too many customers are tempted to spend the money rather than put it in a high-paying savings account in our experience – but for those with iron wills it is a financially smart thing to do.

In practice, initial balance transfer fees and fees for withdrawing cash or making transfers from credit cards have limited the opportunities available to Stoozers to make money but it is still possible in some cases. The bigger hindrance in recent times has been the paltry savings rates available. Nevertheless, Stoozers are a welcome reminder that it is always worth thinking creatively about how to use introductory deals to make money rather than spend it.

Credit Repairers

There is a small but distinct group of customers that product managers tend to call 'Credit Repairers'. These customers have often had trouble with credit in the past, perhaps missing repayments or falling into default on a loan or credit card. They might have the odd county court judgment against their name also.

These customers are therefore in the market for a credit card that helps them 'repair' their credit record. A number of specialist credit card providers tend to dominate this market, offering cards with low credit limits and high annual percentage rates (a reflection of the perceived risk in lending to these customers but also a focus on making returns) that allow customers with bad credit ratings or simply no credit record at all (so-called 'thin file' customers) to start to build up a positive credit record.

For product managers, Credit Repairers represent a high-wire act. The best returns for product managers – the highest interest rates – are to be found by lending money to those that are least price sensitive, those that *need* to borrow and are grateful for any provider able to lend them the money. Yet these customers are often highly likely to default on their debts, leaving the bank at a loss.

Mortgages
FTBs
First-Time Buyers (FTBs) are an important group of customers for mortgage product managers. FTBs made up over £45 billion of the £220 billion mortgage market in 2015. Affordability has been tough for this group, with the costs of raising a deposit and earning enough to borrow the sums required to buy a house beyond many.

If product managers are to compete to win the business of more experienced customers seeking to move house or remortgage, the focus is usually on providing the best price. FTBs, however, sometimes display different motivations and focus. Many are a little unsure what the process of applying for a mortgage entails and are unclear about how much they can borrow, whether they should take a fixed-rate mortgage or a tracker, and whether the rate they are offered is a 'good' rate.

Unlike the homemover and remortgage market, the FTB market is less dominated by brokers. This is because frequently FTBs will approach their bank, at least initially, to see whether they can get a mortgage. Therefore, many banks focus their marketing for FTBs on how approachable and helpful the bank is, stressing how easy the process of applying for a mortgage will be. You've probably seen the branch posters of smiling staff and relieved-looking young house buyers.

FTBs represent good news for product managers in three important regards. First, as they tend to approach the bank directly and not via an intermediary or broker, the product manager doesn't have to pay the broker commission. This means higher margins, keeping the product manager happy. Second, FTBs are, generally speaking, less price-sensitive than more experienced customers so again, this means a higher margin for the product manager. Finally, FTBs offer the product manager the opportunity to build a lifelong relationship with the customer, meaning that they continue to remortgage with the bank when their fixed-term or tracker deal ends. In this way, the product manager can keep the customer away from intermediaries or brokers, who tend not to be loyal to any one brand and therefore are more likely to move the customer to whichever provider is offering the best rate, quickest application process, and highest commission. It's not all good news though as FTBs usually take higher LTV loans and banks have to hold more capital against these loans.

Remos

Remos, short for remortgage customers, are simply looking for a new mortgage on their existing property. To do this they will often change provider, usually to get a better rate or lower fee on the mortgage. This market was worth over £52 billion in 2015. Competition for these customers can be fierce, particularly in key LTV bands such as below 60% LTV (deemed less risky by banks as the house has more equity). There is competition too, albeit of a more specialized nature, in the higher LTV markets, as these customers are willing to pay a higher interest rate on their mortgage in order to secure a larger mortgage. While higher LTV mortgages require banks to hold more capital against the loan, this is more than offset by the additional interest rate these mortgages can demand.

Homemovers

Homemovers are different to Remos – they are in the market for a new mortgage and they are in the market for a new house. Homemovers made up just over £70 billion of mortgage lending in 2015 according to the CML. Behaviourally, these customers are very similar to Remo customers – focused on price, frequently customers of intermediary brokers, and therefore displaying precious little brand loyalty when it comes to which bank or mortgage provider they choose for their mortgage.

Rate Switchers

Unlike Remos, who are staying put but changing mortgage provider, Rate Switchers are moving to a new deal with the same lender and may or may not be moving property. The Rate Switcher market is large, some £100 billion a year compared to the £220 billion or so represented by the rest of the mortgage market, yet they rarely show up in market statistics as for all intents and purposes these customers are simply upgrading their existing mortgage deal with the same provider. Rate Switchers show that banks have learned to invest in their retention mortgage services – offering existing customers a new mortgage deal when or before their current deal expires. Leave it too late and your customer will have made contact with other providers to see what deals are out there. Get in early and many customers think, "I cannot be bothered to go through the rigmarole of a drawn-out mortgage application at another provider, I will simply switch to a new offer where I am."

Product managers know a particular type of pricing strategy is called for when it comes to Rate Switchers. The rate offered needs to be 'there or thereabouts' so that any

Rate Switcher isn't so outraged that they look elsewhere. At the same time, the rate offered doesn't need to be stellar because product managers know that these customers don't really want the hassle of moving to another provider, which entails income verification, identification, and lots of other paperwork that we all hate.

Further Advancers

Further advancers are looking to take on more borrowing from their existing mortgage lender. For example, they might have borrowed £100,000 on a mortgage to buy a property worth £200,000, at a loan-to-value of 50%. In order to pay for an extension for the property, the Further Advancer might want to borrow another £20,000, taking their total borrowing to £120,000 before repayments, a LTV of 60%.

The further advance market was worth just over £5 billion in 2015 and is therefore relatively small when compared to the overall mortgage market. However, for a product manager Further Advancers represent a fantastic opportunity. This is for three main reasons. First, a further advance, that is providing the customer with more money than they initially borrowed on the mortgage, typically carries a different (higher) interest rate from the main mortgage. Thus further advances offer the product manager to make additional margin.

Second, this margin is often deemed low risk, as customers that request further advances have typically been paying an existing mortgage for several years, so product managers can see that the customer is reliable and unlikely to default on any borrowings as long as the overall debt burden doesn't become unaffordable.

Third, a further advance can make customers extra 'sticky', that is, they tend to switch around less than customers with a simple mortgage. This is because these customers are not always sure whether another lender would provide them with the same level of borrowing represented by their mortgage and further advance.

Unsecured personal loans

Purchasers

The bread and butter of personal lending. This is the biggest group of borrowers, seeking to fund things like a house extension or other major purchase. These customers may have other options, albeit more expensive ones, such as overdrafts, credit cards, or, as we have seen, further advances on their mortgages if they are home owners.

Debt consolidators

These are customers who have built up debt balances on credit cards, store cards, or overdrafts. Customers with persistent balances on cards or overdrafts are often paying higher rates than those available on a personal loan. Customers take out a loan to take advantage of both the lower rate, and the structured way to repay the debt. Banks often require customers to pay down debts elsewhere on disbursement of the loan so as not to increase overall debt.

Consolidators can be a significant source of lending for product managers who might well target the bank's own credit card customer base to generate income for his or her department, particularly as they can automatically pay off a customer's credit card or overdraft debt, to ensure that overall indebtedness remains within risk appetite.

Refinancers
Customers refinance primarily for two reasons. First, they may have taken out a loan at a point when rates were higher, and are seeking to pay a lower rate. This is generally bad news for banks if customers do this in large volumes, as it reduces profitability. Second, customers often refinance to borrow more, and take advantage of a new rate and the convenience of having a single repayment, or they might simply be seeking to restructure their loan over a longer period.

Car financers
Customers often take advantage of financing deals offered by car dealerships, which typically include a small repayment and a 'balloon' payment at the end of a fixed time, at which point a customer can make the payment, or return or sell the car. These deals often seem very cheap compared with bank loans, but cheap financing deals are often funded by a higher overall car price.

Point of sale
This is a growing market and one that usually centres on furniture stores or large white-goods retailers where purchases can be paid for in instalments using credit. There are often 'interest-free' or 'buy now, pay later' offers available. These deals are actually financed by the retailer in order to encourage sales – something few customers understand or know.

Payday borrowers
These are people in the market for small amounts of credit, normally less than £1,000, over a short period. Many customers have poor credit scores. These customers tend to be

outside the 'risk appetite' of the banks: sometimes this is driven by credit risk, sometimes the PR risk of taking part in a market with perceived dubious moral standards. Payday borrowers have decreased significantly in recent years, due to the reduction of supply in the market, following greater regulatory scrutiny and price caps.

How they make money out of you
Credit cards
It's free money, right?
Most product managers will tell you that you can't hope to attract new credit card customers today without offering a juicy interest-free offer on card purchases or balance transfers. They have become the 'new normal' in the market. Unfortunately, for those customers that are mired in debt or just don't pay close attention to how they are managing their debt, these offers regularly turn bad.

Paradoxically enough, the aim of these interest-free offers is to get you to pay interest. This is because product managers know that many customers will not pay down their debt before the end of the interest-free period, meaning that customers will either have to switch to another credit card provider (always a hassle and customers are, on the whole, lazy) or suck up having to pay interest on their outstanding balance.

Balance transfer offers are quite straightforward in many ways. Your bank offers you a headline-grabbing, 36-month, interest-free balance transfer offer on a new credit card. You have an existing credit card balance of, perhaps, £3,000 and decide to transfer this balance to your new card to benefit from such a long interest-free period. At this point an interest fee is levied on the transferred balance, usually around 3% but sometimes higher. Straight away your interest-free promotion is anything but – you have paid £90 – 3% interest – on your outstanding balance in order to access an interest-free promotion. If it sounds kooky, that's because it is, and it hoodwinks many a customer. However, after this point the balance on the card does not attract any more interest until the promotional period ends. So for customers looking to pay down large credit card balances this can be a good option, on the proviso that they don't mind paying the initial balance transfer charge.

Sadly, though, life tends to get in the way when it comes to paying off debt and product managers know this. Invariably, customers fail to pay off all their outstanding balance by the time the interest-free period ends. There are lots of claims on our monthly pay packet and paying off debt when you know it is not incurring any interest can seem like a low priority.

Interest charges on the balance return with a vengeance when the interest-free period is up. Your rate might go from 0% to 25.9% APR or higher overnight. With a portfolio of thousands of customers attracted by the original offer, a product manager only needs a percentage of these customers to start paying interest at the end of the promotional period to pay for the costs of the original interest-free offer and to start making a profit overall. Yet again, product managers are taking advantage of the fact that, when it comes to debt, we tend to be slower to pay it off than we hope.

Interest-free purchase promotions on credit cards work in much the same way. A promotional period when any purchases on the card are interest-free sounds like a good deal but when that promotional period ends the outstanding balance attracts a high interest rate and that's when product managers start to rub their hands with glee.

Of course, when interest charges do kick in, it is possible for customers to search around for another interest-free balance transfer offer but an initial transfer fee will be payable again and there are no guarantees that the customer will be accepted by another provider. Life events like illness, unemployment, or simply not keeping up repayments on other debts can have an impact on a customer's credit score, hampering efforts to open another card elsewhere.

Knowledge of how these products actually work is poor among customers. Moneysupermarket.com found in 2016 that 21% of credit card customers didn't even know what a balance transfer fee or balance transfer credit card was. Research from the Co-op has found that around 20% of customers who took out a 0% balance transfer credit card offer in the last five years have fallen foul of the terms and conditions of the deal and consequently had the promotional rate withdrawn early, reverting to standard interest rates and costing them a collective £948 million in additional interest as a result. They found that nearly 40% of credit card holders with a promotional offer will have made such a mistake at one time or another. A 2015 survey by the consumer organization Which? found similar gaps in knowledge on the part of customers, with only one in ten of those surveyed able to correctly calculate the true cost of an interest-free promotional credit card offer.

The evidence that these promotional offers lead to long-term customer detriment is overwhelming. The Fairbanking Foundation found that 29% of people who took out best-buy credit cards for spending or balance transfers in the past five years ended up with more debt. We are all responsible for what we spend, of course, yet it is difficult not to conclude that when it comes to interest-free promotional card offers, product managers have figured out how to get us to live beyond our means in order to deliver handsome returns for banks.

Perhaps rather gratifyingly if you're one of those who has fallen foul of these seemingly attractive promotional offers, banks' reliance on them to make money may be about to bite back. In April 2017, several bank chief executives confided to the *Financial Times* that these offers were a "ticking time bomb". The reason for such hyperbole was the way banks recognize the income from interest-free offers, relying on something called the effective interest rate. Banks assume a customer will hold a card for, say, five years. For perhaps the first three years the card might generate the bank no income in real terms as it has an interest-free promotion. In years four and five, the rate on the card will increase and, assuming the customer is still using the card, start generating income for the bank.

But here's where it gets really weird. Banks then take the income they forecast they will make in years four and five and spread it out across the whole five years of the product as an average. So in year one, when you are enjoying interest-free spending on that card, the bank is still able to claim in its accounts that it is making money.

You do not have to be Einstein to realize that lenders are recognizing income even though there is no cash flow associated with it. If customers decided to cancel their card in year three before the rate increases, the bank may have recognized income – in the accounting sense of the term – that they will now never actually see. The result is a 'hit' or correction to the bank's profit and loss account.

In fairness, banks account for promotional credit card income this way because it is required by international accounting rules. The key point though is that explosive growth in credit card balances combined with some fairly optimistic assumptions about how many customers will actually end up earning the bank income after promotional periods end mean banks could be storing up yet another sizeable problem for the future. We have seen this movie before.

Points mean prizes, right?
Along with balance transfer offers, the other common credit card offer in the market is rewards – in the form of points earned for spending on the credit card. There is something rather nice about feeling that you are earning reward points every time you buy something. It's nice to get a little something back for making card purchases that you need to make anyway.

It is, however, worth pondering why product managers offer rewards-based credit cards. It is most certainly not to be nice to you. Reward credit cards are offered to get you to spend money – lots of it – to both pay for your rewards and also run up as high a credit card balance as possible so that the bank can start to, hopefully, earn interest on any balance carried over at the end of the month.

The key 'trick' product managers play when it comes to reward credit cards is confusing customers as to what a point is worth. You will see many reward-based credit cards claiming that customers will earn "one point for every £1 you spend". Intuitively this sounds reasonable enough. Many customers calculate what they spend on a card each week and then feel rather smug at how many points they are set to accumulate. Surprisingly few customers stop to think – or indeed research – what one point actually earns them.

Depending on the reward scheme in place – whether it's airmiles or vouchers – the relationship between a pound spent and the value put towards the reward can vary wildly. With some credit cards, every £1 spent can actually earn customers as little as 0.5p when taken as high-street vouchers, for example. Few customers would think a deal that offered customers the chance to earn 0.5p for every £1 they spend on their credit card was worth having. Some quick mental maths would show that you need to spend a vast amount to get anything meaningful back. Product managers know this and so they prefer to advertise the 'points per pound' con.

Rewards offers tend to offer paltry value for a very simple reason. As we mentioned above, banks used to earn much more from customers transacting regularly on their card in the form of interchange fees. Since these fees have fallen, cashback and rewards offers have decreased in value. Put simply, the card doesn't earn enough for the bank from transactions alone to provide a great rewards offer. That is unless a customer runs up a large credit card balance in a desperate bid to earn more points and doesn't pay off this balance each month, thereby allowing the bank to charge interest on that balance. This has been the main driver behind card providers continuing to offer rewards-based cards. They know encouraging card spend is positively correlated with some customers not paying that spend off. The number-one question to ask yourself whenever you see a credit card rewards offer, then, is "what does £1 spend actually buy me?" This is especially true as many banks reduce the benefits each pound generates for long-term customers to maintain better offers for new customers.

Minimum monthly repayments

The minimum monthly repayment listed on credit card statements is the minimum a customer must pay on their outstanding balance to avoid penalties. It is usually at least the interest charged every month on the outstanding balance plus around 1% of what is owed. However, researchers at The Wharton School at the University of Pennsylvania in the United States have found that this minimum monthly repayment figure has a powerful behavioural impact on customers, acting as a psychological 'anchor' which customers used to determine how much to pay. They found that having this minimum repayment figure tended to mean customers paid off less than they could afford to if required. Behaviourally, customers often internalize the minimum monthly repayment as what they *should* pay rather than the *minimum* they can actually pay off.

The FCA's credit card market study, whose final findings were published in 2016, found that problematic credit card debt was widespread with around two million people in arrears or default and a further two million carrying persistent debt on their credit card (defined as having an average credit limit utilization of 90% or more while also incurring interest charges). This is actually not good news for banks: having customers in arrears requires them to increase the provisions (a form of reserves) they must hold against the potential for these loans to be written off entirely.

Tellingly, a further 1.6 million people were found by the study to only ever make a minimum repayment each month. The study found that credit cards, instead of being used for one-off and short-term credit needs, were for many people a long-term debt management product. Sticking to the minimum monthly repayment on a credit card has real implications for the total amount of interest a customer pays on their borrowings. The study found that 5.1 million cardholders active in January 2015 would still be paying off their balance a decade later if they maintained their current repayment patterns.

To be fair to product managers, the minimum monthly repayment figure on credit cards is not a clever trick they have thought up to leave customers in debt for years. The FCA's Consumer Credit Sourcebook and other guidance regulates credit card products and includes the minimum amounts and timings of repayments. Nevertheless, it is fair to point out that product managers know that while consumers who default on their credit card are extremely unprofitable for banks, those customers able to pay the minimum monthly repayment represent something of a commercial sweet spot.

Banks have no real incentive to contact customers who repeatedly make minimum payments as these customers are normally profitable – often very much so. The FCA credit card market study considered that firms could and should do more to help these customers to reduce debt burdens before they become problematic and to nudge those customers making minimum repayments to repay more quickly when they can.

Rate blindness and limit stealth

'Rate blindness' is when banks make it difficult for customers to see the interest rate they are being charged. This trick is particularly acute within online banking. Rates are never front and centre of your screen. They make you click around and search for them. Yes it will be shown on any statement but if you're honest you never check your statement closely. Rate blindness means that few customers have any idea what rate they are paying and therefore don't know whether it is an expensive rate or a competitive one. This, in turn, reduces their propensity to shop around.

In a similar vein, product managers make more money out of credit card customers by unilaterally increasing a customer's credit limit, even if they haven't asked for an increase. They are required to give customers at least 30 days' notice and customers are perfectly entitled to decline the offer of a limit increase. Yet few, at least in our experience, do decline the limit increase, seeing a large credit limit as a badge of honour.

Larger limits are broadly and unsurprisingly correlated with more spending – that's why product managers increase them – and the more a customer spends the more likely they are not to pay the entire outstanding balance off each month and therefore drive interest income for the bank.

Perhaps the more sinister aspect to this practice is how product managers go about selecting the customers whose limits will be increased. The customers selected tend to be those product managers assess as likely to drive interest income and not the super-wealthy who they know tend to pay off balances or have a range of other ways to pay.

Product managers are targeting those customers who they think may have a high propensity to revolve balances month-to-month, making interest income for the bank. This point is worth dwelling on: product managers are increasing the credit limits of customers that make the most income for the bank. They are, in a very real sense, targeting those customers that may struggle to pay off debt each month, thereby tipping them into longer-term debt at a high interest rate.

These are not the only tricks and temptations product managers conjure up when it comes to credit cards. Customers sometimes lose benefits like rewards if they do not use their card regularly or get slammed with an inactivity fee after a period, usually six months. Any introductory interest-free period may lapse unless the card is used. As with debit cards, credit cards often charge higher fees for use overseas and fees also apply if monthly payments are late. Taking money out of a cash machine with a credit card (a cash advance) attracts a much higher interest rate, often without an interest-free period.

A credit card plays on our desire to 'buy it now' before making it all too easy to take longer than necessary to clear the resulting debt. And in the process product managers have a plethora of different techniques to make money out of you.

Mortgages
As easy as E, R, C

Ah...Early Repayment Charges (ERC). Product managers love them. An ERC is payable on most mortgage products when the mortgage is repaid ahead of its promotional term. For example, if you took out a five-year fixed-rate mortgage offer for £100,000 and suddenly inherited £100,000 and decided to pay off your mortgage, the mortgage provider would probably charge you an ERC.

The amount the lender will charge you tends to vary and is often determined by when in the term of the mortgage product you repay. Thus in your first year of a five-year mortgage you might be asked to pay 5% of the outstanding mortgage amount as an ERC. In year three of your mortgage deal you might be asked to pay 3% and so on. ERCs tend to get cheaper the nearer the end of your deal you are.

Customers sometimes pay off mortgages if they come into some money or, just as likely, if they spot a much more competitive mortgage offer from another provider and calculate that even with an ERC from their current provider it is still cheaper to move mortgages.

Under the regulations that govern mortgages these ERCs should be a reasonable pre-estimate of the costs mortgage providers will incur for ending a mortgage before its term. In reality, they tend to bear very little relation to the costs a bank or other mortgage provider will actually incur and for large mortgages can run into tens of thousands of pounds. There is paperwork to sort and the bank is likely to have incurred hedging costs for any fixed-rate mortgage through the use of a market swap, but together these operational and interest-rate-risk adjustment costs do not add up to the amount some lenders tend to charge in ERCs.

If big banks are honest, ERCs have come to be viewed as a sort of insurance policy ("If the customer is going to pay off or move their mortgage, at least we recouped some of the costs spent on paying the intermediary broker and marketing the product").

Broker is best?

As any mortgage product manager will tell you, when it comes to the mortgage market, brokers are kings of the castle. Sometimes up to eight in every ten mortgage products sold come via brokers. These brokers are required to search for the best deal for their clients and banks are required to pay these brokers commission for introducing mortgage customers to them.

Banks and other mortgage providers still have to underwrite these mortgages to ensure that the customer can afford the borrowing and to ensure that all the necessary due diligence on identification, anti-money laundering and income verification has been completed – brokers simply tend to package up a prospective borrower's application in a pre-agreed format that makes it easier for lenders to process, typically by entering the applicant's details on a technology platform.

In our experience, brokers tend to have three concerns when it comes to their clients. The first is to ensure that they get a good deal for the client, based on the information provided. The second is to ensure that they earn as much commission as they can. The third is to ensure everything moves as quickly and as seamlessly as possible during the application process. Brokers want their commission as quickly as possible.

In practice, this third factor gives brokers a lot of discretion as to where they place their business. They can justify not sending a client's application to the provider offering the cheapest rate if they believe that the lender would take a more accommodating view of the prospective borrowers specific characteristics, such as bonus payments in any annual income assessment, or if they believe this particular lender will move quickly and the customer is in a hurry.

Brokers use these grey areas – lenders' specific policies on lending and reputation for efficiency – to justify not always choosing the cheapest mortgage product available. More often than not, as with much in the business world, brokers tend to send applications to the banks they have a good relationship with while keeping a beady eye on the commission offered.

With all that said, using a broker can still make sense. Even if the broker doesn't choose the out-and-out cheapest deal in the market at the time, it is often cheaper than the customer walking in to their local high-street bank and going with whatever product they are offered. Brokers offer a 'whole of market' view and can chase down some terrific deals for customers. It just pays to be aware that these terrific deals are often also terrific for the broker too.

Table gaming

One thing is for sure in the mortgage market: price matters. It is one of the most commoditized markets out there with very little differentiation between products. In nearly every way imaginable, a two-year fixed-rate mortgage from Bank A is identical to a two-year fixed-rate mortgage from Bank B. The only difference tends to be price.

Even accounting for the vagaries of brokers, a 'best-buy' mortgage deal will almost always attract a lot more business than a deal that is middle of the pack. And the way for product managers to ensure that a best-buy deal is seen and heard about is by topping the charts of the mortgage sourcing platforms all the brokers use. These sourcing systems, such as Trigold, hold huge sway over the market and often contain specific special deals available only to brokers.

Unsurprisingly, then, product managers are keen as mustard to get to the top of these best-buy tables when they want to sell as many mortgages as possible. And so they set about doing so in ways that are not always transparent. A favourite technique is to offer a mortgage with a very low rate but a high fee. Product managers do this for two reasons. The first is that they know that mortgage sourcing systems tend to rank mortgage deals by headline rate. Therefore having a competitive headline rate makes sense. So, too, does having a high arrangement fee for the mortgage. This ensures that the mortgage product manager earns back some of the margin they may have invested in offering such a cheap headline interest rate on the mortgage.

The second is that they know that customers tend to discount the fees associated with mortgages, or at least do not compare them as readily as they do the headline interest rate. A cheap headline rate means customers tend to think they have got a 'great deal', irrespective of whether the associated mortgage fee is high.

Brokers, in case you're wondering, are required to show their clients how the maths of all this works out and rarely recommend mortgages with exorbitant fees. Nevertheless, the fees don't need to be exorbitant, just enough to allow the product manager to knock a few more basis points off the promotional mortgage rate to get it up to the top of the sourcing system. As is so often the case, it pays to work out the total cost of the product (fees plus interest rate) over its lifetime to work out what the best product out there actually is.

The SVR money hose

Standard Variable Rate (SVR) is the annual percentage rate that mortgage products switch to after any promotional period is over. For example, your two-year fixed-rate mortgage deal offering an introductory rate of 1.99% APR might now be at an end and you will be moved on to your bank's SVR of perhaps 3.49% APR.

Given that SVR is often significantly more expensive than any promotional rate, it is surprising how many customers are on SVR with their lender. Mainly this is because most people have mortgages with promotional periods of two or five years and there are therefore hundreds of thousands of customers whose mortgages are rolling off these promotional deals every year.

Often customers don't spend very long on SVR. Their current mortgage deal ends and perhaps they have been slow getting around to sorting out another one. In such instances they might spend a month or two paying their current lender's SVR until they arrange a new deal.

Yet the fact that lenders' SVRs are so much higher than the promotional deals they offer gives you some clue how important SVR is to the economics of mortgages for product managers. Even a couple of months of a customer paying SVR can earn the bank a handsome return and more than pay for the lower rate the customer enjoyed during the promotional period. SVRs are therefore key to the effective, overall rate a mortgage customer will pay during their time with the bank.

Sometimes it is not just lethargy that means customers pay SVR. Changes in circumstance can mean that customers find it difficult to get another mortgage elsewhere (such as a bad credit rating) or perhaps the value of the property has plummeted leaving a customer in negative equity meaning that remortgaging is impossible or highly costly.

Less occasionally, customers are on SVR for a more positive reason, such as while waiting to receive a significant amount of money from an inheritance or other good fortune. They therefore value the flexibility of being on a bank's SVR as this usually means they don't have to pay early repayment charges if they pay a sizeable sum off the mortgage.

Whatever the reason a customer is paying SVR it is almost always good news for product managers. While the customer is vulnerable to being 'poached' by another lender as there is no contractual commitment to staying put after a promotional deal has ended, product managers know that SVR customers are valuable. The SVR is, by definition, variable, meaning that product managers can move the rate up and down at will, although there is a convention that this is usually done in broad relationship to the Bank of England Base Rate moving up or down. But if product managers feel they can argue that their costs have increased, then they may feel justified in unilaterally moving their SVR north, providing a juicy income boost to the bank. The fact the rate is variable also means these mortgages present low interest-rate risk to the bank.

For many product managers, their book of SVR customers is to be 'adored and ignored': adored because they provide the lender with a fantastic interest-rate income and ignored because they do not want to wake these customers up by sending them lots of letters or other marketing material about the bank in case it stimulates the customer to question what mortgage deal they are on and start searching around for a better deal.

Pay attention to retention

Beware retention offers. For customers, the attractiveness of signing up to another five-year fixed-term mortgage in a few clicks online (lenders make it very easy) can be significant. Much time can be saved collating documents and filling in forms to apply for another mortgage with another lender. It can feel good to get a new deal sorted out with a minimum of fuss.

For product managers, proactive retention like this makes even more sense. Product teams often build quite sophisticated, statistical propensity models to identify those customers with a low likelihood to switch to another provider, typically those with a low LTV mortgage with a small balance where moving to get a better rate will not make very much difference to monthly payments as the mortgage amount is so small. Another group with a low propensity to switch tend to be First-Time Buyers, particularly if they took their first mortgage by entering a bank branch. Product managers contact these customers, sometimes by phone but more often than not via email nowadays, to present a rate of new mortgage offers that can be accessed through a few simple clicks. At all times product managers are focused on getting you on to a new deal before you've had the time, or the inclination, to survey the whole mortgage market and develop any awareness of whether the rates you are being offered are competitive or not. In fairness to banks, retention deals are sometimes very competitive and the process of moving on to a new deal often seamless. But it nearly always makes sense to see what other deals are around before you take one of these offers up.

Unsecured personal loans
When the price you see is not the price you get
When you look at a bank's adverts for loans, you will see a 'representative APR'. The APR is the compounded interest rate, and includes any fees that a bank might charge upfront. Its purpose is to provide a useful rate comparison between providers. But the price you see may not be the price you get, much to the surprise of many customers. This is because the 'representative' bit means that it is the

rate that at least 51% of customers will get. The remaining 49% of customers will be charged a higher rate – sometimes much higher. Banks are not required to display their maximum rates.

There's no getting round the fact that unsecured loan pricing is complicated. The bank's product managers price loans for a customer's personal risk profile. So if a customer has had trouble paying bills in the past, or has defaulted on a loan, the bank will charge more to reflect the higher risk associated with lending to that customer. The bank has to take into account the cost of two types of losses.

The first is expected losses. Expected losses are calculated by understanding, for each 100 customers, how many are likely to default and how much the bank will lose on average from each of those customers. The level of these default losses is a cost line within the profit and loss account for each loan product. Within that group, you will have 'best risk customers', for example the top ten who have the lowest likelihood of default, and are usually graded as risk band A. These customers will usually be offered the best rates (however, the relationship between the cost of expected defaults and price is not linear, as we shall see).

A bank can simply practise risk-based pricing based on expected losses. That is, all customers will have different prices depending on their risk banding, but all risk bands are expected to yield the same margin for the bank.

The second type is unexpected losses. Unexpected losses are how much the bank would expect to lose from customers in the event of an adverse economic shock, like the 2008 recession. Product managers often like to think of this in terms of a loss multiplier, that is, how many times the expected losses could increase, and the bank still break even on the loan. In periods of stability, if a bank takes expected and unexpected losses into account, different risk bands of customers will be expected to yield different margins, after expected losses. Higher-risk customers will yield greater margins than low-risk customers. However, in an economic shock, where a bank had correctly estimated unexpected losses, yield would be expected to even out. This is because higher-risk customers are expected to be impacted more significantly in a negative economic shock. Many banks simply take these two factors into account, and add a flat margin on top across their customer base.

Price optimization

This is less a 'trick' that product managers play than an explanation of how bankers determine what price they can get away with charging customers.

Risk-based pricing is not the only determinant of the pricing you will pay on a loan. Price optimization (or price sensitivity analysis) is when product managers look at the demographic make-up of customers, as well as their financial and spending patterns, and determine the highest price they can charge them at which they will still buy the loan.

The difference between banks and many other industries is that they can charge individuals different prices, and not really explain why. So it is very different from buying, say, a TV (all priced the same) but similar to buying an airline ticket (where pricing is based on demand). In banking, 'risk-based pricing' provides a cloak for the practice of price optimization. Banks protect themselves in the fine print by noting that pricing is also based on 'personal circumstances'.

A simple example shows how price optimization works in practice. A bank's baseline price for a loan is 5%. They might add 1% for expected losses, and another 1% for unexpected losses, making a total of 7%. At a rate of 7%, the product manager knows that 100 people will take the loan. For simplicity let's say each person takes out £10 for one year, and interest is compounded annually. The total income pool for this cohort of 100 customers borrowing £1,000 at 7% for one year is therefore £70.

Here's where the sensitivity analysis comes in. Product managers think that if they charged a higher price of 9%, 90 people would still take out the loan. So they charge the higher price, which gives £81 of income from a smaller amount of lending. Product managers are effectively working out the best price they can charge for the loan.

It's also possible to calculate the break-even point for the price change – which is basically how many fewer customers can buy the loan without the product manager losing any overall income. In this case, 22 customers can refuse to take the loan and the price change still makes sense as shown in Table 9.

Table 9

	Current loan rate and take up	Fewer customers higher rate	Break-even point for price change
Number of customers	100	100	100
Customers choosing loan	100	90	78
Loan size per person (£)	10	10	10
Total bank lending (£)	1,000	900	780
Interest rate	7%	9%	9%
Profit made (£)	70	81	70

In case you're wondering, there are many aspects of who you are and how you behave that suggest how likely you are to accept a higher price. Key factors in the lending market include customer risk, and whether you purchased your loan in store or online.

Price optimization happens after a price has been set based on risk. The riskier a customer is, the more likely they are to accept a higher price, even after taking into account default risk. So riskier customers get charged a disproportionately higher price. There might be several reasons for this, but a key factor is supply – there are likely to be fewer banks that want to lend to higher-risk customers. A bank can add additional margin because these customers have less choice elsewhere.

The channel can also have a big impact. If you go through a broker or financial adviser, you are more likely to be charged a higher price. And, traditionally, it costs more for customers to purchase loans in bank branches than online. This is because customers shopping online are more likely to shop around than those searching in branches.

Other factors might not be so obvious. Banks run complex statistical models to understand which aspects of customer behaviour are more likely to be correlated with accepting a higher price. It might be, for example, that customers who use ATMs frequently are more likely to accept a higher price. Unbeknown to the customer, the price at which they will be offered a loan increases every time they take cash out. It might even be that your bank has seen that you have visited the loan pages on your bank's internet banking service several times meaning they know you are interested in a loan so they amend your price to reflect that.

The problem with all this, of course, is that customers cannot understand what impacts their price, and so cannot change their behaviour in order to reduce that price. So you might put off that new kitchen for a year because the cost of financing is too high. You might make efforts to improve your credit score by getting on the electoral roll, and ensuring your bills are paid on time, but that could be counteracted by seemingly unrelated behaviours that affect your loan price but indicate to product managers that you could be charged more.

Bells and whistles

The draw of a potential loan can make customers blind when it comes to fees. All that they are focused on is getting the loan they need to buy a new laptop or mobile phone and they discount in their minds any upfront fees as just a necessary pain. Yet these charges are an important part of the economics of a personal loan for a product manager and it pays to be aware of them.

- **Arrangement fees:** An upfront fee for taking out the loan. The arrangement fee is included in the APR that a bank offers you. As banks are trying to offer you the lowest possible APR, these fees are rare in the mainstream market.
- **Repayment holidays:** Can be useful if you are in a complete bind in a particular month. But be wary that taking out a repayment holiday will increase the overall cost of your loan, simply because you are taking out the money for longer.
- **Early repayment fees:** Consider this carefully when you take out a loan. You should pick a loan term which realistically matches your ability to pay,

particularly if early repayment fees are charged. If you are expecting to pay off your loan with a lump sum at some point in the future, ensure that you take into account any early repayment fees when selecting your loan.

Flat-interest rate loans

These types of loans are becoming rare (thank goodness) but they can still be found, mainly in the less customer-friendly car dealers out there. The trick here is for the loan provider to make the loan sound cheaper even though it's anything but.

A conventional repayment loan would see less interest charged as the outstanding balance declines. This is because the interest charge is being applied to a smaller outstanding balance. Pretty standard stuff.

Not so flat-interest rate loans. Here you pay the same interest charge on your last payment as your first. Your interest charge doesn't reduce as your balance reduces. Why do car dealers and others go for a flat-rate loan? They make more money, that's why. A £10,000 loan over three years at a flat rate of 5% means you will repay £11,500 in total. A £10,000 loan over three years at an APR of 5% will see you repay £10,789 in total. That's a big difference.

Sadly, the majority of customers that are exposed to flat-rate interest loans don't spot the fact that the rate is not an APR rate.

Bag of tricks

There is a whole host of other tricks and techniques – explicit or otherwise – that bankers use to earn more money from personal loan customers.

Customers are frequently duped into taking a longer-term loan in order for monthly repayments to be lower. Lower monthly repayments sound good. But the longer the loan term, the more interest you pay. A longer loan term might make perfect sense for some customers, but few really understand the additional cost they are signing up to.

As with bank accounts and savings accounts, bankers will look to cross-subsidize across different product categories. The best loan rates will be offered to current account or savings customers. This incentivizes loan customers to transfer their banking or savings, regardless of whether the bank offers competitive deals on either of these products. Product managers are simply taking the extra margin from one product and transferring it to another.

Sometimes the interest rate you will be offered will go down the more you borrow. This is counter-intuitive to most customers who think that a bigger loan should attract a higher rate. Yet the additional interest income that a larger loan will generate can often mean that the product manager can afford to offer a lower interest on the loan. Separately, bankers are wary of customers taking out very small loans – perhaps £1,000 – as it indicates the customer may be struggling financially. These loans tend to be priced at a higher APR as a result.

CHAPTER SUMMARY

- Lending provides banks with interest income and fees, and relies on product managers striking a balance between lending the right amount of money at the right price to customers that represent the right level of risk.

- Scale matters in lending, allowing providers to absorb losses more easily, make better decisions on whom to lend to, and diversify their lending, thereby reducing risk.

- Product managers deploy risk-based pricing to determine what interest rate to charge on loans. The higher the risk the customer presents, the higher the rate charged.

- Banks have to hold capital in reserve against loans advanced to customers to absorb potential losses from customers potentially not repaying their borrowings. Different types of loan attract different capital charges.

- Product managers need to manage interest-rate risk when offering fixed-rate lending, using market instruments like swaps to turn fixed-rate assets into variable-rate assets.

CHAPTER SUMMARY

- Credit card customers usually fall into one of four categories: Revolvers; Transactors; Stoozers; and Credit Repairers.

- Mortgage customers mostly commonly divide into five groups: First-Time Buyers; Remos; Homemovers; Rate Switchers; and Further Advancers.

- Personal loan customers usually split into six types: Purchasers; Consolidators; Refinancers; Car Financers; Point of Sale Customers; and Payday Borrowers.

CHAPTER SUMMARY

Credit cards

- Interest-free credit card purchases or balance transfers encourage customers to run up large balances which can be expensive for customers to repay when the promotional period ends.

- Reward- or points-based credit cards also encourage customers to spend but often the pounds-to-points ratio is low, meaning significant spend is required to earn meaningful rewards.

- Credit card debt can last for years if customers only pay the minimum required payment.

- Product managers often make it difficult for customers to see the credit card rate they are on.

CHAPTER SUMMARY

Mortgages

- Early repayment charges are a money earner for banks, usually charged when borrowers pay more than 10% of the outstanding mortgage deal within a promotional period.

- Brokers are focused on getting a good rate for their clients but also on the amount of commission they will receive from the mortgage referral and how quickly the provider will process the application.

- Mortgage providers often play around with their rates and fees to try and get the best position on the mortgage pricing platforms that the broker industry refer to as this guarantees more business.

- Standard Variable Rate (SVR) is the rate mortgage customers go on to when their promotional period ends. It is usually materially higher than any promotional rate and a big money earner for banks. Most people don't spend very long on SVR.

- Mortgage providers are keen to offer existing borrowers simple and easy remortgage options to stop them searching the market for a new deal.

CHAPTER SUMMARY

Unsecured personal loans

- Customers will not always receive the loan rate they see advertised as this rate need only apply to 51% of customers that apply and is a 'representative APR'.

- Product managers are constantly trying to optimize their loan pricing, to ascertain the highest loan rate they can charge customers while still continuing to hit their lending targets.

- Like mortgages, personal loans tend to come with lots of associated fees, most notably arrangement fees and early repayment fees.

- Extending a loan term can cost customers more in interest even though monthly payments are lower.

- Product managers incentivize customers to take out additional products in order to qualify for the best loan rates.

- Rates offered on personal loans will sometimes get lower the more you borrow as this provides the loan provider with more income overall.

PART 3

Things can only get better

CHAPTER 8

Better banking

Retail banking is expensive, with hundreds of millions of pounds spent each year on IT platforms, branches, bank staff, and the like. At the same time, the retail banking market is growing only slowly and customers are inert – few of us switch banks to get a better deal – meaning banks don't need to try that hard to keep our business. As a result, there is little differentiation in the products they offer. High barriers to entry (regulatory, investment, capital) and the relatively small number of competitors are the main reasons why the big high-street banks have survived in their current form as long as they have. These banks have the advantage of scale – they are large enough to pay for their own costs and still make a profit.

This context explains why product managers inside retail banks work so hard to find new sources of income from customers. Incentivized to hit profit targets in ways that do not lead to damaging public-relations headlines but nonetheless deliver value to the bottom line, they have thought up ever more elaborate products, pricing strategies, fee structures, and promotions in the hope of extracting margin from customers. In Part 1 we saw that product managers come to product design with a set of objectives antithetical to good customer outcomes. Loyal customers are treated worse than new customers. Customers who hold lots of products with the same bank are usually receiving a worse deal than those that spread their banking around. Rates are constantly readjusted on products to make more and more money from customers.

The question then arises: what can I do as a customer to protect myself from all this? How can I set up my personal banking in a way that means I am not exploited by product managers looking to charge exorbitant fees, reduce my saving rate regularly, or charge me high rates for borrowing?

The answer to these questions is not, as you might have suspected, a simple one. But there is an answer. It is based on developing a good understanding of who you are, how you behave in a financial sense, what's important to you, and how you can take sensible steps to reduce your exposure to some of the sharper practices deployed by banks out there. And it starts with asking yourself four questions.

Four important questions

In our experience as product managers, we can all start to benefit from better banking if we answer four simple questions before we apply for any new product or service from a bank. Answering these questions can have a profound effect on how you bank, save and borrow.

Question 1: What do I want to achieve?

It was that reliable source of enigmatic quotes Winston Churchill who said, "Let our advance worrying become advance thinking and planning." We agree and we think this is particularly true when it comes to your finances. It is remarkable how few customers have a plan or know what it is they are trying to achieve.

To be clear, we understand that banking can be confusing, boring, and regularly downright frustrating in equal measure. Be that as it may, this doesn't preclude us all thinking through what we are actually trying to achieve with our personal finances. Unless this is clear, financial products are likely to do more harm than good.

Just a few examples make the point. We often see customers taking out a credit card with a long balance transfer offer because it "looked like a cracking deal", regardless of whether they have an existing balance on a card elsewhere to transfer or even whether they actually use a credit card very often. We've lost count of the number of times customers have opened a fixed-term savings product that comes to an end well after the date they were saving the money for, leaving them in a pickle as many banks won't let them have access to the money without a penalty. Still others will take a fixed-rate, unsecured personal loan as a 'safety net' for when things get tight at the end of the month when this is usually not the right solution.

Asking "what do I want to achieve?" helps to clarify what your personal financial objectives might be – whether that's saving for a car, or paying off debt from your student days – before you think about the best way to achieve this objective. That means before the confusion and temptation of bank product offers enter your head. And before a charismatic employee from one of the high-street banks has tried to convince you that what you really need is the product that gets them the biggest bonus.

Instead, focus on the most appropriate product to suit your specific personal objectives, rather than be seduced by the latest short-term rate promotion or cash incentive. It might sound strange, but many customers turn this logic on its head, rushing headlong for what looks like a good promotion and never stopping to think whether it is the most appropriate product for their circumstances.

The more specific your objectives the better. While 'saving for a house' is admirable, better to know how much of a deposit you need, when you want to buy a house, and work back to the sum you need to save each year, month, or week. The same goes in reverse if you are trying to pay down debt.

Our recommendation is to know what you are trying to do when it comes to your finances and – just as importantly – recognize when your objectives actually conflict with each other. Again, we regularly see customers who are financially savvy yet they have failed to recognize that the way they are using banking products is self-defeating. To use the same example, saving for a house deposit while paying off unsecured debt at the same time is rarely sensible as the rate you are paying on the unsecured debt is likely to far outstrip the savings rate you are receiving.

There is no substitute for starting with the end in mind. It is only possible to choose the right products and the right bank to support your plans if you have some. The 'what do I actually want to achieve?' question is arguably the most important one of the lot.

Question 2: What are they trying to get me to do?
The 'they' here, in case you were wondering, is the product manager sitting at his or her desk at one of the large high-street banks, plotting to make money out of you.

In our view, before taking out any new banking product, and when reviewing the products you currently use for that matter, understanding what the product manager is trying to get you to do is essential. Remember, most product managers are incentivized to focus on just a few things, namely: growing the market share of the product they manage; decreasing the cost to the bank of providing that product; and increasing the income it delivers to the bank. Sometimes they will be focused on just one of these, sometimes all three. The ultimate goal is to enhance the financial return the product delivers to the bank.

This focus is obvious but also helpful. Helpful because it reminds us that the interests of the product manager are rarely, if ever, aligned with our own. This being the case, all that is left to do is work out *how* the product manager intends to take advantage of us. Therefore, asking yourself what the product manager is trying to get me, the customer, to do often elicits some surprisingly helpful insights.

In Table 10 we've summarized just a few examples to illustrate the point.

Table 10

Product/ offer	What are they trying to get me to do?	What is the product manager betting on?
Packaged current account	• Pay a monthly fee for a range of benefits that may cost the bank less to provide than the monthly fee	• You can't be bothered to buy all the benefits separately • You won't check whether buying everything separately is cheaper • You won't use everything in the package, meaning it is cheaper for the bank to provide
Credit card balance transfer offer	• Transfer a large balance, forget about it, and then start paying a high interest rate when the offer runs out • Fail to notice the initial balance transfer interest charge	• You won't pay off as much of the outstanding balance during the promotional period as you'd hoped • You'll forget when the offer period ends
Savings account with introductory bonus rate	• Deposit funds and then forget to move them when the bonus rate runs out, allowing the product manager to drop the rate and benefit from relatively low-cost funding	• You'll forget when the bonus period ends
Current account with a high credit interest rate offer	• Build up a large credit balance in your current account and pay credit interest on only a small proportion of it, perhaps the first £1,000, thereby providing low-cost funding to the bank	• You won't have noticed that the credit interest is only applicable to the first £1,000 of the balance ('inverse tiering')
A new mortgage deal with the same provider six months before your current one ends	• Renew your mortgage before you have had time to look around to see what other offers are available in the market	• You prefer the convenience of moving to a new deal in a few clicks of a mouse than comparing the offer to see whether it is competitive versus the market

You get the picture. While you might think that a number of the tricks product managers pull are obvious, it is surprising how few of us stop to think clearly about what the product manager is trying to get us to do. When a bank writes to us suggesting a new, much higher credit limit on our credit card, few of us stop to think about why the bank has done that, preferring to revel in the fiction that it's because we are special and the bank is somehow rewarding us for good behaviour.

Of course, sometimes it is perfectly fine to understand what the product manager is trying to do and go along with it. You might not, after all, have time to research and source all of the insurances that come as part of a packaged bank account separately to see if you could buy them cheaper elsewhere. But at least if you stop to think about what the product manager is up to you are making that decision consciously.

Asking yourself – during any interaction with your bank – what they are trying to get you to do, then, is a useful way to think critically about the motivations of the product manager. And in our experience, product managers will be trying to get you to do one of four things:

- forget when a deal or promotion ends
- incorrectly assess how you will use a product
- take out more products
- miss something in the terms and conditions.

If you forget when a promotional offer ends you are easy prey for a product manager who wants to ramp up charges or reduce interest paid out. If you don't put an arranged overdraft in place on your current account because you convince yourself you will never run out of money, you are the perfect candidate to get whacked with penalty fees. If you're the sort of person who gets rather flattered when you are offered 'exclusive products for existing customers' you are walking straight into the trap of product managers cross-subsidizing between products, offering good value on one product while extracting margin on another, making money overall from you as a customer. If you don't tend to read terms and conditions then you will probably have missed the fact that you will pay a 3% balance transfer fee on your new credit card before you benefit from an interest-free period, ensuring that the product manager makes a hefty one-off charge from any transfer.

Asking what the product manager is trying to get me to do – standing in the shoes of the product manager – is the easiest way for us all to ensure we do exactly the opposite, usually saving us money, time, and stress.

Question 3: Is it a big number?

This might sound like an odd question to ask but it's a really important one. Whether it is the fault of the great British school system or just a facet of how busy everyone is, in our experience customers are generally bad at putting personal finance numbers in context. Even when they are told a number – such as an interest rate or a fee – they rarely stop to think if that number is a big one relative to the situation at hand. Assessing the *relative* significance of any number is key.

For example, if you are told that a new savings account pays a rate of 5% AER you have no information to judge whether this is a 'good' rate without situating that rate in some sort of context – comparing it to the rates offered by other banks, the Bank of England Base Rate, the rate you are currently earning on your savings, or the rate you need in order to afford that new motorbike in 18 months' time. Whether 5% AER is a good rate depends on lots of factors and by asking whether it is a big number we are forced to think about what those factors might be.

Similarly, if you are told that every £1 spent on your credit card buys one reward point, to be redeemed at a retailer, few of us will stop to ask what that one point can buy. Few of us, in other words, stop to think whether one point is a big number. As we discussed in Part 2, these points can end up being worth pennies.

The 'Is it a big number?' question is particularly powerful when it comes to fees. This is because for reasons of behavioural psychology we tend to discount fees in our heads, convincing ourselves we won't pay them and, if we do, rarely stopping to think about whether they are proportionate.

As we saw in Part 2, a product manager offering a mortgage product with a very competitive headline rate but a large upfront fee is a classic ploy. It means the product sits high on the database mortgage brokers use to find the best rates but still bags the bank a healthy income overall. Adding the fee to the cost of the mortgage overall would mean that the mortgage offers only average value. But few of us stop to think whether a large product fee – perhaps £1,500 or £2,000 – is a big number relative to the interest we will be paying on the mortgage itself.

At a deeper level, asking whether a number is a big number lifts our gaze to think about what we are being offered by our bank and evaluate it more critically. It invites us to *compare* the number to those offered by other banks and sometimes non-banks. It pushes us to reflect on whether a number is *affordable* compared to our incomings and outgoings. It starts us on the journey to evaluating the number instead of assuming the bank must be right and that a rate or fee must just be the going rate.

Question 4: How do I *really* behave?

We're not talking about whether you are a nice person here. We're talking about how you actually behave when it comes to your personal finances.

Product managers make money by exploiting the gap between how we *hope* to act when it comes to our finances and how we *actually* behave. As we saw in Part 1, we all have myriad psychological biases impacting how we evaluate financial decisions. In our experience, one of the most damaging is overconfidence. We consistently convince ourselves that we are going to behave in ways that are unrealistic. From wrongly believing we will have enough spare cash to fund a Regular Saver product to assuming we will never need an overdraft, there are myriad examples where we assume things will work out just fine and they never do.

This question is not just about behavioural finance biases and all that complicated stuff though. In many respects it is simpler than that – it asks us to consider how we actually use financial products. Product managers in banks understand how customers tend to behave *in general*. They have the benefit of being able to continually track the behaviour of millions of customers and they can spot patterns. They then design products and services to make money out of these patterns.

For example, banks know they can slowly reduce the interest rate they are paying you on your savings account because they know, *on average*, most customers rarely check the rate they are receiving and won't move their savings somewhere else. Similarly, banks have made millions of pounds from customers using their debit cards overseas because they know we forget to check the fees the bank applied to these transactions when we get back home. We might convince ourselves we will track a rate or stay on top of what we are spending, but life gets in the way.

It would be easy for us to repeat the guidance you see every week in the personal finance columns in newspapers, encouraging customers to check the best-buy tables and be prepared to switch their banking around frequently. Yet in our experience, relatively few customers do and the reason is plain enough: life is too short. Yes, seeking out the best deals banks have to offer can save (or earn) you significantly more than staying put, but most people are busy and find thinking about their personal finances pretty boring. We confess, we find a lot of banking quite boring too and we work in the industry!

The secret, such as it is, then, is to configure your banking in a way that best suits how you *actually* live your life and is reflective of the time you *really* have available to spend focusing on your finances. This might mean choosing simple products you actually understand rather than those with 'tricksy' promotional offers that come and go and usually end up becoming bad products. It might mean setting up your banking so that things happen automatically instead of relying on you to remember, such as paying bills by direct debit or setting up a standing order to fund a savings account. And it might mean choosing a bank for reasons other than the products it offers. It may be that proximity to a branch, how easy you find the mobile app to use, or whether the call centre is UK-based and staffed by human beings is, in the final analysis, more important to you given how you actually bank.

The 'how do I really behave?' question is a simple heuristic that customers can use to make sure they are being realistic in how they approach financial services providers and the products they sell. Look past the blizzard of promotions and advertising and consider how your finances work each month, whether you are really able – or can afford – to change your typical pattern of behaviour, and whether your bank and the products you use are the right ones.

Brilliant basics

Sometimes, when it comes to your finances no amount of self-examination and soul-searching is a substitute for ensuring that you do a few simple things well. To the extent that we believe there are general rules to live by when it comes to banking, saving, and borrowing, they are as follows:

Check every rate, every six months

Product managers make money from how busy your life is. They are betting you don't check the rates you are paying on debt products or earning on savings products, very often. This offers them an opportunity to charge you more or pay you less than they should. A good rule of thumb is therefore to spend ten minutes every six months checking the rates on your current account (credit interest rate, if any, and overdraft debit rate), savings rate (instant access and any fixed-term products you are currently using) and loan, mortgage, or credit card rates, if you use any of these. Note down whether any of these rates have changed since the last time you checked and see how they compare to other banks and providers in the market. Ask if better rates are available at the bank you are currently banking with.

Put in place a small overdraft, as long as it is free to do so

One way to reduce the likelihood of ever paying overdraft paid- and unpaid-item penalty fees is to ensure you put in place a small overdraft on your current account (assuming your credit rating allows you to have one). It is still possible to find banks that won't charge you anything for putting an overdraft facility in place and only levy a simple debit interest rate if you end up using it.

Is an overdraft right for everyone? Not if you are the sort of person who cannot resist the temptation to spend what you have or what the bank is willing to give you. Clearing out your authorized overdraft to buy that new pair of heels or the latest iPad would be a poor decision. Similarly, if you are in a basic bank account that doesn't offer an overdraft facility, this option may not be available to you.

However, in our experience as product managers, in general it is almost always sensible for bank account customers to have a small, arranged overdraft facility in place, perhaps up to a limit of around 10% of your typical monthly expenditure. Any slip-ups will see you pay debit interest for a short period of time but no penalty fees. By so doing you are saying to a product manager that you are prepared to take control of your finances and they can look elsewhere to make their money.

If you're wondering why more people don't do this, remember that most of us convince ourselves we will never go over our limit. And banks have no incentive to disavow us of this notion as they make many millions of pounds in penalty fees every year.

Get digital

The digital revolution is a wonderful thing. We can now all have a vast record collection in our pocket and check our emails on the beach. But for a product manager, the advent of digital banking is a bit of a nightmare. Product managers, if they are being honest, like you to know as little about what is going on with your finances as possible, in the hope that they can slowly make more and more money out of you over time without you noticing.

Yet digital banking, to a very significant degree, makes banking more transparent. It is now easier to find out the rate you are receiving on your savings or paying on your credit card. It is far quicker to check your balance so you do not pay fees. New payment services, such as faster payments mean it is easier to move money between banks and mobile banking apps make it simple to move sums between accounts. The good old World Wide Web also makes it very easy – often within just a few clicks – to compare the deal you are on with those offered by other banks. Information is most certainly power when it comes to your personal banking and new digital technologies – online banking, mobile apps, the web, sources of advice online such as Which? – provide you with a big opportunity to ensure that product managers do not take advantage of your inertia.

It is for these reasons that in our experience customers who regularly use online banking and mobile banking tend to earn more money on their savings and pay less money in fees than customers who stay offline. This correlation is, perhaps, unsurprising. Yet the number of customers who regularly utilize digital technology to keep track of their finances and what other banks are offering, while growing rapidly, is lower than you might imagine. From keeping track of the rates you are earning or paying to ensuring that transactions are correct, digital banking provides greater visibility of what is going on in your own personal financial universe. It also helps you understand your own financial behaviour that little bit better. Using digital banking services is key to beating the product manager at their own game.

Promiscuity can pay but only if you are organized

Does it pay to shop around? In our experience that depends on two things. The first is what's important to you and that might not be spending large amounts of your spare time checking the personal finance press for the best deals.

The second is how organized you are. You might like the idea of getting the best deals, switching around to take advantage of cash incentives, extra reward points, and the like, but often products offering the best deals don't offer the best deals very long. Long-term loyalty to one bank or financial provider for all your products rarely makes sense – it is the banking equivalent of having all your eggs in one basket – yet it is also important to be thoughtful about just how often you can spend time ensuring you are switching from one leading deal to the next. Particularly as it is often not just about switching – it's about ensuring that once you have the shiny new product you operate it in the right way to qualify for the benefits, such as funding the account regularly. Sometimes it's better to go for a reasonable deal, with a reliable brand, that doesn't tend to change things too often.

Just as importantly, it pays to consider the service you receive from your bank, not just the rates it offers. Switching around regularly can mean you eke out slightly better rates but are left with a bank that has a terrible call centre, no local branch, and a frustratingly complicated online banking service. Choosing a new provider should not all be about rate.

If you need to borrow, or are already in debt, a loan is nearly always right

Many personal finance journalists, and most product managers, will howl in disagreement at this one. They will argue that different types of debt product – be they a credit card, loan, or overdraft – are appropriate for different reasons and at different times. We disagree.

There are very few scenarios, in our experience, where using a credit card to borrow makes a lot of sense. If you fancy yourself as a bit of a personal finance whizz, and feel confident taking advantage of a long interest-free balance transfer or purchase period on a credit card, then good luck to you. This is by definition a cheap way to borrow. The only observation we would make is that whenever we meet someone who has become mired in debt, the reason why is usually down to credit card debt and frequently because a tempting interest-free promotional period ran out before the customer had time to pay off the outstanding balance. Credit cards are, for many, a gateway product into further debt.

It is nearly always right to take a loan if you need to borrow for purposes other than buying a property. This is for two reasons. First, a standard unsecured personal loan normally charges a lower interest rate than a credit card. Second, a personal loan requires regular repayments of capital and interest for a defined period whereas a credit card entices people to pay only the monthly minimum repayment, which means debt can roll on for years, far surpassing the period over which a similar sum could be paid off using a fixed-rate, fixed-term personal loan. Overdrafts have their uses, as a safety net at the end of the month before payday mainly, but rarely make sense as a source of borrowing over the long term as the equivalent annual rates charged are high.

Our preference for loans is not a hard and fast rule – individual circumstances will apply (it makes no sense to take out a loan if you expect to receive some money in a few weeks that could clear the debt, for example) – but it is based on our experience of the numbers of customers that get themselves into a muddle with credit cards.

Pay down debt with savings

It almost never makes sense to build up savings and debt at the same time. This is for an obvious reason – the interest rate you are paying on any debt is likely to far exceed the interest you are receiving on any deposits. If you think about it, that's how banks make money. So, while it may be reassuring to have lots of savings and while those savings might in some weird way make you feel like you can *afford* to run up a little credit card debt or delve deep into an overdraft, financially this is a silly thing to do. You are making yourself poorer.

Ignore awards and star ratings

Banks – all banks – love to advertise the awards their products win. One product might have five stars, another might have won 'Best Provider' in some awards category or other. Mostly these awards are total bunkum. Product managers like winning them because it gives them something to put on a poster in the branch or place in an advert – some supposedly independent corroboration that their products are good.

The problem with awards and star ratings are four-fold. First, often the winners of various product award categories were good products for only a short amount of time. A fantastic, market-beating mortgage product that disappeared as quickly as it appeared. A savings rate that topped the best-buy table then vanished. Awards and star ratings for the 'best' products tend to ignore how long those products were available for and how many customers actually took advantage of them.

The second point to make is that most of these awards are fixated on product pricing. That is, products that offered the best rates often scoop the most plaudits. As we've seen, price is only one factor in how good a product is – there are plenty of products with complex terms and conditions that offer great headline prices to tempt customers in but let them down in lots of other ways. Price is just one determinant of whether a product is right for you. A good product from an unreliable provider is not a good deal. A great price that is quickly repriced is not a good product.

Third, product awards are frequently a function of which product managers can be bothered to nominate their product for an award. As such, the nominations for product awards are not particularly representative of the market as a whole. Rather it is who had a spare Friday afternoon to fill in a long nomination application and pop it in the post!

Finally, and most importantly of all, it is worth remembering why these companies offer awards and ratings. The answer is to make money. The awarding companies rate products or shortlist products for an award and make money by holding an awards night where it costs the nominee banks thousands of pounds to buy a table at the ceremony. Or they charge the bank thousands of pounds if they want to use the logo or kite mark associated with the award on their marketing material. We have heard more than one story of a bank winning an award simply because they bought a table at the awards night. As such, we're really not sure product awards and star ratings tell you very much at all. But if you do choose to rely on awards and star ratings when choosing products, make sure they are ones where the public has voted for them as these tend to be the most reliable.

It makes sense to use a mortgage broker

As we said in Chapter 7 on borrowing, using mortgage brokers can have a few downsides. Brokers occasionally don't choose the out and out 'best' deal for you and they are unsurprisingly fixated on the commission they will earn from arranging your mortgage. But, on balance, it is better to use them than not. Brokers that are part of the big broker networks frequently get access to special mortgage deals that the person in the street cannot get access to, they are often useful if your case is in any way out of the ordinary (perhaps you have irregular patterns of income, for example) and they hurry lenders along if the process is taking too long. Generally speaking, they offer a whole of market view, ensuring the deal you get is at least competitive, and sometimes exceptionally so. By far the most important point to recommend them to you is that, generally speaking, most banks would love it if brokers didn't exist. Brokers contact customers when their deal ends to see if they can find them another deal, even if that means moving to another lender. Most banks hate this. So, think of brokers as your personal mortgage switching support service – one paid for by the banks no less – and make sure you use them the next time you need to arrange a mortgage.

The principle of contingency

Rainy days are inevitable, so prepare for them. We know every book on personal budgeting says this. We also know that putting money aside from the monthly budget can be exceptionally challenging. In our experience, though, it is best defence against needing to rely on what we would term 'bad credit' – that is the need to arrange to borrow money in a hurry or when you might not have very many options available as to which bank or lender to borrow from. There is a wealth of policy evidence to show that having a cushion of at least some savings not only protects you from financial consequences of unexpected events such as illness or the loss of a job, it also changes the way you think and behave. Those with even a small amount of savings are more cautious and tend to make better financial decisions. But the real priority has to be avoiding the use of short-term, highly expensive credit as this is how the spiral of debt starts. The UK has one of the lowest saving rates in the developed world and this lack of any sort of protective buffer for people is one reason we have such high levels of unsecured debt. They are two sides of the same coin – literally.

Ask what your options are when repriced

When it comes to product managers moving the interest rates up and down on your banking products, our advice is not to take it lying down. As we've said many times, bankers rely on the fact you can't be bothered to move to another product when the interest rate on your credit card goes up or your savings account down.

The best thing to do in our experience is to ask your bank what your options are. They don't get asked this very often and can look and sound a little confused when you do. The key thing to remember to ask is what rates are available to new customers and if there is any reason why you can't be transferred to one of these products. It used to be the case that banks actively stopped existing customers accessing the deals available to new customers. Today, under pressure from customers and consumer groups, banks tend to be more flexible and if you ask to be transferred to the better deals for new customers many will oblige. Banks can still rely on the majority of customers not being bothered to pick up the phone or visit a branch to do this – don't be one of them.

Use aggregators wisely

The temptation is to think that price comparison websites – or aggregators, as product managers tend to call them – have taken all the hassle out of finding the best deals. Unfortunately, this simply isn't true and our advice is to use them selectively and with the full knowledge that the deals you are being presented as the 'best' are often anything but.

Aggregators make money in lots of ways but by far the most significant is by earning fees from some banks every time they refer business to them. Often aggregators will work with banks on how best to present or list a new product or promotion to guarantee more applications. The big banks provide aggregators with a lot of income and they therefore have significant bargaining power. Aggregators therefore work hard to ensure that a good deal – but one that might not be the 'best' deal – gets a lot of clicks. Sometimes they only list deals from banks that pay them commission and have in the past used misleading language to describe a promotion. The bottom line, then, is that the league table of rates or deals you are looking at on screen is a highly selective league table, so be careful.

Again, the other point to make here is that the bases on which products and promotions are listed is limited – often centred on rate. Short-term promotional rates can rank highly, even though the rate won't be around for long and you will quickly be repriced. Similarly, products with great promotions can sometimes be the worst for fees. There is therefore no substitute for doing your own research and using aggregators as a useful, but biased, reference point.

Standing up for yourself

Even if you ask the right questions of your bank and the products it sells and even if you make sure you put in place all of the basics described above, there will probably come a time when you need to complain to your bank. Despite what you might think, the odds are not stacked against you, even though we readily admit that complaining to a bank can be downright infuriating. To the extent that it's possible to identify some golden rules when complaining from an insider's perspective, they are as follows:

Be bothered to complain

In an effort to maintain the fiction that they are customer focused, many banks spend a lot of time and money trying to avoid complaints. Complaint volumes are published publicly and frequently picked over by the press in order to identify the 'worst bank for complaints'. Banks are also required to show on their websites the number of complaints that ended up being referred to the Financial Ombudsman Service (FOS), the ombudsman that referees disputes between customers and banks. Nobody likes topping that chart either.

Obviously, banks being banks, many of them spend a lot of time re-categorizing complaints as forms of feedback that are not actually complaints, or summarizing complaints data in ways that not even the most sophisticated statistician could understand – all to avoid their complaint volumes looking too high.

The incentive to re-categorize complaints as feedback has recently increased. Previously banks had to report publicly the volume of complaints not addressed by the end of the following working day but now the FCA makes banks report all complaints, regardless of how long they took to resolve. Unsurprisingly the number of complaints the banks are now obliged to report has increased and therefore banks are on the lookout for ways to get this number down.

Few bank chief executive officers like to be top of the complaints league table. Fewer still like high numbers of complaints that have been referred to the FOS. FOS referrals usually occur when the customer and the bank cannot agree on the outcome of a complaint so the details are sent to the FOS for review. FOS cases are often upheld in favour of the customer. Between April and December 2016, for example, some 27% of cases relating to current accounts and 29% of cases relating to credit cards referred to the FOS were upheld.

Two points merit consideration here. First, it costs banks money when cases are sent to the FOS – several hundred pounds in fact – so by saying that you are willing to take your case to the FOS if you have not received a satisfactory response to your complaint is often effective. Banks will regularly settle a complaint on the grounds that it will cost less to settle than to pay the costs associated with the case going to the FOS.

Second, it pays to keep a careful, accurate record of the facts of any complaint, covering details like how long it took for the bank to reply to your complaint, how much you are out of pocket, what you were told when you took out a product, and any other evidence such as bank statements and letters. This information is important in helping the FOS evaluate your case and helps you fight your corner.

What all this means is that complaining to your bank can be surprisingly effective. While it might be tempting to conclude it's a case of David versus Goliath, if you have been treated poorly, received incorrect information, or been left out of pocket unjustifiably, banks are duty bound to process your complaint in a timely fashion and with due consideration. And you can always escalate your complaint to the FOS if you don't like what you hear.

Retain your product terms and conditions

Nothing panics a bank staff member more than a customer brandishing a copy of the terms and conditions given to them when they opened their bank account, savings account, loan, credit card, or mortgage. This is for a few reasons.

The first is that banks sometimes reprint their terms and conditions several times a year – adding sections, removing sections, updating them for the latest regulatory requirements, adjusting prices, you name it. Terms and conditions booklets are lengthy and complex and many (most) colleagues have literally no idea what's in them. So, while product managers in head offices might congratulate themselves for thinking up a devious little ploy to make money and put this into the terms and conditions of the product, the chances are that the poor branch colleague will neither understand this nor remember it if you raise a query about it. If you take the time to read the terms and conditions you are likely to be far better informed than the branch colleague. Many will refund fees and charges immediately if they feel like you know your stuff as they are sure they don't.

The second reason is that banks make more mistakes in their terms and conditions than they care to admit. A 'current' version of terms and conditions often turns out not to be the 'current' terms and conditions as branches all receive new printed stock at different times. Customers are sometimes given the wrong, outdated, terms and conditions when they sign up to a product and can use this to their advantage when they complain.

So, keep your terms and conditions, do your best to understand them, bring them with you into the branch if you want to complain. You'll be surprised how reluctant bank staff will be to engage you on the substance of your complaint when you hold out the terms and conditions, preferring instead to reverse some fees or change your rate back to what it was previously.

Ask for stuff to be written down

Banks hate it when you ask for stuff to be written down. Not only does it seem to take an inordinate effort for them to do so as your complaint grinds its way through their customer relations teams that often number hundreds of people, it means they need to take the time to research the facts of your case rather than give you a cursory response on the phone. At some point many banks prefer just to give in and refund fees and charges than spend any more operational expense coordinating people to issue you an official letter.

Our advice, though, would be to ask for more stuff to be written down than just a complaint response. You are perfectly within your rights to ask the bank to write down on a bank letterhead what they told you when you opened a new packaged bank account or plumped for a new credit card deal. Branch colleagues in the big banks intent on hitting their sales targets have in the past been economical with the truth, or certainly selective in pointing out the downsides of a product. Getting them to write it all down gives you a clear point of reference and official version of events in case there is any need to complain in the future. If they won't write things down for you, ask yourself why that might be.

CHAPTER SUMMARY

- Retail banking is expensive to provide, leading product managers to look for ways to earn more income, increase market share, or cut costs.

- Asking "What do I want to achieve?" is arguably the most important question of all, encouraging us to have a plan when it comes to our personal finances and ensuring that the products and services we use are aligned to this plan.

- Asking "What are they trying to get me to do?" helps you to think critically about how the product manager is hoping to make money out of you. This is usually achieved through customers forgetting when a deal ends, incorrectly assessing how they will use a product, taking out more products, or missing something important in the terms and conditions.

- Asking "Is it a big number?" helps to evaluate and compare a fee or a rate and put it in context. This in turn helps us to make better decisions.

- "How do I really behave?" is an important question to ask, requiring us to reflect on how we actually use financial services and products to ensure we choose the right ones for our circumstances.

- Checking the rates you are receiving or paying once every six months helps to ensure you know when your deals are no longer competitive.

CHAPTER SUMMARY

- Taking out a small overdraft facility – as long as it is free – often makes sense if you are keen to avoid penalty fees.

- Signing up to and making use of banks' various digital banking services means that you can more easily keep track of your finances, avoid fees, and move money around more easily.

- Moving your banking, savings, and borrowing around from one provider to another can save you money but only if you are highly organized and ensure you don't get tripped up by specific terms and conditions along the way. Be realistic about how much time you have to compare and contrast deals.

- In our experience, for those with existing debt or who need to borrow, a personal loan is often the safest way to borrow as it has set repayments ensuring you don't slip deeper into the red.

- Ignore banks when they claim to have won awards or star ratings for their products. These awards may not go to the most deserving products or banks. Use your brain instead.

- Using a mortgage broker nearly always saves you money and keeps banks on their toes.

CHAPTER SUMMARY

- Putting some money away for a rainy day ensures you have a safety buffer and negates the need to take out short-term, expensive unsecured lending.

- If your savings rate goes down or your borrowing rate up, always ask your bank what your options are and what rates new customers are being offered.

- Use aggregators wisely as they earn money by referring applications to financial institutions. Sometimes the way they list promotions and deals is less than objective.

- Banks try to keep complaint numbers down, particularly referrals to the Financial Ombudsman Service. This means you should always complain if you have been mistreated as banks may well settle any dispute to avoid you complaining further.

- Always retain the terms and conditions given to you when you opened your product. Bank staff are often unfamiliar with them and they frequently contain errors, strengthening your hand during any complaint.

- Always ask for things to be written down during any dispute with your bank as this can be a useful reference point, and evidence, if you need to complain.

CHAPTER 9

Better banks

What about the banks themselves? While we can all take sensible steps to bank, save, and borrow more effectively, there is no getting round the fact that banks need to step up to the mark, too, if retail banking is to really improve.

The changes the banks need to make are vast, multifaceted, and likely to take a considerable amount of time. They also traverse many different areas – from the underlying economics of banking to the types of employees banks hire. Here we focus on the practical steps banks can take right now to make things better for customers and restore trust, before going on to look at the transformative prospect of digital technology on banking in the next chapter.

Many of the recommendations below come with a price tag attached – they will cost banks money to implement – but doing the right thing often does. In the long term, however, ensuring banks are more transparent and straightforward to deal with means that the income the banks do earn is 'earned' in the truest sense of the term – a fair value exchange for services provided – rather than gained from customers through confusion and sharp practices. It has become increasingly obvious to us that for banks to survive – let alone thrive – they need to provide customers with things they want, at fair prices, in ways they understand.

Putting the economics of retail banking on a solid footing
The end of 'free' banking
Today, a relatively small number of customers, paying high penalty fees and charges, go a long way to enabling banks to offer 'free' banking to everyone else. Millions of customers enjoy very low cost banking, potentially just

the opportunity cost of keeping their deposits in a non-interest paying current account, because banks are raking in lots of fees from a small minority to pay for it. Perhaps unsurprisingly, many of us see no reason why we should pay for our banking, believing that those who are paying penalty fees and high interest charges have no one to blame but themselves.

Yet this cross-subsidization effect leads to a deep level of cynicism on the part of customers, the media, and regulators. Hammering those customers that make a mistake to pay for free banking for others seems both unfair and punitive. The charges this group pay are often disproportionate to the offence committed – a few pounds over your limit and you can get hit by fees ten times that figure. Banks continue to charge these fees, of course, because they need this income if they are to provide free banking to everyone else. Not to charge it would have a material impact on the profitability and viability of many services they provide. Moreover, many charge it simply because they can, knowing that few customers will switch to another provider.

In our view, so-called 'free' banking is a key driver behind many of the bad features of retail banking in the UK. It incentivizes banks to charge customers high fees for making mistakes rather than charging everyone fees proportionate to how they use a bank's services. It encourages banks to be opaque in how and when they charge customers via labyrinthine terms and conditions and complex product structures and requirements. Banking cannot survive if a significant proportion of the income it earns is unrelated to the services it provides.

Free banking is not just unfair, it is also unsustainable for banks. As digital technology improves it will be easier than ever for customers to avoid paying things like penalty fees through alerts and notifications and automated transfers from one account to another. Regulators are likely to continue to tighten up on complex fee structures which lead to people paying over the odds for particular services such as overdrafts. It seems obvious that, over time, banks will have a decreasing line of income to pay for free banking for everyone else.

To put the economics of retail banking back on solid ground, banks need to devise fairer, more proportional ways of structuring their income. They might consider transitioning to a revenue model where customers pay a few pence for different types of transaction or an 'all-in' monthly fee and remove penalty fees. This won't be easy – or popular – but it has the virtue of being transparent, straightforward, and understandable. It should also lead to subtle changes in the relationship between banks and their customers – from a game of cat and mouse to one of a fair value exchange for services provided. It would take a bold CEO and a great, sustained marketing campaign to make it work but our bet is that if one large bank moved, others would soon follow.

Getting lean

Banks need to take a long, hard look at their operational costs and try to be more efficient in how they provide banking services to avoid the unholy alliance of bad fees paying for poor business models. Despite earning billions in profit over the years and spending decades trying to become more efficient, the big banks have made little discernible progress in driving efficiency when compared to other industries such as retail. A KPMG report found that the cost-to-income ratio, the relationship between how much income a bank returns and its costs, for the Big Five UK banks was

63% in 2014. This compared to 53% for smaller challenger banks who benefited from simpler business models and product sets. Keeping things simple reduces costs.

We saw in Part 1 that the big banks have laboured under high cost bases for decades. Large, expensive IT infrastructure, a sprawling, poorly chosen branch estate resulting from many episodes of merger and acquisition, and vast numbers of back office colleagues marshalling bits of paper across the organization have combined to leave banks needing to make high levels of income to make ends meet. This inefficiency is ultimately paid for by the customer in the form of higher fees and, historically, from a 'product pushing' sales culture in branches.

If banks cannot afford to pay for their cost bases without charging customers exorbitant fees in less than transparent ways they need to cut their cost bases. There is good news and bad news here. The good news is for the first time there is a sense that banks can make real progress thanks to new technologies. Process automation offers the potential to make customer experiences quicker, intuitive, and more reliable, cutting out the additional time and errors associated with processes that require human intervention. 'Digitizing' back office processes, such as payments and account opening, and using things like machine learning to better route telephone calls to the right teams, offer banks the chance to save millions of pounds of operational expense.

The bad news is that getting costs under control will not come without pain. It seems inevitable that the banks with branches in the wrong locations will need to close them. This will be controversial and have real social impacts. Closing the last bank in town has consequences for those that rely on and need face-to-face financial advice. Alternatives, like mobile branches, should be employed to help customers, particularly vulnerable customers, with the transition. Yet the social detriment caused by banks needing to pay for unproductive real estate are arguably worse. Banks recover these costs in other ways, principally through products that cost consumers more than they bargained for and charge disproportionate fees when they slip up.

Self-service

Irrespective of whether you think the growth in digital technology will herald radical changes in banking, most people agree that providing customers with the ability to self-serve – that is undertake simple transactions and processes themselves using their mobile phone or online banking – should be the 'new normal'. The trouble is, few banks have a clear self-service strategy meaning that while it's possible to do a *few* things it is rarely possible to do *many* things yourself. Again, the villain of the piece here is the legacy IT systems the big banks continue to use. Knitting together all those wires can mean that providing customers with what sound like simple self-service options is actually rather complicated.

In our view, banks need to commit to a more extensive range of self-service options to give customers choice and – just as importantly – make them feel empowered over their own financial lives. From changing address securely to ordering a new debit or credit card, it shouldn't be as hard as it is to undertake simple financial housekeeping tasks.

To make all this happen, though, banks need to invest in their customer authentication processes: making sure that when you want to open a new account, or log in to service an existing account, the bank is able to verify that you are you. Too many banks still rely on different passcodes and types of identification that differ by channel, meaning that a customer has a passcode for online banking, and a different set of credentials altogether when they phone up to speak with an adviser. Fingerprint scanning, voice recognition, and simple, secure, multichannel authentication technology is now available to ensure that customers are able to log in and get on with whatever it is they want to do – but too few banks are making use of them currently.

Restoring trust through greater transparency
Better rate visibility

Customer awareness of the rate they are being paid on their savings or paying on their borrowing is notoriously poor. We are all busy and banks change rates all the time anyway. Banks take advantage of this lack of interest and confusion as they know that the less aware you are of the rate you're on, the less incentive there is to move to a better deal because, by definition, you won't know whether another deal is actually any better. Witness the quarter of customers typically still languishing on bad interest rates two years after a bonus savings deal runs out.

In an effort to prove to customers that banks are not, in fact, set up to frustrate and obfuscate, there is much more banks could do to enhance the visibility of the rates they are paying to or charging customers. There is no reason why banks should not adopt a 'first page/first screen' commitment to show the rate of every product on the first screen when a customer logs in to online banking or the first page of any monthly statement. An annual 'rate reminder' for all the products a customer holds could become standard practice.

Of course, rate visibility is not, on its own, enough to make you move your banking. But such awareness is correlated with better rate recall ("I know my savings rate is 1%") which in turn is correlated with people recognizing a better deal when they see it.

Changing rates the right way

Banks sometimes need to change their rates. A move up or down in the Bank of England Base Rate, the need for more bank funding in the form of savings deposits or the need to reduce lending by putting rates up – the reasons why banks move their rates are many and varied. Yet while the need to change rates might be perfectly reasonable, as we've seen, the way banks go about informing customers rarely is. In our view, a few simple steps would make all the difference to customers.

First, when banks change pricing they should be more proactive in how they inform customers. For rates that negatively impact a customer, banks usually send an email or a letter and hope that customers ignore it. We would like to see banks putting in place prompts that alert customers to rate increases or decreases when they log in to online banking, access their mobile app, or call to speak with an adviser. These 'interstitial' prompts are easy to do and would ensure that customers are aware their rate is changing.

Second, banks should calculate what any rate change will mean for a customer in pounds and pence. If a credit card rate is to increase and someone had an outstanding balance of £100 on their account, banks should calculate how much interest each month a customer might pay if they do not clear the balance. Similarly, if a customer has £1,000 in a savings account and the rate is to fall, banks should be forced to quantify what the reduction in monthly or annual interest received will be. This will take price changes out of the realm of abstract percentages and make changes tangible and real for customers. Seeing your credit card rate rise from 15% APR to 18% APR sounds bad but is hard to quantify. Realizing that unless you clear the balance this is going to cost you another £20 a month is more likely to get you to sit up and take note.

Third, when banks notify customers of a change in rates they should include information on any alternative products available with the bank. Customers should be offered information on the features of these alternatives and there should be a straightforward process to move balances to new products. This would helpfully nudge customers towards a proactive choice between products, rather than sticking with the status quo because they haven't thought about it.

Fourth, all banks should be forced to publish the interest rate of the product the customer was offered when they first opened the account, their current rate and how the Bank of England Base Rate has changed over that period. Customers would be able to see how badly their savings rate has been cut over time or their borrowing rate increased relative to changes in Base Rate, which would encourage customers to look around for a better deal. Of course, the same goes the other way round. If banks have actually increased savings rates or decreased borrowing rates since a customer took out a product this can be made clear too.

The best rate available, for all

It would be easy for the industry to remove one reason why so many customers are cynical about banks overnight. Banks should be forced to ensure that all existing customers are offered the savings rates available to new customers. In other words, banks should not be able to restrict the best paying savings accounts for new customers only. This destroys trust in banks ("they're only interested in new customers, loyalty doesn't pay") and provides options for customers that may not wish to move banks entirely to find a competitive rate but are not happy at being slowly margin-managed at their current bank. It creates a level playing field where new and existing customers can take advantage of the bank's best available rate.

Importantly, this is not the same as saying that banks should pay all customers the same rate. Banks need to be able to move their pricing up and down to meet their short- and long-term funding needs. But it is saying that as they offer new products and new rates they should ensure that these products are available and offered to existing customers as well.

Timely notice of charges

One of the areas that generates genuine customer rage is when banks levy charges for services customers feel they were never given any choice but to incur. The best example here is again overdrafts. Banks decide themselves whether to extend unauthorized overdrafts to customers (often called 'shadow limits'), leading to paid item fees which customers have little choice but to pay. Information on fees and charges might have been provided at account opening, but as most customers stay with their bank for many years, these costs aren't front of mind. Banks should show customers what their potential overdraft fees and rates are *before* they reach their account limit, so that they can make a proactive choice as to whether they use other forms of lending, or sweep cash across from a savings account to avoid going over their limit.

It's not just overdraft fees either. Banks should remind customers of their overseas card transaction fees as they land in a new country or try to make an international transaction – perhaps via a simple text message. Where a customer makes anything less than full repayment on their credit card, they should be given information on how much more it might cost them to maintain an additional balance on their card for the next month.

Providing notifications – be they emails, text messages, or even letters – ahead of the fee event actually happening would promote active choices by customers, rather than leaving them feeling that charges are slipped in surreptitiously by banks.

A monthly bill

Banking is one of the few long-term relationships we all have with a company where we are not provided with a monthly bill for the services provided. Gas, electricity, water, mobile phone, broadband, and satellite television providers all produce monthly bills, making it easier for us to understand what we are paying and how this might compare to other offers out there.

While the bank statements we receive detail the transactions on each of our accounts, and let us know of any upcoming fees we are due to pay, we do not receive a consolidated monthly bill showing us what all our banking has cost us in pounds and pence in the last month or quarter. Paul Pester, Chief Executive Officer of Spanish-owned TSB, has led the charge on calling for such monthly bills, and we agree with him.

One of the reasons why banks have not traditionally offered monthly bills is because calculating them would send most of them into meltdown. While it might be easy enough to add up the fees and debit interest a customer might have paid on a current account each month, banks would then struggle to calculate all the other charges and interest paid on other products a customer might hold with the bank to provide one, consolidated, monthly bill. This is often because banks have many complex product IT platforms that all work in slightly different ways – there is no single view of the customer and all their product holdings. So, getting to a point where your monthly bill shows all the fees and interest charges you paid on your bank account, credit card, loan, mortgage, travel money order, and debit card use abroad, for example, is likely to be some time away. Only when banks sort out all their old, legacy IT systems and get their customer data into better shape could such a monthly bill be produced. But that doesn't mean they shouldn't try.

Over time, we would like to see monthly bills include the opportunity costs of banking, such as what you might have earned on the money currently sitting in a current account if you had put it into a savings product. This is, after all, the true cost to us of placing our money in a bank. It is possible to imagine a dynamic monthly bill that gave you this information, potentially with a link offering to sweep the excess funds from your current account into a savings product for a better return.

Safer sales
Removal of sales incentives

Retail banking has a long and tortuous history of selling bad products to customers in the wrong way. From endowment mortgages to payment protection insurance, banks have consistently filled their boots on highly lucrative products that turn out to be a bad deal for customers. A key factor in such scandals is usually the incentives that staff are provided with to sell them.

There was a time when all banks had schemes in place that rewarded staff in different ways depending on the value of the products they managed to sell. Banks even 'gamified' this to the point where they awarded a higher number of 'points' for products sold that provided the bank with more income. Points made prizes for the colleagues with the highest totals at the end of the month, quarter, or year. Branch managers would hold morning 'huddles' with their teams and fire them up to sell "at least 20 credit cards today!" At no point did anyone stop to consider whether the poor customer needed a credit card, or indeed whether it was appropriate for them to have one.

While most banks have now amended their incentives schemes to take into account conduct risk measures and customer service scores, product sales still remains a part of many compensation schemes for front-line colleagues.

Yet in our view the moment a staff member is incentivized to sell one product over another, or hit a certain number of sales of any product, the customer is in a perilous position. The solution is obvious, if unpalatable, for many banks. No front-line colleagues should have sales incentives. Instead, banks should consider measuring staff by how well they treat customers through customer experience surveys. Would banks sell fewer products if they adopted this approach? Almost certainly. That tells you all you need to know.

Recorded sales

No matter how hard banks try to simplify things, individual circumstances can mean that the process of finding the right product for a customer can sometimes be complex. Mortgages are a case in point, which is why the sales process for a mortgage is a regulated process, subject to a lot more scrutiny than the process for selling a customer a savings account, for example. Yet modern technology means that it is now much easier to record the sales process for every type of banking product to ensure the process is fair. Banks can record the screen flow and attestations a customer or colleague clicks through on screen, which can be shared with the customer and stored by the bank to ensure a common understanding. This provides customers and the bank with a clear record of the product application process, the information disclosed, and the decisions made. If there are any disputes in the future, the recording can be accessed, making resolution that much easier. This approach would also, of course, have the handy effect of making banks clean up their acts when talking to customers in the first place.

Culture and organization
A balanced scorecard – really

While most of the large high-street banks claim to place customer outcomes such as complaint volumes and customer experience scores on an equal footing with financial performance, in reality it is the numbers that do the talking. The glossy annual reports from the banks all window dress the hard numbers with commitments to investing in new technologies and more convenient banking, yet the reality tends to be long wait times on the phone and branches that are always closed. We think banks need to become as fanatical about customer service – and monitor it just as closely – as they are about financial performance. Only when this performance scorecard is truly balanced will banks become genuinely customer focused.

Until you've worked in a bank – and in a product team in particular – it's difficult to imagine what this might mean in practice. Yet for a product manager any move whereby your employer becomes as interested in customer satisfaction as the bottom line would completely transform the job. While the need to develop and distribute products that earn the bank a return would not change, the ways to achieve this end most certainly would. Focus would shift from trying to make rate and fee changes in ways that few customers notice, to thinking about products and services customers would be willing to pay for. While plenty of banks give this idea lip service, most of them equate better customer service with higher costs or lower fee income. In our view that is looking at things the wrong way round – it is customer satisfaction that drives more income because happy customers are willing to pay for the bank's services.

A different type of banker

As we will see in the next chapter, the relentless demands unleashed by the digital economy mean that banks also need to attract a different type of banker if they are to remain relevant. Traditionally, the teams that build new products and services for customers have largely come from a commercial background, experienced in fiddling with spreadsheets and building complex revenue and risk models. While these skills will still be needed, banks now need to also invest in a wider array of talent, ranging from graphic designers and data analysts through to user journey specialists and agile project managers. As the delivery and design of retail banking products changes, so too must the bankers that build them.

Processes not products

Technology giants like Apple and Google are slowly stepping into markets that banks have traditionally owned – such as payments. Financial start-ups are chipping away at high-fee-generating services like foreign currency – offering cheaper, easier, and faster alternatives. Ask a bank CEO what keeps them up at night and it is usually the prospect of a technology company announcing they are going to enter the banking market. These companies have better data, and smarter ways to interrogate that data, than banks do. They have prioritized designing convenient, fast, and secure customer experiences. But by far the most significant factor in their success is how they organize themselves – around the customer.

As we said in Part 1, banks have traditionally organized themselves in silos. The credit card team doesn't have much to do with the mortgage team. The call centre rarely chats to the branch team. Such an organization structure and way of working will become untenable in the future.

Banks need to start organizing themselves around specific customer experiences, like account opening or payments, rather than by channel or product, to ensure that these processes and services work for different types of customers across every touchpoint in the bank. Banks need to move to a model where they rapidly iterate and launch new products and services as proofs of concept. The principle of a minimum viable product (MVP) – effectively a 'suck it and see' approach to putting something out there to see how customers find it – sits uncomfortably with many financial institutions who are risk averse and highly regulated. Yet few will have a choice since their competitors – not all of whom will be banks – will do just that. Speed of delivery, flexibility, security, and excellent design are the new competitive battlegrounds requiring new talent and new ways of working.

Committing to competition
Faster switching and account number portability

The UK has made great progress in creating a seven-day current account switching service that, once a customer requests to switch bank, moves all their direct debits and regular payments automatically. This kind of service doesn't exist in a lot of countries. But it's not enough.

The problem is, in a world where you where you can buy a toaster with one-click on Amazon and have it delivered to your door a few hours later, seven working days for a banking switch just doesn't cut the mustard. It feels slow, old, and screams 'it's complicated', making customers think that something might go wrong. We think customers should be able to shift their direct debits at a click of a button on the same day. It may be difficult, but it is doable. If the regulator and the industry want to improve competition, speeding up switching is vital.

The answer might be account number portability. Bankers have been chewing this one over for years and convincing regulators it would take too long and cost billions to do. Yet account number portability would do just what it says on the tin – offering customers the prospect of being able to transfer their banking to another provider but keep the same account number. It's already possible in the mobile phone industry and there seems little reason why it couldn't work in retail banking.

A major reason people worry about switching banks is they don't want payments to go astray. That's why we believe account number portability – where payments don't move because your account number doesn't change – could be a game changer when it comes to encouraging people to switch banks.

Overdraft switching

When we talk to customers, one of the other big impediments to switching is overdrafts. Most of us are not too sure whether another bank will give us the same overdraft limit as we have with our current bank. Even if we want to switch everything somewhere new, we wonder whether we might lose out if we do. Yet the benefits of overdraft customers switching to a better deal are real. The recent CMA report into retail banking found that those who regularly use an overdraft could save anywhere between £70 and £140 a year if they switched, with big overdraft users potentially saving even more.

Some banks get around this challenge in customers' minds by committing to match an overdraft a customer has elsewhere, as long as they bring in proof of the facility in place at the other bank and that the facility has been kept in good order. Yet such overdraft matching is not, in percentage terms, very common. Banks tend to keep their credit appetite – how willing they are to lend you money – fairly close to their chests as it is proprietary information. It determines how good a bank is at lending, which is commercially valuable information. As a result, banks have historically been fairly unwilling to let customers see how much they might be able to borrow *before* deciding whether to switch bank accounts. The seven-day Current Account Switch Service also doesn't let customers switch an overdraft, which can mean they end up being disappointed when the new bank will not accept their borrowings.

One solution would be for banks to make a customer's transactional data available to a prospective new bank (with their permission), allowing the new bank to make a better credit decision and, all being well, let the customer know the potential overdraft they will be provided with. By allowing their data to be evaluated by another bank before deciding whether to move, customers can have their cake and eat it – switching if the new bank can give them what they need, sitting tight if it can't.

The role of the regulator in driving competition
Capital requirements for new banks

One of the most challenging aspects of being a new bank is having to be part of the standardized approach to capital management rather than being able to use the 'advanced internal ratings-based' approach (AIRB). If you cast your mind back to Chapter 2, banks must hold a certain amount of capital against the lending that they make, to ensure that the bank won't crumble if there is an economic shock and customers can't pay back their loans.

The standardized approach uses external ratings agency data to determine the risk weighting of certain types of lending, which then helps calculate how much capital the bank must hold against different types of asset (75% on personal loans, for example). The riskier the asset, the greater the amount of capital the bank needs to hold against it.

The big high-street banks do not use the standardized approach, which can be a fairly blunt tool. The AIRB approach, by comparison, is a more nuanced approach which allows banks to determine their own ratings based on their calculation of the riskiness of their lending and their exposure. Developing and maintaining an AIRB model is a complex task – and a heavy investment for a new or small bank to make. To move to an AIRB model, banks must prove to the PRA that they have met certain standards.

The key point here is that AIRB is significantly less conservative and allows banks to hold less capital against their lending: sometimes many times less. It follows that additional capital requirements put new, challenger banks at a serious competitive disadvantage to more established banks, despite there being precious little evidence they are any better at lending. For challenger banks to make income, invest it, and grow they need to lend, yet the current capital guidelines make it disproportionately hard for them to make the same return on the same type of loan as the big banks.

In early 2017, the PRA launched a consultation to address the disparity between the two approaches, which, if delivered effectively, will improve competitiveness for smaller and newer banks. We are keeping our fingers crossed.

Authorization of new banks

Starting a new bank is hard. You need a truckload of investment to create a capital base for the bank, to build infrastructure capable of handling banking products and to attract experienced talent.

But on top of these significant barriers to entry that exist in retail banking, banks need to go through a fairly arduous authorization process with the regulators. While this has been made easier in recent years, and is now led through a single institution (the PRA, rather than the PRA and FCA), it is still slow, costly, and rather cumbersome. In order to take any would-be start-up bank through the process, backers need very deep pockets. Thus, the authorization process itself can add a further barrier to entry since the risk and payback time for investors is greater when authorization takes a long time and, in some cases, may not happen at all.

Of course, we support a thorough authorization process – it ensures new banks are properly set up to handle people's hard-earned cash. However, the aim has to be to create an authorization process that does not in and of itself dissuade entrepreneurs and investors from giving it a go.

Payments infrastructure

In order for new banks to process payments, they have to clear them through one of Barclays, HSBC, Lloyds, or RBS. You read that right. At the time of writing, there are only four clearing banks in the whole of the UK and all of them are stuck on 'old bank' infrastructure. This means that new challenger banks have to rely on the payments processing of the old banks they are trying to compete against – including having to take it on the chin when their systems go down. It is a significant inhibitor to competition in the market and adds more cost to new banks struggling to grow. Only when the UK's payments infrastructure is managed as a common industry infrastructure which all banks can 'plug in' to will we see this barrier to competition removed.

Things are starting to move in the right direction. In 2017, we will probably see the emergence of the first new clearing bank for 250 years, which will offer clearing services to new challenger banks and fintech companies, without being a competitor in the consumer banking space. The new Payment Services Regulator has also stated that it is focused on ensuring that the payments infrastructure is not an inhibitor to retail banking competition. So far, so good.

CHAPTER SUMMARY

- Banks need to end the process of cross-subsidization, whereby a small number of customers pay disproportionately high fees to enable others to receive 'free' banking.

- Banks need to reduce their operational costs by simplifying their business models and product ranges.

- The ability for customers to 'self-serve' via smartphones and online banking is still too patchy and requires banks to get their authentication technology right.

- Banks can increase customer trust through giving customers better visibility of the rate they are receiving or paying on a product and ensuring that when rates are changed customers understand the full implications and are provided with alternative options.

- Banks should commit to ensuring that existing customers are offered the same product rates as new customers.

- We think a monthly bill for your banking is a good idea, helping customers to understand what their banking actually costs.

- Banks can enhance the sales process by removing sales incentives from front-line colleagues and recording sales conversations with customers.

CHAPTER SUMMARY

- Placing customer satisfaction and experience on an equal footing with financial performance is necessary if banks are to regain customer trust.

- Banks need to ensure that they hire a new type of banker, who reflects the need for banks to design user-friendly products and processes.

- While the seven-day current account switching service has been a good start, we think switching should be instantaneous just like it is when you change mobile phone provider. Account number portability would help.

- Helping customers with overdrafts switch by showing them the limits available to them elsewhere is important in driving up switching.

- The regulatory authorities have an important role to play in driving up competition in the retail banking market through more proportional capital requirements for new banks, a swifter authorization process, and by opening up the UK's payments infrastructure to new entrants.

CHAPTER 10

Future banking

Retail banking in the UK is in a dreadful state. Competition for the big incumbent banks has for many years been muted by high barriers to entry, the absolute need for scale to succeed and a regulatory regime that has failed to deliver a level playing field in terms of capital regulation. Banks' profits have been impacted by a combination of ultra-low interest rates, endless refunds to customers mis-sold products, and massive regulatory fines. Banks continue to be hamstrung by inefficient business models and vast cost bases. Little wonder that many of the big high-street banks have been posting annual losses.

This environment has proven toxic for the consumer as the big banks have been focused far more intently on survival, regulatory compliance, and capital ratios than they have on delivering customer service. That management focus away from the customer, coupled with the day-to-day incentives and pressures within product management teams, has led directly to a cultural stagnation within the banks as well as a series of scandals where customers have lost money – from the headline dominating PPI scandal to the more mundane tricks played in the course of everyday business, such as continually changing customers' rates.

We think we're now at a bit of a fork in the road. Down one path lies the long, slow death of the big banks as we know them. Their ancient systems, cost pressures, and male/stale/pale cultures mean they will likely *never* change for the better but will (very) gradually die out, to be replaced by a new breed of financial services business.

Down the other path lies the forced evolution of the big banks – and their redemption – as they drive change through their own organizations to become more customer focused and ultimately triumph over (or assimilate) the upstarts of the fintech scene.

Ultimately, we think that both possibilities are actually likely to happen together. The old way of banking – involving massive cost bases, sprawling IT and property estates, and labyrinthine processes – is certainly becoming unsustainable. Every industry with those features has been, or is being, transformed by technology and the internet. Cars are now built on increasingly automated production lines by robots and will soon be driving themselves. Record shops have given way to streaming services that can predict your musical tastes and suggest tunes you might like. Online retail is growing at a pace that physical site retailers cannot comprehend, with personalized shopping suggestions and special offers tailored to your individual search history the absolute norm. It would be arrogant in the extreme to expect banking to be any different, and existing banks that fail to react to this new reality will very probably see their business eroded by other banks who have moved to adopt new technologies more quickly.

That said, we do not see the nature of what banking is, or how it functions in society, changing very much at all – as it actually hasn't really changed for hundreds of years. Customers will still require banks (or bank-like institutions) to provide the same three basic things they always have: deposits (a place to store money safely); payments (a means to access and use that money to pay for things); and lending (a source of funds when they need to access more cash than they have themselves).

Therefore any organization attempting to do all three will continue to have to manage the complexities inherent in this activity, principally liquidity and capital. So, if the basic elements of 'financial services' are not going to change, the only remaining questions are 'who will provide these services' and 'will they make life any better for beleaguered banking customers?'.

In the long run, the answer to 'who will provide the services' does not include the big banks *as they are today*. It is very difficult to imagine that these businesses can survive in their current form. To our eyes at least they look increasingly anachronistic – giant beasts from another era, out of place in a modern world and needing to adapt or face extinction. Their cost-to-income ratios are unsustainable, the sheer complexity of coordinating day-to-day operations consumes too much management focus, and they are prone to failure. They are also subject to a range of environmental pressures (regulation, a degree of competition, shareholder economics) that are driving them to change. But we do think that the existing banks that are able to evolve will continue to dominate the market.

At heart, banking remains a *scale* industry and will continue to be so. Even if set-up and running costs fall over time as technology penetrates the industry, income lines will continue to be characterized by small sums of money being made on a very high number of transactions. In other words, banks and other financial services firms are always likely to need *loads* of customers to make enough real money to pay for the infrastructure and skills required to run their businesses, even if the costs of that infrastructure fall over time.

We believe that as a result there is an inherent tendency in the banking industry towards market concentration (if not oligopoly) and we don't really see that changing much. If anything, the industries that have experienced the most intense transformation through technology are now dominated by one or two giant firms (just look at Google and Amazon), not diverse ecologies of small and medium-sized businesses.

Therefore, we don't believe that big banks will die off like dinosaurs, being replaced by a cleverer, cuddlier class of mammalian fintechs who are better able to adapt. Instead we think the big banks have had a terrible decade or so, but that the stimuli of sustained losses, regulatory fines, and customer fury is evoking a Darwinian response. They are evolving, but it is happening (as much evolution does) so slowly as to be nearly imperceptible.

Predictions are a dangerous game, of course, but our money is on retail financial services continuing to be dominated by a small number of very large institutions for many years to come and we'd be quite surprised if the majority of those institutions weren't well-known bank brands already.

Evolution of existing big banks

The incumbent big banks aren't just 'big', they're massive. Even if they invested nothing, ignored digital, and delivered the same old service then it would still take years (at current switching rates) to reverse their dominance. If they do nothing in that time then eventually they are likely to die out as other firms take over, but they are all taking steps to respond before this comes about. Today, they are spending billions to address legacy technology and regulatory challenges, and in some cases even redefining their organizational structures and working practices to better compete for business in the future. The changes they are pursuing can be broken down into a few key trends.

Digital transformation of the retail experience

The smartphone was recently described to us by a management consultant as, "The greatest demand aggregation tool in the history of the world." Hyperbolic consultant-speak aside, he had a point. In the old days if you wanted to sell stuff you needed a shop. The people who walked in to your shop were your customers. If you wanted more than passing trade then you had to advertise and get people to want to come to your shop especially. The most recent figures estimate that 37% of the world's population now has a smartphone. That's 2.7 billion people. Most of them use Facebook and Google. So, any product placed on Facebook – for example – can be viewed by a staggering number of customers. Thanks to aggregators like Amazon, *global* demand is accessible to sellers at very low marginal costs. Banking cannot be excluded from this revolution – we can't think of another suitable word for it – in *retailing*.

At the very least, banks will need to build their own 'shop windows' in mobile – allowing customers both to buy new products as well as service existing ones. A reasonable analogy to consider is an airline app. These days it only requires a few moments to search for a flight, enter a few details and a credit card number, and buy a flight. Once bought one can check-in on the app, get a boarding pass, and even scan through the gates at the airport all on a phone.

Similar experiences can and will be delivered for banking. A quick Google search for a new credit card could lead to a simple, mobile-friendly application journey resulting in the 'purchase' of a new financial product that can then be readily accessed and managed via the app.

Mobile banking technology is still relatively nascent. Some smaller banks are yet to build an app, and while the bigger banks might be on their second or third generation apps by now, the functionality is limited and many products are not available via mobile. Things continue to develop quickly though and once each bank has established a mobile 'base camp' the only way is up, since successive app releases with new functionality emerge at an increasing pace.

A good mobile app is only the beginning, though. Major retailers of consumer goods: clothes, shoes, handbags, toys, etc. have already made giant strides in the digital shopping experience more generally. Websites are glossy libraries of high-quality photos of products, searchable and filter-able with ease. Cookies ensure the products shown to you are optimized by algorithms to suit what the analysts perceive to be 'your' taste, and offers are similarly tailored to, and targeted at, your digital profile.

The big banks aren't really doing this in the same way... yet. How often have you noticed that the product you just googled (that new handbag you really *love*) suddenly appears in your Facebook feed, or halfway down an unrelated Google search – or even just in a banner advertisement on the side of an unrelated website. Banks have only just begun to offer their products in the same way, such as by embedding mortgage advertisements in estate agency websites. They are likely to go a step further and show you that handbag inside your online banking and mobile app with a 'click here to purchase' button that would have the same effect as typing your credit card details into the handbag website – but a whole lot easier. This kind of *embedded* digital experience is becoming ever more pervasive in the world of retail but banking still has much to do to catch up.

Digital ways of working

Banks have historically been organized like old-fashioned manufacturing businesses. Raw materials (deposits) come in at one end of the factory, processing occurs (managing liquidity and capital), and finished products emerge at the other end (such as mortgages advanced to customers to buy houses). Teams of people were dedicated to each stage and largely didn't care about what happened in other parts of the plant. Until recently, automation of these processes was an ideal outcome for banks – like a car manufacturer pursuing a Henry-Ford-style manufacturing revolution, banks wanted to automate the steps in the process to get to the end quicker with less manual intervention. But fundamentally the process steps were the same, in the same order, just being done faster by machines instead of people. The result was always the same – the bank designed the product, it made the product, then it went looking for people to buy the product.

Things could not be any more different in a digital design world, where the desire is always to 'design from the screen down' with the 'user experience' and 'user interface' of critical importance. No longer is a paper loan file created and passed from team to team around a building until a loan is advanced. Now the information required for a loan application can be captured, scored, decided, and processed in seconds with a binding offer – or even the advance itself – back with the customer in a few minutes. There are teams forming inside the big banks now with the aim of building these new 'customer journeys'. These teams have to be multidisciplinary and able to bring *all* the required banking expertise to bear at once on the process. As a result, old divisional silos are breaking down, with whole teams of people being introduced to one another for nigh on the first time and made to work together – often in an 'ideation lab' replete with whiteboards for walls and beanbags for chairs! This is a cultural shift and requires new skills to be learned and old prejudices to be abandoned – and it is happening already, albeit relatively slowly as old banking dogs try to learn new tricks.

These multidisciplinary teams are also aiming to build fast-paced change environments where new ideas can be prototyped rapidly and released in days or weeks instead of the more traditional bank change cycles measured in months and years. The big banks are working really hard to change their underlying technical infrastructure to support this rapid innovation cycle. Having realized that building more and more layers on to old, legacy systems each decade was yielding unsustainable complexity and a glacial pace of change, they are engaged in massive architectural shifts in IT to provide a firm foundation for continuous, high intensity digital innovation. We're still very much in the infancy of this transformation to a more digital way of working inside the big banks, but as the underlying architecture shifts conclude, the pace of digital change they are capable of will probably increase.

Ultimately this new way of working may well alleviate some of the day-to-day pressures faced by the beleaguered product manager. Of course, banks must make money – they are businesses after all – but part of the digital way of thinking is to prioritise customer-focused performance metrics throughout the end-to-end customer journey *as well as* profit measures. Analysis of click-through rates, how users navigate around a web page, the elapsed time from process start to process finish, the number of customers falling out of the standard process as exceptions requiring special treatment – all these things reinforce the view of the customer experience as something to manage holistically, and are also a lead indicator of more value-related measures like applications for products.

Increasingly product managers are looking to compete on how easy products are to use, instead of focusing solely on pricing and promotions. Product managers will in the future need to think about using and analysing customer data to deliver personalized offers via digital advertising, targeted to very small subsets of customers. While banks can't become technology businesses valued for their 'customer base' irrespective of income generated like Snap or LinkedIn, the influence of this way of thinking is rebalancing the way banks operate in favour of placing customer experience first. Given that banking is – and always has been – a scale exercise, building this 'user base' is as important as ever. If banks can learn the lessons of how the digital giants succeeded in winning customers this will probably be beneficial overall for the customer experience.

Rethinking branch banking

For all the fuss about digital, banking still needs branches and people as not everything can be done remotely. Amazon is building shops, Apple already has them. John Lewis has very successfully married a fine digital experience with what seems like logistical sorcery to deliver online orders to your nearest Waitrose within a matter of hours. The trendy term is 'bricks and clicks' – not our favourite phrase by any means, but it is a pithy encapsulation of how we think retail is evolving towards a marriage of the digital and the physical. Banking has too much physical and not enough digital at the moment, and the physical sites most banks have are not being utilized any differently from how they were before the digital revolution occurred. As the investment in, and adoption of, digital technology increases, we think the physical aspects of banking will evolve to better suit a seamless experience across channels, as well as remaining the only option for some services.

We therefore most certainly do not believe that the concept of branch banking is dead. A study by EY found that nearly 60% of consumers want to visit a branch to purchase a new product or get advice. The consumer trust that branches engender make them both worthwhile and important for brand identity. Even if there was no practical reason for banks to have branches (such as to sell products to customers face-to-face), they might still choose to have them anyway for the goodwill (in the accounting sense of the word) alone. In reality we think that branches will continue to exist for both reasons of practical necessity, and also as drivers of either tangible or intangible value for the banks. The challenge for banks is to monetize their real estate more effectively to ensure that the cost of covering the necessities is more than matched by the income they generate. Clues as to how this might happen are to be found in the examples of where a branch is a necessity:

- **Physical cash and cheques:** the rise of digital payments is plain to see, but many people still use cash and cheques and will continue to do so for many years. In Metro Bank the free coin-counting machines are a constant draw for both customers and non-customers. In 2016, the bank processed coins worth tens of millions of pounds.
- **Advice:** money is often an emotive topic for people, particularly when large sums are involved – such as

transferring a deposit for a house purchase, or applying for a mortgage. Many customers want to look someone in the eye and talk through such transactions. Online, automated or so-called 'robo' advice is, of course, another nascent innovation which is likely to remove some demand from branches, but ultimately, we see banking as a service based on trust and we therefore expect to see a continued demand from customers for *human* contact with their bank.

- **Documentation:** banks must by law 'know their customers' in order to comply with anti-money laundering legislation. There are many 'electronic identification' tools out there which offer varying degrees of digital confirmation of identity. But none are foolproof and many people continue to need to supply physical proofs of identity and address in order to access financial services. Doing this via post is very slow, and risks crucial documents (like passports) getting lost. Having a branch offers a practical, faster, safer alternative.

The role of branches will not be limited to simply handling cash, opening accounts, and processing documentation. The banks that will succeed will look to use their branches to deliver more value to the customers they are serving. Potential examples here include:

- **'Click-and-collect':** it seems inevitable that banks will become fulfilment locations where customers can pick up a bank card or travel money ordered in advance, just the same as we pick up orders from other high-street retailers. Banks seem likely to become drop-off points for other companies' packages – they are secure locations after all. Of course, there are challenges to this: site access and parking availability, liability for the goods prior to collection etc. But if the banks are going to occupy the space anyway, it makes sense to explore whether these challenges can be overcome so the bank can do more things that customers value.

- **Community engagement and shared space:** one of the hallmarks of the best high-street retail brands is how easy they make it to engage with the brand. From wandering round the Apple store to sitting down to work for the day in your local café or book store, brands now actively seek to become 'engagement destinations'. Although today it might seem like a stretch of the imagination, there is no reason why local high-street bank branches cannot do the same. From hosting community events after hours to offering free (or at least cheap) space for start-up businesses, banks will probably rethink how they use their physical space to ensure it supports their overall brand much better than it does today.

- **Offering non-financial products:** Banks will probably not limit themselves to offering just banking products. A physical branch offers the opportunity for banks to offer and distribute physical products easily. We expect that more banks will start to offer things like the physical hardware that small businesses use to take card payments, or safe-deposit boxes, to provide additional value to customers.

At the moment, the incumbent banks see their branch network as a problem – a cost anchor weighing them down. If they flipped this thinking around and asked "how can we use these sites to deliver more value to our customers?" they might come up with some interesting ideas that help to make the banking experience that bit easier for customers.

Open banking and the enigma that is PSD2

It might sound like a character from Star Wars but PSD2 – 'Payment Services Directive 2' – is a piece of European Union legislation published in 2016 which is required to be enacted into UK domestic law by January 2018. PSD2 will be either the single largest evolutionary stimulus banking has had in the last 50 years or a niggly bit of administrative hassle from Brussels that will have little effect. The exciting thing is that no one is quite sure which one it will be.

What we do know for certain is that PSD2 is all about *payments*. It has nothing directly to do with the other two services banks provide: deposits and lending. The many aims of PSD2 are to: contribute to a more integrated and efficient European payments market; promote competition through a regulatory framework which encourages the emergence of new players (e.g. fintechs) and the development of innovative mobile and internet payment services in Europe; improve consumer protection against fraud, possible abuses, and payment incidents through enhanced security requirements including the use of strong customer authentication for electronic payments; and encourage lower prices for payments.

The context for the regulation is that payments services have changed dramatically in a very short space of time, driven by an increasingly global payments landscape. Retail payments used to be a *local* activity. Our grandparents paid the butcher, the baker, and the candlestick maker, in their local high street, usually with cash. They definitely didn't pay a t-shirt shop in Sydney, a bookshop in Ohio, or an airline in Geneva using a debit card or PayPal. While payments are global now the infrastructure through which payments are transmitted and effected is still local – or regional at any rate. The payments to Sydney, Ohio, and Geneva started life in a UK bank, which talked to the UK debit card system (such as Mastercard), which then talked either directly to the banks where the t-shirt shop, bookshop, and airline have their accounts, or via an intermediary bank along the way. Eventually the payments will end up being recognized for value via the domestic clearing systems in Australia, the USA, and Switzerland respectively.

Within Europe, the original Payment Services Directive (2007) and now PSD2, aim to create central standards that make payments within Europe much simpler. That simplicity and commonality of infrastructure and messaging delivers the aims above: lowering barriers to entry for new providers which increases innovation and competition, reduces costs, and makes it easier to spot and control fraud.

From a neutral perspective, PSD2 is a 'good thing'. Standardization, security, and efficiency – the great hallmarks of the digital revolution. Who wouldn't want those? It's the unintended consequences of one aspect of PSD2 in particular that might prove to be fascinating though: the concept of 'open banking'.

For hundreds of years banks have worked on being secure, and the traditional way of doing that was to be secretive. Knowledge was restricted wherever possible and physical barriers were erected between the bank and the world – not just doors, walls, and vaults, but digital perimeter security, too, involving things like firewalls and so-called demilitarized zones (or DMZs). PSD2 forces banks to open up, requiring them to provide a means for third parties to effect payments from a customer's account, and also to obtain the customer's transaction history and account balance.

An example of what this might mean could be something like this: you buy something on Amazon. At the checkout, instead of entering your card details (which may well be prestored by Amazon) you can click a button that says something like 'Bank-Pay'. After entering some security details – say a thumbprint on your smartphone and a one-time passcode via text, Amazon will generate an instruction to your bank to debit your account directly. This cuts out card scheme providers like Mastercard and Visa completely, shortens the route the payment has to take through the clearing pipework and therefore makes the payment cheaper and faster to process. The effect is the same as if Amazon had logged into your online bank account, keyed in a payment to itself, and hit send. Under PSD2 this is called 'payment initiation'. Amazon could also – with your permission and security input – show you *all* of your bank account balances in one place to make it easier for you to manage your money, and decide how much to spend on Kindle books. PSD2 calls this 'aggregation'.

Just how much will payment initiation and aggregation change retail banking? On the one hand the impact might be really negligible. I can buy stuff from Amazon now with a single click based on stored credit card details. While the payment process behind the scenes might be cheaper, faster, and more secure, the 'Bank-Pay' option actually makes life harder for me as a customer as now I have to go through yet another layer of security to effect payment. Therefore, adoption of the new payment initiation service by third parties might be low. Also, the aggregation won't necessarily encompass all products (savings accounts for example), just accounts that you can make payments from like bank accounts. So, the value of aggregation is questionable. Again, take-up might be low.

On the other hand, though, it might be possible for giant technology companies to insert themselves in between banks and their customers. If, say, Google or Facebook built an absolutely killer personal finance app, able to access and use your personal bank account data, with loads of whizzy tools to help you manage money, buy what you wanted online etc. then why would you ever go to your bank's online banking page ever again? One theory is that from this point you then have no allegiance to your original bank anymore and that you can point and click to get a credit card, or a loan, or a mortgage within an aggregated view without caring which bank is actually supplying the product. At that point, not only have the banks lost control over payments, they've also lost a great deal of brand value, reliability of demand, and control over price. Their ability to win deposits and sell loans is boiled down to the twin pillars of price competition and their ability to surface their products online in a really effective way (e.g. coming top in a Google search for 'new credit card').

If this happens, it will be because customers want it to happen. While it will undoubtedly disrupt banks' current business models, it might eventually be really good news for banks too. Instead of every individual bank having to spend millions on their online banking platforms and their mobile apps, and maintaining connections to a range of complicated bits of payments infrastructure, there might just be one or two digital platforms with standardized methods of integration that all banks can access with one common (technical) language for payments.

Banks are therefore facing a key decision point right now – do they build infrastructure to become aggregators (of other banks' data) to enable their customers to see all their accounts in one place and create payments directly against current accounts in other banks, or not? Ultimately this is a judgement call – will customers value aggregation and payment initiation or will it take years to become mainstream given how attached customers are to banking the way they do today? Time will tell.

The new kids on the block

We have suggested previously that we think existing banks will continue to dominate the market. This idea runs contrary to the apparent zeitgeist which heralds the disruptive power of 'fintech'. This buzzword – short for 'financial technology' – is used to describe an ecosystem of new-start, non-bank companies that are aiming to use technology to 'disrupt' the way the existing banking industry works. Mention of fintech in the mainstream press has reached near-epidemic proportions and has been variously described in the media as the industry on which a post-Brexit Britain can be built, the solution to Britain's banking woes, an alternative to fossil fuels, and an approximation of the meaning of life (OK, we made up the last two). You get the idea though: the hype around these companies is really substantial.

Under the general header of 'fintech' are different strands of activities, each focusing on different aspects of financial services. A huge amount of effort is going into payments innovation at present, especially around international payments. Similarly, trade finance (a crucial component of business banking for firms buying or selling goods overseas) is also receiving a lot of attention. As a rule of thumb: wherever traditional banks are running the most complex, most obscure, most high-cost processes, 'fintech' is focusing on building solutions to these problems and make everything transparent, efficient, and just brilliant for customers. Yet while we absolutely agree that technology can solve many problems within banking, we simply do not believe all of the hype surrounding 'fintech', especially when the term is being used to describe every small start-up with two or three graduates who can write some code and make big promises.

Fintechs are undoubtedly incorporating the latest thinking in online and mobile customer experiences: beautiful apps, easy log-in authentication, and clear pricing structures. However, while they offer some really great new services and ideas, we think most will struggle to reach scale and in the end very few will end up challenging banks outright. Even if they do not ultimately challenge banks they will still be extremely important as motivators for banks to be better, since fintechs are setting new standards in process design and digital banking services. Most likely some will end up *enabling* banks to be better in their own right, either through providing more efficient and secure central payments infrastructure that all banks can access, or alternatively through being acquired by banks that want to internalize their practices and products, which cannot be produced inside the stifling systems architecture and security apparatus of the banks themselves.

Payments fintechs

Payments fintechs have shaken up the financial services industry by identifying underserved gaps in the market, like payments processing for people selling their wares on eBay, or by providing cheaper alternatives to high-cost payment types, like international remittances.

These companies have radically different business models from banks. Rather than making money from money (i.e. through deposit-funded lending), these companies charge fees for a service – be that a pound fee or a percentage rate for each transaction they execute. This kind of model works particularly well in the payments space because of the regular usage and relative predictability of payments flows and the ability to apply a small charge to every payment flowing through the system without impacting a customer's decision as to whether to use the service. It is a business model – skimming small amounts from large payment flows – we have seen many times over from fintechs.

The challenges of this business model are that the margins are very thin, and therefore the only way to make a large amount of money is to capture a big slice of the market (many millions of customers). If you only make £0.01 (i.e. 1p) for every transaction processed through your system or platform, you will need to push a lot of transactions through it to make enough money to run the business, let alone make a profit.

Banks themselves don't make serious money out of payments. They make money out of taking and managing risk – liquidity and credit risk specifically – through the paying and charging of interest on fluctuating balances of deposits and loans. To compete, payments fintechs need to participate and 'win' in as many markets as possible, so that they can capture enough scale to support the cost of running their business. The challenge also is to avoid being a one-trick pony, vulnerable to the next whizzy payments company coming along and taking their one line of income.

Given how rapidly the payments market is changing, payments fintechs must therefore work hard to diversify their proposition to customers so that they are not overly reliant on one piece of technology or pricing approach.

Peer-to-peer lending

One of the highest profile groups of fintechs in recent years has been the 'peer-to-peer' lenders. These businesses introduce customers with money to invest to customers who want to borrow. Investors expect higher returns than they get in a savings account, but they are also taking on the risk associated with unsecured lending.

The peer-to-peer lender runs the marketplace and manages the liquidity of investor funds. They provide a loan application, do the underwriting, and fulfil the loans via an online platform. Peer-to-peer lenders therefore make their money by charging a fee to every customer that takes a loan (and sometimes charging the investor too), taking little or no risk themselves, since the money for the loans is provided by other customers.

One of the most extraordinary – and telling – things about peer-to-peer lenders in recent years is that they have had to turn to institutional lenders – hedge funds and, yes, banks – to access enough funding to keep lending. Why did this happen? Quite simply, demand for loans outstripped the supply of willing investors.

As peer-to-peer fintechs usually only get paid when transactions have been completed, they need to make sure that everyone who wants a loan and has sufficient credit quality can get a loan. Leaving demand unfulfilled means these companies are leaving money on the table, as well as annoying potentially good-quality borrowers of the future.

Little surprise, then, that one of the leading peer-to-peer lenders in the UK, Zopa, applied for a banking licence in 2016. In one sense this was a natural progression since Zopa was already doing much of what a bank does in relation to consumer lending. By obtaining a banking licence Zopa can get access to a steady, reliable source of funds by raising ordinary customer deposits to fund loans. So why not take a bank licence and make more money by doing it?

The example of how Zopa's model has evolved over time is a neat encapsulation of the limits of much of the fintech sector. Fintechs can undoubtedly make customer experiences better by creating slick online journeys and short-cutting some of the complexities of old-fashioned bank processes. By doing that, they create a wave of innovation across the industry as old banks replicate to keep up.

But for all the talk of 'disruption' and the 'remaking' of the financial services universe, many can't replace the fundamental elements of how to make money out of money – something banks have vast experience in. It is too early to tell if a banking licence will work for Zopa and, if it does, what that will do to its original peer-to-peer strategy over time. However it works out, we strongly suspect that Zopa is unlikely to be the last peer-to-peer lender applying to become a bank.

Neo-banks

Neo-banks are the newest guys in town, most having entered the scene around 2015 and several are still awaiting their banking licences. They are jumping in with both feet, promising to create full-service, digital-only banks, powered entirely by state-of-the-art technology platforms and unencumbered by the high fixed costs of a bank branch estate.

In the UK, the likes of Atom, Starling, Tandem, and Monzo are in the very early stages of their development. Awash with buzzwords, they are surfing down the digital zeitgeist, building 'platforms' and 'communities' under distinctive branding that is a world away from traditional banking. They seek feedback from their customers on product ideas, publish their development roadmaps for all to see and allow developers to link in easily to their platforms. Many encourage their early customers to invest in their company so they feel a sense of ownership.

Life won't be plain sailing for the neo-banks. They have received (or are in the process of applying for) full-banking licences that enable them to take deposits. However, with limited brand awareness, no physical shop window, and hardly any customers, to grow their deposit funding will require them to offer high – if not market-leading – savings rates. This is an unsustainable strategy because, as we have seen, the higher your cost of funds, the harder it is to lend money out and make a good net interest margin. During the time taken to write this book Atom Bank has in fact offered to lend mortgages at a rate *lower* than it was willing to pay on deposits. In other words, it openly accepted a loss-making position in order to grow its book of deposits and lending. This is entirely unsustainable as it is fundamentally at odds with running a profitable business.

The second big problem these banks face is replication. Despite all the inefficiencies and high cost bases of the big banks, if they really put their minds to it – particularly if they feel they are losing market share – they could build pretty much everything these digital banks offer in a matter of months. We have already seen this start to happen.

Many digital banks are still riding the wave of early adopters and media buzz, attracting customers keen to be able to talk about being part of the latest technology trend. These banks are betting that their app, and the attractiveness of their brand, are significantly better than big banks can offer. Yet the real challenge is to see whether these groups can attract a critical mass of regular customers, who are going to be less impressed by being part of something new, and much more difficult to attract, for all the reasons described in this book.

Building banking technology from scratch is hard and slow work. Getting customers to move their banking based on small product and service improvements is even harder. These digital banks need investors that will stick by them during the marathon. They will, we hope, gain some market share and continue to nip at the heels of the big banks. Their success will inevitably nudge the industry towards transparency, better designed processes, and the sense that the big banks are not actually masters of the universe.

But as pressure grows from their investors to attract customers and make money, we wonder how many will stick to their guns and how many will fall back on the tried and tested techniques that all the big banks use to make money.

Other neo-banks are taking a different route. Where they are unable (or unwilling) to provide a product or service, their platform will present a product from a carefully selected alternative supplier. In a very real sense, many are looking to become product supermarkets. But we're not convinced about this business model either. Do customers really want a bank that operates, say, their bank account but offers a platform with hundreds of other financial and non-financial products on it for them to choose from? And, more to the point, will the companies touting their products on the platform really pay these banks enough for introducing them to new customers for them to survive?

The technology behind 'platforms' is relatively straightforward. What matters is scale, and the network effect that scale brings. While functionality is important – it's what keeps people on your platform once they've got there – for every winner when it comes to platforms there are many losers. Even oligopoly isn't really sustainable when it comes to digital platforms: monopoly is required. There was only one winner out of MySpace, Bebo, Friends United, and Facebook, after all.

These banks do not appear to be competing with old banks at all. Instead, they seem to be building a new digital channel where everyone will go to see their existing financial products and to get new ones – even to the point of encouraging existing banks to sell products via their channel. One of these banks might succeed over time but there will almost certainly be many losers along the way.

What happens next?

Banking is – ultimately – a trust enterprise. Depositors trust banks will give them their money back, banks trust borrowers to repay the loans the bank has granted. Prudent bank management teams, and regulators, know that ultimately some degree of scale is required to build safe banks. Certainly, banks can be too big – the credit crisis of 2008 taught us that – but the crisis also taught us that smaller banks and building societies may be unable to survive major shocks that the bigger banks can withstand.

In the UK, we have a few very big banks. Many of us *dislike* them, but few of us actually *distrust* them – in the sense that they would not give us our deposits back when asked, or would fail to calculate our loans correctly. The dislike – we think – is based on a combination of persistent service failures and a history of rip-off product scandals.

The service failures are driven by layers of aged or ageing technology that make it very hard for bank colleagues to deliver really good customer service. Indirectly, the same legacy problems are also behind the product scandals that have plagued the industry as banks flail around looking to drive income in order to cover their spiralling costs. Banks are so focused on keeping the lights on that they've forgotten why they need lights in the first place.

So, banking has a problem, and that problem is being thrown into the sharpest possible relief by the rapid proliferation of digital technology and its transformation of retail experiences across multiple industries. The legacy technology at the heart of the largest banks has caused the adoption of new technologies to happen only slowly where in other industries it has been rapid. This has been compounded by inevitably long timelines required to create an industry-wide response to building new payments-clearing infrastructure – on which much technological innovation depends – that is fit for purpose in the digital age. Consequently, banks have been slow to react to consumer demand for seamless, multichannel banking, clear information, and 24/7 service.

But, banks are now starting to change, and at an increasingly rapid rate. The dangers of obsolescence – extinction even – is receding as banks spend billions updating their technologies, cultures, and ways of working to catch up with the digital age. But technology alone is not a substitute for the skill and discipline required to take a bunch of deposits and turn them into 25-year mortgages.

What the big banks have today is scale in the form of millions of customers and deep expertise when it comes to asset and liability management, maturity transformation, and managing liquidity risk and credit risk. They know how to do *banking*, in its most real and practical sense, and many fintechs and neo-banks do not. Being able to bank customers and businesses really, really well is a source of deep and enduring competitive advantage.

We see the innovations in the fintech space (well, some of them) as hugely positive, and in some cases potentially transformational in their impact on the financial services infrastructure. Undoubtedly cool new things are being built right now. But the fastest broadband speed imaginable along the whizziest fibre optic cable is of no use if the internet service provider who owns the cable and sells the broadband package has no customers. The whizzy fibre optic cable service provider will be an acquisition target for a big, old copper-wire provider with loads of customers and a desire to buy innovation rather than create it in-house. The same is likely to happen with many – if not most – fintech companies and digital banks.

Our big blind spot though is 'open banking'. We do not know what kind of organizations will try to walk through the door that the PSD2 regulations have opened. Disintermediation – banks getting cut off from their customers by other companies planting themselves in between – is a real risk for banks in the next decade. And that disintermediation could come from the most unlikely sources. Consider this example: at any given moment, Starbucks has about $1.2 billion sitting on its store cards, where its customers have added money to their cards to fund their daily coffee habit but not yet spent it. That's around $1.2 billion of what a bank would call 'deposits' and it's bigger than most building societies in the UK. Most interestingly of all – it's an *accident*. Starbucks is a coffee retailer, not a financial institution. But imagine what they could do in financial services if they actually *tried*. They could – for example – start offering loans to their supply chain funded by the excess cash floating on their store cards.

Ultimately though, Starbucks itself needs a banking partner (or partners) because it's a coffee business, not a bank. And even if it had the strategic desire to launch a financial services offshoot, the global coffee company itself would still need access to the scalability, reliability, security, and advanced financial products that only big banks can deliver. Therefore, while we can see that some degree of disintermediation at the retail level is possible the big banks' natural defences against this are the inherent complexities of retail banking in general as well as the ability to pick up deposits and lending from business and corporate customers.

Even with the benefit of better technology, banking needs to be a full-time job, not a side-of-the-desk strategy for a technology company or retailer. We therefore struggle to see non-bank operators (like Apple for example) evolving quietly into this space one product at a time. If one of the big technology players does enter the market it is likely to be in the form of a clearly identified new entity (e.g. Apple Bank) making a 'big bang' entrance after significant research and development. For now, banks are safe.

CHAPTER SUMMARY

- Banks are increasingly likely to focus on the digital transformation of the retail banking experience in the coming years. This will require banks to invest in their mobile banking offerings and make digital purchases seamless and convenient.

- Banks will also need to change the way they work, moving from product and channel silos to integrated businesses focused on discrete customer journeys and key processes. Teams will be multidisciplinary and release new products, services, and process improvements more often.

- Branch banking is also likely to go through something of a transformation in the near future, with banks focused on identifying better uses for branches, such as offering click-and-collect services and providing flexible work spaces for local businesses and community groups.

- 'Open banking' and the Payment Services Directive 2 have the potential to transform the retail banking industry, providing customers with new ways to view all their accounts in one place ('aggregation') and initiate payments in new ways. Open banking will also probably see more third-party, non-bank companies enter the market, building services and products for customers that utilize the data banks are required to make available to comply with PSD2.

CHAPTER SUMMARY

- The number of financial technology ('fintech') companies has grown significantly in recent years, offering new financial services to customers such as peer-to-peer lending and new payment technologies. These companies lack scale and in many cases, have unproven business models. Many still rely on banks or seek to complement – not compete with – them.

- Neo-banks have also grown in number in recent years, adopting a low-cost, all-digital, zero-branch business model. They have so far struggled to scale, offering limited products and services, lacking a high-street presence, and having to pay disproportionately more to attract customers' savings and deposits. Some want to become product 'supermarkets' offering everything to everyone from a financial services perspective.

- Banking is a trust enterprise and while customers dislike the big banks today they do not, on the whole, distrust them. Service failures have been the fault of aged and ageing technology. High cost bases have led banks to develop and sell products that leave customers short. Yet banks are turning things around, working in different ways to deliver new technologies that offer the prospect of a more customer-centred form of banking. Banks are therefore likely to continue to dominate in future.

CHAPTER 11

Conclusion

In this book we have tried to show you how retail banking really works and the inherent challenges in running a successful bank. We've tried to explain why these challenges can make it hard for banks to remain customer focused, deliver really great customer service, and provide good value products. Our intention was not to make excuses for bad service and poor products, but rather to be clear on the reasons why banks find it so hard to do the right thing.

We've seen there are many reasons *why* retail banking as an industry disappoints so many of us: high barriers to market entry and a lack of competition yielding an oligopolistic market; legacy IT and property portfolios that act as cost anchors dragging banks down; product managers incentivized to make money rather than make customers happy; and the underlying scale advantages big banks enjoy, crowding out smaller players that might offer something better for customers.

We've also tried to outline *how* bad banking manifests itself for ordinary people, every day: the large number of product design and promotional tricks banks play and the way they exploit customers' psychological and behavioural biases. Both are made possible by the reluctance on the part of customers to switch their banking somewhere else.

But it's not all bad news. We think banking is now changing at an unprecedented pace. After decades of virtually no change, the 2008 financial crisis and the advent of mass digital technology have triggered a fundamental re-evaluation of what banks are for and how they should work. Regulators are deliberately lowering barriers to entry and allowing more competition into the market. In response the incumbent banks are investing in new technology and new ways of working to drive down costs and improve the experiences of their customers.

There's still a long way to go. The legacy IT architectures and property portfolios look like ageing nuclear reactors to us – once cutting edge, now redundant, hugely expensive, and dangerous to decommission. New solutions and business models have yet to emerge to any great degree. Left to the big banks alone, change will take a long time to come. Customers must therefore play their part. Asking our four very simple questions – "what do I want to achieve?", "what are they trying to get me to do?", "is it a big number?", and "how do I really behave?" – would dramatically improve customers' chances of picking the best financial products for their own circumstances. It would also propel the big banks to simplify their products and increase the transparency of their sales processes. An increasing willingness on the part of customers to read terms and conditions, to complain, and to demand better service generally, and ultimately to be willing to switch to a new bank, would also force the banks to become more customer focused.

Banks themselves could choose different paths that, almost overnight, would radically improve customers' perceptions of the industry, such as by ensuring all products are available to new and existing customers equally, removing sales incentives, recording all sales conversations and making the rates on all products easily visible to customers. But these would be brave decisions to take unilaterally as they cut across decades of ingrained industry practice and may impact a bank's ability to make money in the short term. In the absence of industry consensus, public pressure, or regulatory compulsion, we think many of these recommendations are unlikely to be adopted quickly.

As with many other industries the best hope for radical change appears to rest with technology. As online banking and now mobile banking proliferate, they improve customers' ability to self-serve, to consume real-time data about their finances, and to access competitive financial products quickly. This must breed an increasing awareness of financial products, promote greater transparency, and drive industry competition. All of these things will act as catalysts, driving the incumbent banks to adapt or face gradual extinction.

Technology cannot replace the fundamental alchemy of banking though – taking deposits, transforming them into lending, and managing the liquidity and capital risks inherent in so doing, continue to be very specialist activities. Deep experience in this business is an enduring competitive advantage, much more so than technology, which can be increasingly easily replicated. So while PSD2 and the whole regulatory push towards 'open banking' has the potential to open the industry up to vastly greater competition than exists today we cannot see big banks dying out completely and being replaced by fintech firms. We think it's far more likely that many of the successful fintechs will end up either supplying central utility infrastructure (such as new payment systems) that all banks can access for a very low marginal cost, or alternatively being acquired by individual banks looking to accelerate their own transformation from traditional caterpillar into digital butterfly.

Even with all the wonders of technology, in our view banking remains a 'trust' business and that as such the humble branch has a crucial role to play: giving physical presence to a brand, as a place to seek out financial advice and increasingly as convenient locations for banks to provide physical fulfilment to digital journeys.

Epilogue

Our intentions in writing this book were manifold. Partly we wanted to bring together in one place all of the insights we've developed in the course of launching and growing the first new high-street bank in the UK for over 100 years. In that sense, this book represents something of a pause for breath in the middle of building our own bank for customers and a record of all the lessons we've learned and thoughts we've had along the way. Getting all these ideas down in one place has provided us with the opportunity to test our own assumptions, acknowledge and challenge our own ingrained biases, and refine our views on how to build a bank that delivers really great customer service.

We also wanted to justify to ourselves that the industry we work in isn't the source of all evil in the world. Part of that meant calling out the many damaging existing practices of the big banks as well as highlighting the bits we think are poorly understood and should be changed.

Most of all, though, we wanted to explain, in words that everyone can understand, how retail banks actually work – naked banking if you will. Why? Because we think banking is important and therefore deserves to be understood by everyone. At heart it is a social necessity – payments, deposits, and loans are required to help society function. If banking is done really well it can be a social good. If it's done badly – as we have seen over the last decade – it has profound social consequences. By building an understanding of what banks do and how they operate we hope that the dialogue around banking – between bankers, customers, regulators, and commentators – can be improved.

Ultimately, we wanted to go beyond the one-dimensional 'evil bankers' narrative of newspaper headlines because we sense that change is in the air. It seems clear to us that many banks are now trying very hard indeed to change how they operate for the better; most regulators are simultaneously attempting to drive that change home; and millions of customers are more empowered than ever before by technology to reward the banks that do the right thing. As such, for the first time in a very long time, there are reasons to be optimistic. A fairer, more transparent, and better value banking industry might be just around the corner.

Acknowledgements

We had never written a book before and getting to the finishing line has only been possible due to the help, generosity, and encouragement of many. Chief among them are our respective partners Emma, Sal, and Rami, whose tolerance for us sloping off to furiously type away for hours on end has been unending. This is particularly true given that no fewer than two babies arrived during the course of this project. Daniel and Amber, welcome to the world.

It was the Metro Bank family and its commitment to doing things differently that inspired us to write this book. Thanks to Sam Walker for reading through chapter drafts and Menis Nikolaropoulos for providing some technical guidance along the way. Thanks also to good friends Gerald McLarnon and Jeremy Cross for their ideas at the start of the project. LID Publishing have been unwaveringly enthusiastic and unfailingly professional as our publisher – thank you.

Final thanks go to Craig Donaldson, current or former boss to us all, who has supported this project from day one, pushing us to stick our heads above the professional parapet and say what we really think.

Sources

Chapter 1: Introduction

Arnold, Martin. "Lloyds Banking Group sets aside further £350M to cover PPI claims." *Financial Times*, (March 10, 2017).
http://on.ft.com/2mJnn3K

"How Financial Services Lost Its Mojo – And How It Can Get It Back." PriceWaterhouseCoopers LLP, (October 2015).
http://www.pwc.co.uk/financial-services/financial-services-risk-and-regulation/how-financial-services-lost-its-mojo.jhtml

"Making Banks Work Harder For You." *Summary of the Final Report Conclusions from the Competition and Markets Authority Market Investigation into Retail Banking*, Competition and Markets Authority, (9 August 2016).
https://www.gov.uk/government/uploads/system/uploads/attachment_data/file/544942/overview-of-the-banking-retail-market.pdf

"Who Are You Calling a 'Challenger Bank?' How Competition is improving customer choice and driving innovation in the UK banking market." PriceWaterhouseCoopers LLP, (2017).
www.pwc.co.uk/challenger-banks

Branch closure figures compiled by the BBC from Lloyds Banking Group, Royal Bank of Scotland, HSBC, Santander, Barclays, and Co-operative Bank, *BBC News*, (13 May 2016).
http://www.bbc.co.uk/news/business-36268324

Chapter 2: Why retail banking isn't working

Lowest instant access savings deposit rate found at Royal Bank of Scotland, www.personal.rbs.co.uk, correct as at 29/05/17. The rate is for their "Instant Saver" product.

"Bank IT Meltdowns: Bank of England Must Do More to Prevent Bank IT Failures, says Treasury Committee chair Andrew Tyrie." *Computerworld*, (25 January 2016).
http://www.computerworlduk.com/applications/hsbc-outage-is-first-bank-it-fiasco-of-2016-but-unlikely-be-last-3632901/

"Barclays customers experience problems with online banking and debit cards after payday technical glitch." *The Independent*, (30 October 2015).
http://www.independent.co.uk/news/business/news/barclays-customers-experience-problems-with-online-banking-and-debit-cards-after-payday-technical-a6715796.html

"HSBC still trying to repair online banking system." *BBC News*, (4-5 January 2016).
http://www.bbc.com/news/business-35231632

"RBS fined £56m over 'unacceptable' computer failure." *BBC News*, (20 November 2014).
http://www.bbc.com/news/business-30125728

"*Best and Worst Banks.*" Which?, (March 2017).
http://www.which.co.uk/money/banking/bank-accounts/guides/best-and-worst-banks

Retail Banking market investigation: provisional findings report, Appendix 5. Competition and Markets Authority, (28 October, 2015).
https://assets.publishing.service.gov.uk/media/5630c4b4e5274a59dc000002/Appendix_5.pdf

Chapter 3: Costs – the heaviest cross to bear

2016 Annual Report. Lloyds Banking Group, (2016).
http://www.lloydsbankinggroup.com/globalassets/documents/investors/2016/2016_lbg_annual_report_v2.pdf

Centring the Computer in the Business of Banking, Barclays Bank & Technological Change, 1954–1974, Ian Martin, Doctoral Thesis, Manchester University, (2010).
https://www.research.manchester.ac.uk/portal/files/54594634/FULL_TEXT.PDF

Financial Inclusion data/Global Findex. The World Bank, (2017).
http://datatopics.worldbank.org/financialinclusion/country/united-kingdom

Statistics. Faster Payments UK, (2015-17).
http://www.fasterpayments.org.uk/statistics

Chapter 4: The truth about us and the truth about you

"UK banks should cap overdraft fees, says watchdog CMA." *Financial Times*, (May 17, 2016).
https://www.ft.com/content/cb9d0240-1bf6-11e6-b286-cddde55ca122

Ausubel, Lawrence, M., *Adverse Selection in the Credit Card Market*. University of Maryland, (June 1999).
http://www.ausubel.com/creditcard-papers/adverse.pdf

Ru, Hong and Schoar, Antoinette, Do Credit Card Companies Screen for Behavioural Biases? *National Bureau of Economic Research.* Working Paper No. 22360, (June 2016).
http://www.nber.org/papers/w22360

Melzer, Brian, The Real Cost of Credit Access: Evidence from the payday lending market, *Quarterly Journal of Economics*, 126(1), (February 2011): 517-555.
https://academic.oup.com/qje/article-abstract/126/1/517/1902774/
The-Real-Costs-of-Credit-Access-Evidence-from-the

O'Donoghue, Ted and Rabin, Matthew., Doing It Now or Later, *The American Economic Review*, 89(1), (March 1999): 103-124.
https://www.aeaweb.org/articles?id=10.1257/aer.89.1.103

"Payday Lenders Given Reform Ultimatum." *The Guardian*, (6 March 2013).
https://www.theguardian.com/money/2013/mar/06/payday-lenders-reform-ultimatum-oft

Detailed Rules for the FCA Regime for Consumer Credit. Financial Conduct Authority, Policy Statement, 14/3, (February 2014).
https://www.fca.org.uk/publication/policy/ps14-03.pdf

"FCA to Review if Payday Lending Cap Feeds Loan Sharks." *Reuters*, (29 November 2016).
http://uk.reuters.com/article/uk-britain-credit-regulator-idUKK
billion13O0IM

Treasury Select Committee minutes, *Competition and Choice in Retail Banking.* Examination of witnesses Eric Daniels, Helen Weir, and Patrick Foley, (7 December 2010).
http://www.publications.parliament.uk/pa/cm201011/cmselect/
cmtreasy/612/10120702.htm

Stango, Victor and Zinman, Jonathan. "What Do Consumers Really Pay on Their Checking and Credit Card Accounts? Explicit, Implicit, and Avoidable Costs." *American Economic Review.* 99(2), (2009): 424-429.
http://www.dartmouth.edu/~jzinman/Papers/Stango&Zinman_AEA09.pdf

Bertand, Marianne., Karlan, Dean., Mullainathan, Sendhil., Shafir, Eldar., and Zinman, Jonathan., "What's Advertising Content Worth? Evidence From a Consumer Credit Marketing Field Experiment." *Quarterly Journal of Economics*, 125(1), (2010): 263-306.
http://isps.yale.edu/research/publications/isps10-006

Which? Financial Product Selling Survey. December 2012.
http://www.comresglobal.com/polls/which-financial-product-selling-survey-december-2012-part-1/

Erta, Kirstine, Stefan Hunt, Zanna Iscenko and Will Brambley., *Applying Behavioural Economics at the Financial Conduct Authority*. FCA Occasional Paper No. 1, (April 2013).
https://www.fca.org.uk/publication/occasional-papers/occasional-paper-1.pdf

Thompson, Leigh. *Mind and Heart of the Negotiator*. 5th edition, (Pearson Education Limited, 2015).

"*Best and Worst Banks*", Which?, (March 2017).
http://www.which.co.uk/money/banking/bank-accounts/guides/best-and-worst-banks

Edelman Trust Barometer. Edelman, (2016).
http://www.edelman.com/insights/intellectual-property/2016-edelman-trust-barometer/global-results/

Fincham, Richard., Rebecca Reynolds, and Nicky Spicer. *Engagement With Current Accounts and the Switching Process*. Optimisa Research for the Financial Conduct Authority, (March 2015). https://www.fca.org.uk/publication/research/cass-qualitative-consumer-research.pdf

Chapter 5: Banking

Personal Current Accounts: Market Study Update. Competition and Markets Authority, (18 July 2014).
https://assets.publishing.service.gov.uk/media/53c834c640f0b610aa000009/140717_-_PCA_Review_Full_Report.pdf

Current Account Switching Data, Bacs, (2016/7).
https://www.bacs.co.uk/NewsCentre/PressReleases/Pages/CurrentAccountSwitchServiceJuly2016.aspx

"*Overdrafts charges more expensive than payday loans*". Which?, (9 July 2016).
http://press.which.co.uk/whichpressreleases/overdraft-charges-more-expensive-than-payday-loans/

Packaged Bank Account. Financial Conduct Authority Thematic Review. TR16/8, (October 2016).
https://www.fca.org.uk/publication/thematic-reviews/tr16-8.pdf

Chapter 6: Saving

Factbook 2011-12, London: Organization for Economic Co-operation and Development, (2012).
http://www.oecd-ilibrary.org/content/book/factbook-2011-en

Cash Savings Market Study Report, Part 1: Findings, Part 2: Proposed Remedies, Market Study MS14/2.3, Financial Conduct Authority, (January 2015).
https://www.fca.org.uk/publication/market-studies/cash-savings-market-study-final-findings.pdf

Review of Barriers to Entry, Expansion and Exit in Retail Banking, Office of Fair Trading, OFT1282, (November 2010).
http://webarchive.nationalarchives.gov.uk/20140402142426/http:/www.oft.gov.uk/shared_oft/personal-current-accounts/oft1282

Cash Savings: Sunlight remedy, Financial Conduct Authority, (8 December 2015).
https://www.fca.org.uk/news/news-stories/cash-savings-sunlight-remedy
https://www.fca.org.uk/publication/market-studies/sunlight-october-2015.pdf

Individual Savings Accounts (ISA) Statistics, HM Revenue and Customs, (April 2017).
https://www.gov.uk/government/uploads/system/uploads/attachment_data/file/547217/Full_Statistics_Release_August_2016.pdf

Chapter 7: Borrowing

The Money Statistics, The Money Charity, (2017).
http://themoneycharity.org.uk/money-statistics/

Key UK Mortgage Facts, Council of Mortgage Lenders, (2016),
https://www.cml.org.uk/industry-data/key-uk-mortgage-facts/

"Interest-Free Credit Cards a 'Ticking Time Bomb' Bankers Fear",
Financial Times, (April 20, 2017).
https://www.ft.com/content/a7df4432-2daa-11e7-9555-23ef563ecf9a

March 2016 Figures for the High Street Banks, British Bankers Association, (26 April 2016).
https://www.bba.org.uk/news/press-releases/march-2016-figures-for-the-high-street-banks/#.WJrgEBicau5

December 2016 Figures for the High Street Banks, British Bankers Association, (26 January 2017).
https://www.bba.org.uk/news/statistics/high-street-banking/december-2016-figures-for-the-high-street-banks/#.WJrkAhicau4

Council of Mortgage Lenders data:
https://www.cml.org.uk/industry-data/

"The Credit Card Knowledge Gap", Moneysupermarket.com (2016).
http://www.moneysupermarket.com/credit-cards/credit-card-knowledge-gap/

"Costly credit card mistakes add £948m in annual interest charges to bills", Co-op Bank, (November 2016).
https://www.co-operativebank.co.uk/news/2017/costly-credit-card-mistakes

"Balance Transfers Misleading Consumers", Which?, (22 September 2015).
http://www.which.co.uk/news/2015/09/0-balance-transfers-misleading-consumers-416500/

"Zero per cent credit cards 'lead to a worrying increase in people's level of debt'", The Fairbanking Foundation, (July 2015).
http://www.fairbanking.org.uk/Press%20Release%2017%20November%202015.pdf

"The Peril of Making Minimum Payments on Credit Card Debt", Knowledge @ Wharton, Wharton, University of Pennsylvania, (26 December 2016),
http://knowledge.wharton.upenn.edu/article/perils-minimum-payment/

Chapter 8: Better banking

Savings Ratio UK, Economics Help, (9 February 2017).
http://www.economicshelp.org/blog/848/economics/savings-ratio-uk/

Statistics, Financial Ombudsman Service, Issue 139, (January/February 2017).
http://www.financial-ombudsman.org.uk/publications/ombudsman-news/139/chart_issue139.pdf

Chapter 9: Better banks

UK "Big Five" High Street Banks Face "Too Big to Compete", as Small Challenger Banks Secure Stellar Returns Says KPMG", KPMG, (22 May 2015).
https://home.kpmg.com/uk/en/home/media/press-releases/2015/05/uk-big-five-highstreet-banks-face-too-big-to-compete-as-small-challenger-banks-secure-stellar-returns-says-kpmg.html

"TSB's Paul Pester Plans a Big Push Into Small Business Banking",
The Telegraph, (25 July 2015).
http://www.telegraph.co.uk/finance/newsbysector/
banksandfinance/11760690/TSBs-Paul-Pester-plans-a-big-push-into-small-
business-banking.html

"CMA proposes better deal for bank customers", Competition and Markets
Authority, (22 October 2015).
https://www.gov.uk/government/news/cma-proposes-better-deal-for-
bank-customers

"CMA proposes UK retail banking changes 'worth £1 billion'",
Financial Times, "May 17, 2016)
https://www.ft.com/content/0d3b99bc-240d-3faa-93e0-317f2dd803a3

Chapter 10: Future Banking

The Relevance Challenge, EY, (2016).
http://www.ey.com/Publication/vwLUAssets/ey-the-relevance-
challenge/$FILE/ey-the-relevance-challenge-2016.pdf

The Second Payment Services Directive (PSD2): A Briefing From Payments UK,
Payments UK, (July 2016).
https://www.paymentsuk.org.uk/sites/default/files/PSD2%20report%20
June%202016.pdf

Smartphone Ownership and Internet Usage Continues to Climb in Emerging
Economies, Pew Research Center, (22 February 2016), (based on survey
data from Spring 2015 Global Attitudes survey) http://www.pewglobal.
org/2016/02/22/smartphone-ownership-and-internet-usage-continues-to-
climb-in-emerging-economies/

2015 World Population Data Sheet, Population Reference Bureau, (2015),
http://www.prb.org/pdf15/2015-world-population-data-sheet_eng.pdf

"Starbucks has more customer money on cards than many banks have in
deposits" *Market Watch*, (June 11, 2016).
http://www.marketwatch.com/story/starbucks-has-more-customer-money-on-
cards-than-many-banks-have-in-deposits-2016-06-09

About the authors

Paul Riseborough

Paul is Chief Commercial Officer at Metro Bank, the first new high street bank in the UK for more than 100 years. He leads the bank's product, digital, change and communications teams. He was educated at Nottingham, Oxford and Warwick universities and is a trustee of Making The Leap, a social mobility charity.

Karolina Morys

Karolina led the Retail Products team at Metro Bank, and previously worked at Lloyds Banking Group and Deloitte Consulting. She was awarded an MBA with Distinction from London Business School in 2015. Passionate about creating a new model of banking that puts customers first, she now works in Silicon Valley helping banks use technology to innovate their customer propositions.

Stephen Hogg

Stephen leads Metro Bank's Business Banking Products and Corporate Transactions teams, with responsibility for developing Metro's proposition for small business customers as well as leading strategic acquisition activity. He graduated from St Catherine's College, Oxford with a first in English Language and Literature. He has spent 12 years building businesses and technology platforms for a range of financial services companies and private equity funds.

About Naked Banking

We all depend on banks. They help us save and they help us spend. Yet for many they represent everything that's wrong with the world of finance. Poor service, high fees and a market controlled by just a few providers have combined in recent years to create a personal banking crisis every bit as severe as the global financial crisis.

How have things got so bad? Why are banks unable to balance providing good customer service with making a profit? And what can we do to protect ourselves from the tricks banks play to part us with our hard-earned money?

This ground-breaking book, written by three industry insiders, reveals why banks do the things they do. From designing products they know will rip customers off, to cutting branches they know their customers rely on, they explain how many banks' failing business models force them to make the wrong choices again and again. Naked Banking makes a rallying call for us all to be better informed about how everyday banking products actually work, so we can stay one step ahead and make the most of our money.